Life with Lowry

LIFE WITH LOWRY

Tilly Marshall

Hutchinson
London Melbourne Sydney Auckland Johannesburg

Hutchinson & Co. (Publishers) Ltd
An imprint of the Hutchinson Publishing Group
3 Fitzroy Square, London W1P 6JD

Hutchinson Group (Australia) Pty Ltd
30–32 Cremorne Street, Richmond South, Victoria 3121
PO Box 151, Broadway, New South Wales 2007

Hutchinson Group (NZ) Ltd
32–34 View Road, PO Box 40-086, Glenfield, Auckland 10

Hutchinson Group (SA) Pty Ltd
PO Box 337, Bergvlei 2012, South Africa

First published 1981

Set in Linotron Plantin by Input Typesetting Ltd
Printed in Great Britain by The Anchor Press Ltd
and bound by Wm Brendon & Son Ltd,
both of Tiptree, Essex

British Library Cataloguing in Publication Data
Marshall, Tilly
Life with Lowry.
1. Lowry, Laurence Stephen
2. Painters – England – Biography
I. Title
759.2 ND497.L83

ISBN 0 09 144090 4

For my husband Micky,
who knew Lowry so well,
and for my grandson Tom,
who never knew him
at all

ILLUSTRATIONS

Lowry celebrating his birthday in the Stone Gallery, 1 November 1971, with Micky, Ian, Lenny Jacobson and Simon

Astarte Syriaca, Dante Gabriel Rossetti, 1877. (Manchester City Art Galleries)

Proserpine, Dante Gabriel Rossetti, 1877

ACKNOWLEDGEMENTS

I should like to express my gratitude to Robson Dring, my brother, for the encouragement he gave me in writing this book.

My thanks must also go to Edwin Mullins for his thoughtful advice.

I am indebted to Mrs Carol Spiers, L. S. Lowry's heir, for her permission to quote from the artist's correspondence.

I wish to acknowledge permission from the City of Manchester Art Galleries to quote from Sir Arthur Elton's foreword to the catalogue of the 1968 exhibition 'Art and the Industrial Revolution', and to quote from Miss Sandra Martin's introduction and notes in the catalogue of the 1977 exhibition 'A Pre-Raphaelite Passion'. Also for permission to reproduce the photographs of the paintings *Astarte Syriaca* and *Proserpine* by Dante Gabriel Rossetti.

The majority of the photographs in the book are from my own collection, but I am indebted to Tyne Tees Television for one or two, and to Pat Cooke for allowing me to include the only photograph in her possession of herself with L. S. Lowry.

I gratefully acknowledge permission from Frederick Muller and Co. for allowing me to use two 'Beachcomber' quotes.

For permission to use short quotes from reviews or reports, which will be found attributed to their source in the context of the book, I am indebted to the following: *The Times*, the *Guardian*, the *Observer*, the *Sunday Telegraph*, the *Daily Telegraph*, the *Listener*, and the *Sun*.

1

I got off Lowry's bed and pushed my feet into my shoes. 'What's the time?' I asked him.

He looked at his boastfully inexpensive H. Samuel watch and replied, 'Seven-thirty.'

'Oh, splendid, not so late as I thought. Where shall we go for dinner – the usual?'

'Yes, yes, we can't do better than the Midland,' he agreed with alacrity. The Midland Hotel, Manchester, was about fourteen miles from The Elms, Mottram-in-Longdendale, Lowry's home, so about eight o'clock should see us in the French restaurant.

Whenever the painter urged me to write a book about him, I promised that, in the event of my doing so, that would be my opening. He would throw back his head and laugh, then splutter through his merriment, 'Don't add at that point that you'd only been on m'bed to take one picture down from above it and hang another in its place!'

I have kept the promise made in fun – now I must go back to the beginning.

The first time I met L. S. Lowry was on 5 August, 1960 in Harrogate. The town was holding an arts festival which included an exhibition of his work on loan from Salford Art Gallery. My husband, Micky, had left our son Simon with me at the exhibition hall while he went off to view the latest oeuvres of a local primitive painter, who was hopeful of an exhibition at our gallery, in Newcastle. While he was gone, I was introduced to Lowry by W. E. Johnson, a northern art critic. I found I had little alternative but to spend the remainder of the afternoon with this well-known painter.

Moving around the hall with him from work to work and back again, while he told me, with blue eyes sparkling, how he had come to paint this or draw that, I was impressed not only with the art, but also with the artist. I was of course familiar with Lowry's industrial scenes, with their myriad small figures scuttling hither and thither, but some of his earlier works, particularly certain landscapes, were eye-openers to me. In one or two oils I fancied the texture could hardly have been surpassed by Constable. When I said so he glowed with obvious pleasure. At the same time he had a delightfully modest air.

Lowry was a tall man, a gangling figure, with thick, once sandy-coloured hair, now silvering and cropped very short, and strong features. Hands in trouser pockets, he leaned slightly back while he talked. As time wore on and his brilliantly blue eyes continued to sparkle and smile, I realized that not only was he flirting with my opinion of his work, but his whole manner was becoming gently flirtatious. Here, I thought with some small surprise, was a man used to his own kind of success with women. Much later I was to recognize this technique when I saw him turn it on for others. It crossed my mind that blue eyes such as these often denote a person of enormous courage, great self-will, and a considerable interest in the opposite sex.

Controlling my wandering thoughts, I heard Lowry telling me how much it disturbed him when the art critics habitually described him as a 'primitive' painter. He had, he said, undergone many years of academic art training, hence he was particularly interested in my observation of the texture he had achieved in some of his oils. Nor did he care, he went on, for the figures peopling his mill scenes to be called 'matchstick' figures. 'I paint them that way because that's how I see them in my mind's eye . . . always moving. But look, they've got weight. Take that fellow – his front leg is maybe no more than one stroke of paint, but he's got all the weight of his body on it. And you know that's only achieved by years in the life class.'

I looked – it was as he said.

Lowry's attention was suddenly focused on the door, as he murmured, 'Ah! Now I wonder who this is? He looks rather an important gentleman.'

'That's only my husband!' I disillusioned him, as Micky smilingly crossed the hall towards us. He is of stout build which he likes to maintain is due in some measure to large bones, rather than only to a surplus of flesh. He has a happy, humorous disposition, but perhaps his stalwart figure conveys a misleading air of importance. When the painter Anne Redpath was introduced to him at an Edinburgh Festival she exclaimed, 'Oh, when I saw you at the reception last evening I imagined you were some frightfully imporant impresario!'

On the way home from Harrogate, as we consumed fish and chips in the car in the company of the art critic who had introduced me to Lowry, the critic suggested that, as I had apparently got on so well with 'L.S.', as he referred to him, it might be a thought to write and ask him for an exhibition in our own gallery. However, my husband did not entirely share my admiration of Lowry's work, and I never cared to oppose his judgement. Eighteen months were to elapse before we met the painter again.

At the age of twenty-one I had been a professional actress for five years. I was impatient, despite the fact that I had been playing juvenile leads when most girls of my age were still at school. On impulse I bought a fine art shop in my home town of Newcastle-upon-Tyne, deciding to make a lot of money which would enable me to open my own repertory company. I could then thumb my overlarge nose at all producers in search of baby dolls, who reminded me upon occasion that I would really come into my own as an actress when I reached middle age. Middle age seemed a lifetime away.

During the war I married one of my customers. He was a naval officer passing through Newcastle on his way home to Chatham. He was set to work upon some secret weapon, about which, for years, I naturally knew nothing. Micky (his name is really Ronald, but as Millers are known as Dusty, so Marshall is known as Micky) was unconventional and, although apparently sometimes at odds with his immediate superiors, at the age of twenty-four he became a staff officer in South Africa and then with the Pacific fleet. His war ended at the Admiralty. Afterwards he became a potter and we went to live in the Cotswolds. We left another ex-naval officer friend of Micky's in charge of the art shop. Eventually this good friend left us to start up on his own, and rather than suffer the anxieties of remote control we returned to live in the north-east.

I had not seen fit to change the old-established trading name of the business – Bernard Stone, the name of the original owner – so when in 1958 my husband decided he wanted to open an art gallery next to the shop, it naturally became the Stone Gallery.

He and I were in agreement that the British public has an instinctive sense of discrimination – whatever market researchers would have us believe to the contrary. My husband had faith in an area which had, after all, pioneered the way from sail to steam and developed the basic industries upon which Tyneside, and indeed the country as a whole, had built its greatness. But, after the hardships of the twenties and the Great Depression, it was thought by some that the north-east had become tired of struggling; that now it was being held back by outdated social, cultural, and commercial values. Education was the nation's religion; throughout Europe and the less tired parts of Britain the 'old order' was changing. If the north-east were to survive, it must change too. One cannot separate the living arts from life, or ignore the pulse of social evolution. With this in mind Micky decided to adopt a policy of internationalism in the running of the gallery. We hoped to contribute to and work for a society capable of facing the challenges of the future, and this determined Stone Gallery policy for the next seven years.

There were powerful forces in opposition to Micky's aims. Regionalism had become a political catch-phrase, and the most prominent local politician was Mr Newcastle himself, T. Dan Smith. As PRO for the Labour Party, Leader of Newcastle City Council, first Chairman of the North-Eastern Economic Development Council and a constant visitor to 10 Downing Street during the Wilson government, he wielded great power, not only at local, but at national, level. He was also the subject of countless TV films, newspaper articles, the founder of the prototype Regional Arts Association (which became part of his 'empire'), associate of John Poulson, and much later a guest in HM prisons.

In June 1958 our first exhibition was one of 'Modern British Painters'; it seemed a logical first step. In the 1950s British painters were rapidly establishing themselves in both Europe and the United States. Many of these painters readily cooperated: we showed new works by Graham Sutherland, Peter Lanyon, William Gear, John Piper and others. Local reaction was mixed: there was the expected opposition from painters not included – Victor Pasmore was Master of Painting at Newcastle University, but he was busy cooperating with Dan Smith on designs for the new town of Peterlee (whose houses today present such a desperate problem). There were mutterings from the regionalists, and from local amateur painters. As we widened our net in future shows to include artists from all over the world – many of whom had never previously exhibited in Britain – these mutterings became quite noisy. We ignored them and made many enemies. Micky made more enemies through his frequent television appearances on the local channels. A controversial character makes good telly but poor public relations. With hindsight we should have been much cleverer, but neither Micky nor I was adept at compromise. We met the challenge by becoming more adventurous.

At first it was difficult to persuade the national press to send art critics to review exhibitions in a place inadvertently referred to by one editor as 'Newmarket'. But, eventually, the quality of the exhibitions could no longer be overlooked; *The Times* covered eighteen consecutive shows – I believe a record for a private gallery. People visited the gallery from all over the country. One day it might be Philip James, then Director of Art for the Arts Council, or its Secretary General, Sir William Emrys Williams – a jovial gentleman. The fascinating Sir Philip Hendy, Director of the National Gallery; the courteous Sir Trenchard Cox, Director of the Victoria and Albert Museum; Benedict Nicolson, son of Sir Harold Nicolson and Vita Sackville-West; the forthright actress Dora Bryan; Irene Worth and Sir John Gielgud; the charming Jo Grimond; the delightful Jon Pertwee; the awkward Clement Freud and ex-miners' leader Lord Lawson were also among our visitors. There was even a party of East German miners, who owing to visa trouble were too late to attend the Bedlington miners' gala, and came to the gallery instead.

The reviews often included photographs, of course, and the *Guardian* gave us six half-pages on six consecutive shows. (This was Lowry's home newspaper – and it was these particular articles which I suppose later brought him to us.)

By 1960, the Stone Gallery was referred to in the House of Commons during a debate calling for the government to appoint a Royal Commission to inquire into the fine arts. Dame Irene Ward paid a special tribute to the gallery and stated that the most appreciative visitors to it were miners and industrial workers from Durham and Northumberland. We knew nothing of this until it was reported in the press; we were not friends of Dame Irene, but applauded at the time her plea that only the best in art was good enough for the provinces, and that the provinces were not satisfied with the Arts Council.

The late Nevile Wallis wrote in the *Observer*:

> A centre of activity which I have visited outside London is the Stone Gallery in Newcastle . . . it is remarkable. When Ronald and Phyllis Marshall opened it with greater missionary fervour than expectations in June 1958, the level of interest in painting in the North-East was confined to Birket Foster and Russell Flint. A standard had to be set. It seemed essential to show significant living art that could be seen in London or foreign capitals so that the Tyneside public could form its first-hand judgements. The latest exhibition . . . is no mandarin's choice for fashion's sake . . . this gallery does more than provide for its owners an unprofitable living. It offers an expanding life.

A typical review from *The Times* stated:

> American and European works, representative of most contemporary styles and techniques, are placed side by side, their diverse imagery strangely in harmony . . . the emphasis here is placed on non-figurative work . . . Louise Nevelson, Vasarely, Jaag Wagemaker – who set the standards of craftsmanship, visual inventiveness, and joy in the materials handled that characterize all the works on show.

The *Guardian* critic wrote:

> . . . the enterprising directors of the Stone Gallery have at last gained a precarious footing on the international scene . . . they have mounted a show that would be eagerly received in London, Paris, or New York.

Two exhibitions at the gallery in one year were compared more than favourably with two on current themes at the Tate Gallery, and in its first annual report, the North Eastern Association for the Arts (today Northern Arts) stated that the Stone Gallery had caused a renaissance of the visual arts in the north-east.

Our exhibitions were by no means all non-figurative or cerebral, but it was against this background that my husband considered that Lowry's popular work did not fit in with his scheme of things. Lowry's industrial scenes were very familiar to the public; they were evocative of the nineteenth century rather than the twentieth – and my husband's undoubted aim during the first seven years of the Stone Gallery was to help prepare the north-east for the twenty-first century. A tall order, which was to fail.

Owing to city centre redevelopment in Newcastle-upon-Tyne, we had to move our gallery four years after its opening from its original site between Woolworth's and Fenwick's to St Mary's Place, a nineteenth-century terrace designed by John Dobson; this was higher up the town, nearer to the university and new civic centre, and directly facing an attractive green surrounding St Thomas's Church.

This house (which later Lowry delighted in referring to as Number 10) had been unoccupied for five years and was in a derelict condition, with pigeons flying happily in and out through the roof, until we renovated and converted it into an art gallery, with the help of a grant from the Gulbenkian Foundation. Directly behind this building, across a narrow lane – with the back of one facing the back of the other – we had a second fine art shop.

The day arrived when, with enthusiasm, Micky and I were about to start hanging some of the many works of art in the new gallery for the first time. A young sales assistant from the adjacent shop approached through the back entrance, to ask, 'Can you see a Mr Lowry?'

'Oh no, Thelma,' I replied a little impatiently. 'I told you all – I'm much too busy today to see any sales reps. Who on earth is it? Just a minute – a Mr Lowry, did you say?'

'Yes,' she answered, turning to leave.

'Does he paint by any chance?'

'Yes, I think he's the chap who did those things we had at school – town scenes with lots of little figures.'

'Oh heavens! He must have gone to the shop by mistake, I suppose. You'd better bring him over.'

'What a nuisance!' Micky exploded. 'Still, he won't stay long, I shouldn't imagine.' (How could he have known that Lowry was to stay on and off for fourteen years?)

A few moments later Thelma returned, ushering through the back entrance of the Stone Gallery the tall, rain-coated figure, wearing a battered trilby, walking-stick tucked through one arm, blue eyes now only questioning and shy – L. S. Lowry.

Laurence Stephen Lowry was born in Manchester on 1 November 1887, the only child of Robert and Elizabeth Lowry. So long as his parents lived, Lowry lived with them. His father, an estate agent, died in 1932, leaving widow and son comfortably off. Hence it was never necessary for Lowry to work at anything but his art – which for long years met with no success. Often he considered giving up painting, but his mother encouraged him to continue by telling him that one never knew, some time someone might like his work.

In 1938 she was proved right, when A. J. McNeil Reid, a director of London's Lefevre Gallery, saw some of Lowry's paintings for the first time, at a London picture framer's. Mr Reid immediately offered Lowry his first one-man exhibition in London, which took place in 1939, and thereafter the painter exhibited his work at the Lefevre Gallery on thirteen occasions.

In 1941 Salford's City Museum and Art Galley gave the artist an exhibition, and two years later he had another at Liverpool's Bluecoat Chambers. In 1945 Lowry was made an honorary MA by the University of Manchester, and three years later he was elected a member of the London Group.

Also in 1948, nine years after his mother's death, he moved from Pendlebury, Salford, to The Elms, Stalybridge Road, Mottram-in-Longdendale, Cheshire. By now Lowry was represented in the Tate Gallery, and later in the collection of the Museum of Modern Art, New York. He was made an Associate of the Royal Academy in 1955. In 1959 he had a Retrospective Exhibition at the City Art Gallery, Manchester and, six years after it had first honoured him, Manchester University gave him an honorary LL.D. The year we met him for the second time, he was elected a Royal Academician, and he was now extremely well known as a painter. His work first came to the notice of a wider public when, towards the end of the war, and from then on, it was reproduced by various print publishers. These coloured reproductions became bestsellers, both for homes and for schools.

The public's attention was also drawn to Lowry when John Read (a son of Sir Herbert Read, art critic and writer) made a film about the Manchester painter for the BBC in 1956. This film set Lowry on his way to fame.

Now it was early afternoon on 3 May 1962 as I took the artist's finely boned hand in mine to greet him. I little knew that this was the beginning of a friendship which would only end as we stood beside his bed watching him die fourteen years later.

Micky had just placed a Henry Moore sculpture on its stand before Lowry walked in. 'So you like Moore, do you?' Lowry asked after a few minutes. From the tone of his voice we realized that he did not. So I went on the attack, reminding Lowry that about a year previously Micky had written to him, at the particular request of a client who wished to acquire one of his paintings, but he had merely referred us to his London gallery. The matter had been left there, as one could not buy at his gallery's asking price to sell again.

'So yes, you'll see some Henry Moore here,' I said. 'Because he supplies us direct. You'll see Picasso, Klee, Hepworth, Fontana, Vasarely – you'll see just about the lot! But alas, nothing of your own, of course.'

'Well,' countered Lowry, 'you've got to understand, I don't paint so much now. Nothing, after all, like I used to. I'm seventy-four.'

'Are you really? You don't look it,' I laughed, and indeed he did not. He talked on for a while, until I said, 'You know, the paintings of yours I seldom see, but prefer to any others, are those single figures – very black on white. I like them much better than your mill scenes.'

He turned abruptly, and looking me full in the face exclaimed in amazement, 'You don't!'

'Yes, Yvonne Mitchell has two tiny ones. They're wonderful.' I did not know it then, but I suppose that, after that one statement, Lowry was bound to us for the rest of his days.

'Good heavens,' I heard him saying, 'well, that makes three of us. Me, of course – or I wouldn't be painting them – Mr Bloom, and now you. Oh, I simply can't believe it! No one likes those, you know. London won't show them. Personally, I think they're my best. I'm *saying* more in those than I've ever said in the mill scenes. But London's got used to selling the mill scenes, so that's all it wants – but I'm not doing them now. I like doing what I call m'single figures . . . everyone seems to think they're sordid – well and so they are I suppose – very sordid.'

'They're very dramatic – we'd show them,' I replied, feeling carried away by Lowry's obvious pleasure and surprise.

But he answered me quickly, 'Oh no, I've nothing at all. I haven't any finished work. Of course you could have a talk with Mr Bloom.'

I had no idea to whom he was referring and did not pursue the matter.

There was no picture or sculpture in the gallery that Lowry did not look at, examine and discuss. He went through all the framed canvases stacked against the walls in readiness for hanging, drawing out a work here and there which pleased or interested him, or which he wanted to look at from a distance.

On the gallery's third floor he eventually found a Rowlandson watercolour. I cannot imagine how it came to be there, but at some time it must have taken Micky's fancy. Lowry asked if he might take it downstairs and continued to admire it at intervals over tea in the office.

Hours went by. Inwardly I began to despair, wondering when on earth he was going to take his departure. I was unprepared for his stamina. Eventually, business finished in the city, I heard Simon make his entrance through the back and give vent to a surprised and hefty shout. 'Bloody hell! A fat lot of work you two have got done – what *have* you been up to?'

I looked hesitantly at the conventional old boy, sitting comfortably with a cold cup of tea at his side, and was rather relieved to see his eyes twinkle when our son entered the room.

'I'm afraid you must blame me, sir!' said Lowry.

Simon was just eighteen, tall, of a happy disposition like his father; and we delighted in his recent choice to join us in our working world. Perhaps because he was only about twenty years younger than his father, they behaved more like equable brothers than father and son. Whatever the reason for it, the three of us managed to have a lot of fun together.

Time was passing, and still Lowry sat on. Eventually I found myself explaining that our home was fifty-five miles south of Newcastle – I could not invite him back for dinner, but would he care to eat with us at the restaurant just around the corner? It was a far from inspiring meal. Lowry, it transpired, was a teetotaller, which was unconducive to an outstandingly merry evening. Out of courtesy we too refrained from anything stronger than orange squash. The wine waiter eyed us with some surprise. Perhaps I should add that this was the only occasion we chose to suffer.

I still recall the painter's choice of tomato soup followed by plaice and mashed potatoes, then a banana with a pint of cream poured over it. Later he was to confess that he didn't feel he knew us well enough to demand his usual chips. But it was not to be long before the restaurant unfailingly offered him 'french fried', which unfailingly amused Lowry, who would murmur, 'Ah, yes now, let me see – shall I have chips or french fried? So different – which d'you think are the best, Mr Marshall?

But that first evening he was on his best behaviour. He relaxed with us little more than we did with him. It was heavy going.

However, he dropped his guard for a while when he learned that Simon was in charge of reproductions. On being told that colour reproductions of his paintings hung in virtually every school throughout the north-east, he inquired whether Simon had noticed anything odd about one called *Church Steps*, featuring a dog in the forefront? This particular dog was a focal point of the composition. Neither Simon nor we had ever been aware of anything odd about it.

'You've never noticed that the dog has five legs?' asked Lowry. We didn't believe it. 'Well, it's true enough – and, d'you know, I looked at that painting to see that it was as perfect as I could make it before it went to the publishers – and not until years later, looking at it in the window of a shop, and then only when a friend said, "Here, what have you been up to?" did I see it. Look – like this.' Taking the cover from an empty cigarette packet lying on the table, Lowry opened it out, drew a dog with five legs and another small sitting one, signed and dated the masterpiece, and with a laugh handed it to Simon with, 'There, keep that – and don't tell anyone until I'm dead!'

Simon could not believe it. He had sold many reproductions of that particular painting. He excused himself, he had his keys, he was off to the shop round the corner, he must see for himself – there was a print in stock. He returned to ask, 'How could we never have noticed?'

'Ah, you didn't notice,' replied Lowry very seriously, 'because I got the balance right. Four legs would have unbalanced the whole painting. Anyway, why shouldn't a dog have five legs?'

It was late when we dropped him off at the Seaburn Hotel. Seaburn is south of the river Tyne, but nevertheless half an hour off our normal route home. No such inconvenience to ourselves ever meant anything to Lowry. This we had yet to discover.

On the afternoon of 15 June, about five weeks later, the painter landed in to see us a second time. The gallery looked very different from the occasion of his first visit. He nodded appreciation as he went from room to room. He much admired the one-man exhibition of Sir William MacTaggart, PRSA.

'My word – you've sold him out,' he murmured. Again tea was taken in the office, again Lowry lingered on, and again we took him to the restaurant around the corner.

'You know,' I heard him saying to Micky, 'I've been thinking about it, and I can't get it out of my mind – I'd better have that Rowlandson.' During the afternoon he had inquired whether we still had it; it was brought to the office, and during tea his eyes constantly flickered towards it. 'I'll put a proposition to you,' he now addressed me, 'I'll exchange the Rowlandson for one of mine – the kind you like. I'll bring it with me next time I'm over.'

Smiling, I replied, 'Fair enough.'

Five days later he was back. Simon and I were spending a welcome day at home; we were busily gardening when I heard the phone ringing. Micky informed me that Lowry had just arrived at the gallery, had brought his painting but refused to open it until I got there. I do not drive: this meant Simon had to take me to Newcastle. Upon our arrival, Lowry promptly handed me a very small brown paper parcel with, 'There. One of my best!'

Opening the tiny unframed oil, I hid my disappointment. I felt it was too studied – it lacked something of the artist's usual freedom of execution. But he appeared delighted with it, recounting the story behind the composition. He felt he had got just what he wanted in the painting. Alas – I hadn't got what I wanted, but I went off to fetch the Rowlandson.

As we stood around the reception area of the gallery nattering, there arrived a young industrialist; a slight, fair-haired boy, highly strung, and a very enthusiastic collector of modern British paintings. After being introduced to Lowry, whose work was insufficiently avant-garde to interest him, the young man moved away to study a painting of William Johnstone's, whose work he admired; he went on to sing the praises of an Alan Davie, eventually to turn to us with a disparaging comment about a Henry Mundy. He fancied this was not up to the standard of two he had in his collection . . . it was a poor work.

Lowry broke in with, 'Nonsense! There's no such thing as a poor painting,' and indeed went further. 'There's no such thing as a bad painting.' With peals of mirth, the young man fell on him, but Lowry got into his stride, thinking up his arguments as he went along, and finishing with, 'I'll give you five pounds if you can find me a bad painting!'

Promptly we joined in the game, urging Micky to produce the key to a certain store where there were a few works by aspiring painters. Returning triumphantly in a short while with an appalling oil, our young client exclaimed, 'There! You can't tell me there's anything good about that one!' But Lowry could. Vividly, I see him in my mind's eye propping it up on a window seat before he took it verbally to pieces to put it together again; before long we might well have been convinced that the awful work was a masterpiece.

We tried a few more but, needless to say, no one got Lowry's five pounds.

One might put it down to his Irish ancestry but, whatever the explanation for it, Lowry could, if he chose, argue the hind legs off a donkey – and a donkey Lowry had decided this young collector was, when he found himself and his work of no interest.

The restaurant to which we were so frequently to take Lowry was a splendid old establishment called Tilley's. The third time we entertained him there we sat at what came to be looked upon as 'Lowry's table', a major enjoyment of his later years. Large and circular, it had around one side a very comfortably upholstered golden beige banquette upon which the artist always sat. Having a wall behind him, he could never feel any kind of draught – for nothing put him out more. Two others might also sit on the banquette, while the remainder of the party would be in comfortable armchairs. That evening Lowry and I sat together, with Micky in a chair facing us. Lowry's loosening-up with us dated from this time.

The manager of the restaurant was a certain Mr Redman – in Lowry's eyes something of a Dickensian character. From the moment we introduced them, they instantly recognized each other as fellow Mancunians. Mr Redman promptly became a great favourite with our friend, as indeed he deserved to be, for nothing was ever too much trouble in that establishment, and it must be admitted that Lowry could cause trouble. Indeed, he thrived on making trouble, and the worst of it was that the better one got to know him the more awkward he became about his food; as the years passed, he went through the most extraordinary likes and dislikes, passions and hates.

At that time he was favouring either fish or cutlets and, if he chose the latter, then they must be dry, frizzled and without garnish, and very unappetizing they appeared. Heaven help the waiter who inadvertently put a spot of cress, tomato or vegetable other than chips on Lowry's plate, for he would often promptly push the whole lot off on to the table. Very occasionally he would suffer a few peas or a couple of mushrooms.

On the evening in question Mr Redman saw to it that the restaurant really did its stuff in honour of a fellow-Mancunian, and Lowry's cutlets arrived decorated with nice little paper frills around the bone. He whipped these off and flicked them across the room, where one landed in an astonished lady's soup. Suppressing his own surprise at his remarkably good aim, and to cover his amusement, Lowry started an earnest discussion with his host, and the lady never knew whence the foreign object came.

The artist had one particularly intense dislike – mint sauce. He was unable even to tolerate the smell of it. As I learned that evening if any unsuspecting fellow diner dared to partake of mint sauce, Lowry would pull faces of disgust, glower, and demand that the sauceboat be taken from the table. But red-currant jelly – that was a different matter altogether; it went down with his cutlets by the dishful.

It was now we heard for the first time and at length what we were to hear from Lowry on countless occasions over the years to come; he felt that *everyone*, without exception, wanted something from him for nothing. And his manner of telling us this made us feel extremely uncomfortable. It was almost an accusation. Personally, we wanted nothing from him; given his choice Micky would have been happily back at home, while I would have chosen not to have left my home all that day. We live in a small and ancient castle in Teesdale; every moment spent there is relaxing, and an enormously pleasurable contrast from city business.

Nevertheless, we did own an art gallery, and Lowry was a well-known painter. But after he told us on his first visit that he had no work available, we had looked for nothing from him. Then and in the years to come we leaned over backwards to prove that we were the exception – we wanted nothing from him. As a consequence, we continued to pay for every meal we ever ate together, and we bore every expense, including his hotel bill, on the occasions we stayed away together. No moment in our company cost Lowry so much as a cent.

A waitress who now brought something to the table had apparently been told by Mr Redman who the elderly man with us was and she smilingly informed him that her name was also 'Lowry'.

The painter glowered and said, 'But I dare say you spell yours with an e – e-r-y.' She told him that was so.

'Well, I don't have an e in mine – mine's L-o-w-r-y.' And that was that. The girl moved out of earshot. 'You know,' said Lowry, 'I've had three different lots of people claim relationship with me. I've looked into it each time – but I only have one living relative, my cousin May. I had three cousins, all daughters of my mother's only sister, but there's only May left now; a silly old fool she is too. Lost most of her money.' I murmured something sympathetic, to be blasted in no uncertain manner. 'Well, Mrs Marshall, I haven't any sympathy for her. She wouldn't take advice. Her second husband left her pretty well off. It was an estate in Rhodesia; when he died she was sure she could go out there and see to things herself. But I told her, and her solicitor told her, to get a good man out there to act for her. But, oh no, she knew better. Out she went, saw to it all herself, and was diddled. I go and stay with her sometimes. She lives near Burford.' His cousin May had a most remarkable cat. 'I stay with her because of her cat. . . . Charles she calls it. It was wild, and she used to put food out for it near the back door, and then one day when she was busy in the kitchen she felt something rubbing round her legs, and there was this wild cat. Remarkable – it became quite tame, but only with May. And there it will lie on a cushion as good as gold, until it wakens up, when if I'm there it'll give me a look, and I shout, "May – get hold of that cat, it's going to attack me," and sure enough, you know, it would; but she can do anything with it. My word I'm very fond of Charles – he certainly doesn't like me though,' Lowry chuckled at the picture in his mind's eye.

After a while he went back to his original train of thought, and he came at last to the third claimant. Suddenly there was an undercurrent of excitement in his voice which I had not previously noticed.

About four years ago, he had received a letter from a Mrs Martha Lowry. Taking out a bulging notecase he added, 'Look, I still carry it.' He waved a tatty piece of paper and promptly put it away again. He went on to tell us that this Mrs Lowry had left her husband, and could no longer afford to keep her fourteen-year-old daughter at private school. She fancied they might well be related, and could Mr Lowry see his way to doing something to help them? Incidentally, her daughter was extremely fond of, and good at, art. Her mother very much wanted her to remain at school.

Lowry maintained that he had looked into the question of any relationship. He had a young friend called Ann, who took him to Cheltenham to visit a distant relative of his mother's – an aged man of about ninety and a retired solicitor. Having written in advance the reason for calling upon him, Lowry rang the old gentleman's door-bell, and was greeted with the words, 'No, oh no, they're no relation – just trying it on.' Lowry said that he and Ann stayed three days in Cheltenham and thoroughly enjoyed their time there.

Keeping the woman's letter in his pocket book – 'just like it is now' – he did nothing about replying until nine months later when, finding himself by accident in Heywood, about nine miles out of Manchester, he called at the address on the spur of the moment and simply out of curiosity, he said. The daughter was at home playing with a friend. She said that her mother would not be back from work until about six o'clock. Lowry said he would return to see her then. At the end of the road, just as he was wondering how to get back into the centre of Manchester in time for tea at his favourite café, a car pulled up beside him, and a friend inquired what on earth he was doing there. Lowry explained, and the friend gave him a lift into the city; after partaking of his favourite hot-buttered potato scones, he returned to call upon Mrs Martha Lowry.

He said that he did not care for the woman a great deal. She talked incessantly, and he was not surprised that the marriage had broken up. Her husband had been a cotton spinner and she had been a weaver. She was an ambitious lady, wanting for her daughter all the things she had never had. Her world revolved round her daughter, Carol Ann, who was born on 24 April 1944.

Lowry was so impressed with the child he felt he could at least see her through the rest of her schooling. And that, he sighed with a sort of relish, was how he had come to meet Carol Ann Lowry.

The strange underlying excitement was still in his voice – here was an emotion he was incapable of controlling. This was something I did not fully comprehend, or was unable to reconcile with the little I knew of the painter at that time. I sensed the reality of the emotion, but was it the outcome of a natural or an unnatural feeling for a young girl? I asked him more, and he was delighted to continue. He had been as good as his word and seen the child through school and on to Hornsey College of Art, but after a year she had been considered unsuitable – he supposed she had not worked hard enough. At any rate she had to leave. He admitted his great disappointment. A friend who had assisted him in getting Carol Ann to Hornsey told him that he was spoiling the girl and giving her far too much money. Lowry had taken his friend's advice, leaving her to find her own way in life, and for the past year Carol Ann had been earning her living as a chambermaid in a hotel. At the moment she had a ginger-haired boyfriend for whom neither he nor Mrs Lowry cared. Carol had knitted the boy a sweater and her mother was of the opinion that that was going too far altogether and that she would put an end to it. If I recall correctly, the boy's name was Archie – but there he goes out of the story.

Lowry still considered 'the child' had great talent as a painter. 'Oh, enormous talent, Mr Marshall.' It was years later that he had to admit his mistake on that score. But that evening over dinner Lowry became ever more enthusiastic about Carol Ann's extraordinary talent. He might have been staking a claim for an exhibition for her there and then. As we asked one or two more questions, suddenly Lowry's enthusiasm took off anew, and he decided that he would take her up again. He later did so and got her into Swansea College of Art, where she obtained a teaching diploma.

But that evening, once on the subject of Carol Ann, there was no getting him off it. 'She has a shocking temper, I can tell you. I once thought I would take her to see some friends of mine, and all the way there in the car she sat never speaking a word – just like a little pot-pig!'

'A little what?' I asked him, startled.

'A little pot-pig. Oh, you've no idea how awkward she can be. Even the taxidriver winked at me, saying, "You've got a right one there." Fortunately the friends were not at home; on the journey back she changed completely, chatting away; you'd have thought butter wouldn't melt in her mouth. Since then I've never let her meet any of my friends. But I shall never forget the first time I took her to London – she'd be about fourteen, I think. After the first night she said, "Shall we go home?" I said, "Yes, if you like," so as she got into the train and I remained on the platform, she said, "But you're coming too?" And I told her I certainly was not. "Well, what shall I tell mother?" she asked, and I told her she could tell her what she damned well pleased. Oh yes – Carol Ann can be very awkward.'

Micky, with a twinkle in his eye, remarked upon the mother's not objecting to her fourteen-year-old daughter going off to London to stay with an elderly painter. Lowry said no, why on earth should she? Micky reminded him that artists do not always have the best of reputations.

In the early days of our friendship Lowry always arrived unannounced in the gallery. Later, when he considered his position in our family life was assured, he would make very precise arrangements in advance. Writing from The Elms, 25 March 1966, 'It is very good of you to come for me next Thursday; it would be very nice – be what you might call a day off for me. I shall expect you about 1.00 on the 31st – and you can tell me all the news on the way back. I will stay at Seaburn for at least a month, but probably longer.'

On 4 March 1967, 'If I hear nothing to the contrary I will be coming this Wednesday and due to arrive Newcastle 3.35 – The Turks Head . . . you've booked I hope for I haven't. I take it you have.'

And again from the Elms on 13 December 1967, 'Thank you very much for fixing up the Seaburn. Looking forward to hearing your news on Saturday. I have none myself – letters and callers, oh my God nothing but letters and callers – oh this weather is misty and nasty. This is a terrible place.'

After his telephone was installed he invariably rang up instead of writing.

When we had not seen him for a little while, after greetings were over, we now never omitted to ask first after his cousin May, and then after Carol Ann. But there came the day when he decided that he was fed up with his cousin, and he did not think he would be going to stay with her again. Firstly, Charles had died, and oh, he was going to miss Charles (far more, apparently, than he was going to miss his cousin) and then May would send him on errands to Burford, and he disliked being bossed around by her. And she had just committed the final folly by objecting to his friendship with Carol Ann. He then surprised us by announcing that Carol Ann would enjoy meeting us. He had been telling her about the gallery – 'She's very fond of pictures, y'know. Oh yes, all this would interest her enormously. I'll bring her over some time. She'll behave shockingly, I expect.' And he roared with laughter.

It was early afternoon in summer when Lowry brought Carol Ann to the gallery for the first time. Looking back, I was more than a little nervous at the prospect of meeting this girl with the awkward temperament. But I found I had no cause for unease – I have never seen any sign of the difficult girl of Lowry's description. (Many years later she was to write to me, 'I'm very fond of the Gallery in St Mary's Place – seems a part of my growing-up somehow! Fondest Love, Carol.') From the beginning we seemed to get along very well.

My first memory of her is as extremely young and vulnerable, short and slightly dumpy (nowadays she is much slimmer), with a fine, pale complexion of the type which never suntans, a very retroussé nose (hence I supposed the description of 'little pot-pig') and dark straightish hair to her shoulders in a casual style with a fringe across her brow.

Quite shortly after arriving she asked if she might change her shoes, as Mr Lowry had taken her to Atkinson's (Newcastle's exclusive shoe shop), where she had brought some lovely new ones. I showed her to my office in the basement, telling her to make herself at home – there was a mirror and she could tidy herself in peace.

Upstairs again in Micky's office, Lowry clutched me excitedly by the arm, asking, 'Now what do you think of her, eh?' I told him she seemed a very nice girl indeed, 'Ah,' he chuckled, 'she likes you all – I can see that, you'd have known it by now if she didn't.'

Carol Ann returned, and shortly a delightfully amusing friend and client of ours happened to look in. This was Dr Chalmers Burns, head of the music department of Newcastle University. He was a bachelor, well into his fifties but something of an eternal undergraduate and a great collector of paintings by Scottish artists. After introducing Chalmers to Lowry, I left it to the painter to introduce his protégée. 'This is Miss Lowry.' I watched with interest as the old man hestitated for a moment or two, wondering what was coming next 'My er . . . niece.' The die was cast. Carol Ann had become Lowry's 'niece'.

But this was by no means good enough for Dr Chalmers Burns, who prided himself on knowing everything about everybody of note. As soon as the opportunity presented itself, he took me into a corner to whisper overloudly, 'Tilly, Tilly – what's all this about a niece?

The old boy has no brothers or sisters!' Chalmers was a great genealogist, claiming that he himself was about fiftieth in line to the throne. He was undoubtedly a great-great-nephew of William Dyce, the highly valued nineteenth-century painter, and possessed a charming portrait of his grandmother by this ancestor.

In an effort to subdue his excitement – for no one loved a little gossip more dearly than he – I said, 'Do shut up, Chalmers, of course she's not really his niece – but her name is Lowry.'

'Spelt the same?'

'Yes.'

'How very odd, I never expected it of him!'

'Expected what of him?'

'Never mind – you're too young.' All agog, Dr Burns made a very hasty departure, only to return with a number of his students, each of whom he delighted in introducing to 'Mr Lowry's niece'. This interlude created a welcome diversion, helping to break the ice for, by the time Chalmers had shepherded his flock back to the university, we might have known Carol Ann for years. Carol Ann had been getting along remarkably well with one and all and Lowry was enjoying himself hugely in consequence.

In those days the gallery was much blessed by the services of a wonderful housekeeper called Ella Phillips, who kept both it and, incidentally, us in order. Often during the business day it was necessary to entertain visiting scholars and critics, as well as potential clients. Ella would provide luncheon or tea, and see throughout the day to endless cups of coffee. We left every detail of entertaining to her, and over the years she spoiled Lowry to an incredible degree – nothing was ever too much trouble for her. A splendid cook, she arranged her menus, whenever possible, to suit the company. Very rapidly she became familiar with Lowry's likes and dislikes; when he was with us she always kept clear of steaks and salads, as he ate neither. She was aware that he enjoyed chicken and had a passion for bread sauce; he often declared that he could make a meal of that alone, and Ella was often threatening to take him at his word. Knowing that I had a partiality for it also, he loved his little joke: 'You don't care for it, do you, Mrs Marshall? So I'd better just finish it up.'

He also revelled in hot puddings, and goodness knows how many steamed 'puds' Ella turned up for him; or for a change it would be rice pudding, another of his favourites. But when he arrived unexpectedly Ella would rush out for ice cream and quickly make a fruit salad. One shudders to think how many gallons of cream Lowry must have consumed over the years. In winter he preferred strawberries – in midsummer hot pudding.

He was not the cleanest of eaters, to put it mildly, and during a few weeks' visit his suit would become horribly food-spotted, if it wasn't already in a dreadful state when he arrived. If Carol Ann was with him he tended to make a little more effort, but as a rule he did not care tuppence for his appearance. Sometimes Ella would wrest his jacket from him with, 'Come along now, sir, this won't do. I'll have to press and brush this up a bit.'

And Lowry would sigh, 'I suppose you'd say I could do with a new suit, but I'm getting near the end you know – yes, very near the end. It's not worth it, I'm afraid.'

'Don't be daft,' Ella would answer. 'You want to get yourself to your tailor's.'

'Oh, do I madam – eh?' he would counter. 'And have you any idea how much a new suit costs?'

Once she said, 'Yes, I know only too well, our Harry paid twelve pounds at Burton's for one the other day.' When she went out of the room, Lowry smiled ironically, 'Our Harry's a lucky fellow, I wish I could get one for twelve pounds. D'you know my last new suit cost me a drawing? And I'm sure the fellow didn't appreciate it – but he'd said he wanted one . . . everyone wants something from me.'

So, on that first afternoon of Carol Ann's appearance in the gallery, Ella met her as she met most people and, as I went out to the kitchen to suggest that we might have tea as soon as she pleased, Ella murmured with reference to the new shoes, which had been proudly displayed, 'She's a very lucky girl.' Ella had worked for her living for most of her life since she went into service at fourteen. Now she had three grown-up children and an invalid husband.

As the years passed, Carol Ann would always go and have a word with Ella, delighting in showing off her latest acquisition of shoes, boots, sheepskin jacket, or whatever. And Ella would murmur to me, 'What a very lucky girl. I wish I had an Uncle Laurie. Somewhere I seem to have missed the boat.'

2

There have been many fine presidents of the Royal Scottish Academy, but none in recent years has made such a contribution to Scottish painting as Sir William MacTaggart. His friend Sir Compton Mackenzie wrote of him in one of our catalogues, 'He is such a modest man that many people do not realise how much he has done. I love the man, and I have no doubt whatever that the City of Newcastle, which has already recognised his great gifts, will accord him further recognition now.' Long before the RSA seriously considered including non-figurative works, Willy accepted and encouraged the younger generation of painters. Like Sir Compton, we loved Willy – and we loved his wife. Fanny MacTaggart was the daughter of a great Norwegian general, and she met her husband when she came to organise the first Munch exhibition in Britain. She had the social graces to perfection, she never erred in making an introduction, she could cope with the most unpronounceable names, and her know-how gave her a cosmopolitan approach, not only to the arts, but the art of living. Charmingly kind, she was kinder to no one more than to Simon, who had known her since he was fifteen. I would state unhesitatingly that these two friends are the greatest gentleman and the greatest lady it has been my pleasure to know. I use old-fashioned terms – but no other term will do.

We had become MacTaggart's English agents in 1959. In 1962 Sir Compton was right, Newcastle did indeed recognize Willy MacTaggart's great gifts. *The Times* in a long review of his second one-man show with us wrote : 'rarely does an exhibition seem to have been timed better to coincide with the richest output of a mature artist.' Every picture sold.

Scotland did not at that time have many collectors of contemporary art. In 1962 the Sonja Henie–Niels Onstad Collection was the

Edinburgh Festival Exhibition, and the MacTaggarts asked Micky and me to attend the private view, as they felt we had the sort of knowledge necessary to talk about their paintings with Sonja Henie and her husband.

At the Caledonian Hotel in Edinburgh (where we always stayed, having an affection for it since Micky had stayed there while Simon was born around the corner) a hasty telephone call requested us to take the MacTaggarts' place at the opening festival concert at the Usher Hall. Disaster struck when we discovered I had left behind the back band for Micky's white waistcoat. A kindly floor waiter produced a delicate-looking piece of laundry string and we set off, I in fear and trembling lest Micky took too deep a breath and came apart. The conductor's baton was raised as we entered the Usher Hall – he put it down again while we took our seats. The reception at the RSA later that evening was a memorable one – I always enjoyed these receptions but the works on exhibition that night were 'a magnificent confession of faith in the resources and strength of free invention'.

Like others of our generation, Micky and I remembered Sonja Henie's incomparable skating, and had enjoyed the films she made with Bing Crosby and others. We expected to hear again the sweet little voice, only to find it disconcerting when this most beautiful woman (wearing a wonderful dress covered with more rhinestones than I thought existed and emeralds that Fanny assured me outshone the Queen's) began to talk. Her deep, resonant voice was more akin to northerly gales than glittering snow crystals. But she and her husband, a man of great charm, belied the popular idea that the very rich only collect to amass objects. They knew their pictures, each had a place in their lives, and they would certainly have been poorer mentally without them, just as we, and the many thousands who have enjoyed and will continue to enjoy their collection, would undoubtedly be the poorer for not having seen them.

I thought Sonja Henie a sad lady – I did not know that she was dying of cancer. In a year she was gone.

After meeting two of the world's great collectors we returned to Newcastle, which was not without some rich men and women – but would they ever collect? Certainly in a small way they were beginning to – but they bought only what they liked, of course, and what they understood.

I remember a happy lady of undoubted respectability looking

with a sense of revelation at some Appels, Mathieus and Crippas, before pausing at a piece of sculpture by César – it was a sheet of rusty metal punctured with holes and fixed to a black metal background. 'Oh,' she exclaimed rapturously to my husband, 'that's wonderful! I feel I have experienced that!'

'How interesting,' said Micky with some small surprise, and tactlessly presented her with a catalogue. Upon studying the title of the recently admired work – *Rape* – she fled.

Where, the reader may well ask, did Lowry fit into all this? At times he didn't. He would often say, 'I don't understand modern art,' and left it at that. Micky was putting on eleven exhibitions a year, which entailed a great amount of work. When it came to the days for hanging exhibitions (which he always did himself), he was quite unbearable. Even our dear Ella Phillips, who understood him better than most, would say, 'For God's sake, leave the bloody man alone!'

So when Lowry arrived unexpectedly it fell to Simon to get him out from under our feet, and I would take over Simon's work. Our son enjoyed driving, and until his best friend was killed motor racing he went in for it in a little way himself. He had various sports cars at various times, but became enamoured of TVRs. He could not get Lowry into these, however, so they always used our larger vehicle. They would drive around the derelict parts of Blyth – the coal staithes and the station there were particularly favoured haunts of Lowry – or maybe to the pleasanter Newbiggin-by-the-Sea; or gaze for hours at the docks and shipyards in which our area abounds. They would be back and forth across the ferry at South Shields, and then on to Seaton Delaval Hall – Lowry had a great love affair with this place, designed by Vanbrugh, for whom he had enormous appreciation. Or they would go off for the day to Bamburgh, and on to Holy Island. Only recently when we were there, Simon pointed laughingly to an upturned hulk to exclaim, 'Look – it's still there – Lowry's very public convenience. They should put a plaque on it – he could never wait a moment longer – he always had to stop there!' Sometimes they only got as far as Amble – it had a certain sordidness which appealed to Lowry. They lunched often at the White Swan at Alnwick. He liked the hotel – but never gave the magnificent castle a second glance.

Occasionally they would pick me up in the late afternoon, and we would take Lowry to have tea with my parents. From the first, however, I became aware of a slight lack of courtesy on Lowry's part, until it became obvious that he had no use for elderly people. Old age bored him. He had a continuous obsession with his own death – more so than anyone I have ever met. Whenever Lowry arrived to see us we would inquire immediately, 'Well, and how are you?' until we dreaded putting the question, for the reply seldom varied. Whether we had parted from him only in the small hours of that morning, or had not seen him for a few weeks or months, it was still the same. Thumping himself into his favourite chair in the office he would moan 'I'm dying – my God, I'm dying,' and then expand upon how near to death he was, looking all the while the picture of health.

My father was not far short of ninety when we first took Lowry visiting. He was a retired clergyman, energetic, of youthful appearance. He was not a conventional clergyman. A north-easterner by adoption, he had come to love the area dearly. He had been called to Peter Lee's death bed; he visited the miners' leaders in prison during the 1926 strike, and these men remained his friends. The following year he had been asked to leave the north-east and go to London, but he declined. 'My miners need me,' he announced to his family. He had been a personal friend of Frank Buchman, founder of the Oxford Group (later Moral Rearmament), but when my father took two miners' leaders to meet Buchman, Buchman, on discovering they were Communists, showed them the door, and my father never met him again. Father was not a Communist at any time, but he was a Christian Socialist, and forever interested in what was going on in the world. He had come to love non-figurative painting and his drawing room was hung with some of the more reasonably priced American abstract painters and a couple of Jim Dines, which Lowry viewed with disapproval.

Nor was my mother a conventional clergyman's wife. In her younger days she had been fond of producing amateur dramatics for charity and, during the years we lived in Liverpool, her great assistant in this activity was David Webster – later Sir David, of Covent Garden fame. She was a little 'trendy' in her dress, always full of fun, with an irreligious sense of humour, which, offset by my father's more serious approach to life, as a rule proved rather irresistible. They had a multitude of friends, and were much loved. So I was surprised by Lowry's total boredom with them – they made both him and Carol Ann very welcome.

During Lowry's first visit, as mother was dispensing tea, she unfortunately inquired about his painting. He fell on her like a ton of bricks – and when Lowry turned violent he could be quite terrifying. 'Good God, madam! Whatever age d'you suppose I am? I'm seventy-four. *Painting*! Why should I still be painting?'

'Oh,' laughed mother, 'you're a mere chicken. Why, you're nothing like Tom's age there, or mine. And we've got lots of work in us yet!'

'*Well*! Your husband's was only a one-day-a-week job. I'm a Sunday painter who's painted every day of the week.'

'Oh? Tom's was only a Sunday job, you think? Well, that's all you know. You can take it from me, he was a Sunday preacher who preached every day of the week!' Lowry was not amused. (My father's parish was two counties, not just one church, so he had been a busy man – and indeed he still was). They fell to comparing ages – again Lowry was not amused. And certainly, looking at both men, it was a little difficult to accept that the artist was so much the junior, as he sat there, ungainly and bad tempered, in his food-spotted suit – endlessly complaining of his taxation. For the subect of his painting invariably led to the subject of his income tax.

Many times over the years I was to wonder at Lowry's preoccupation with his own affairs to the apparent exclusion of any compassion for others. When, a long time later, Ella was taken very ill, for instance, Lowry never once inquired after her. It never occurred to him to send her a message of good wishes despite all the kindness she had shown him. Often at his request she had put a stitch in his jacket, sewn the band on round his trilby when it parted company with the hat, done a repair job on his raincoat. Once she even replaced a missing fly-button when the need became desperate, and, having gone to Woolworth's to buy it, she would have remained out of pocket had I not recompensed her; and for all the good meals she made for him over the years she never received the smallest recognition or thanks from him.

How then reconcile his obsession with the down-and-outs, the cripples and the deformed who people his paintings? Was he only a voyeur? Was his sole purpose to make a picture? Or to make money? Easy for him to say, as he so often did, 'There but for the grace of God . . . ' and reap the reward, albeit an insufficient one, as he would complain when pictures he had sold were resold by the owners at a profit to themselves in later years. It is possibly merely a matter of every man to his job. My father had spent a lifetime trying to make other lives more bearable while Lowry, recording the lives of others, made his own more bearable as a consequence.

Of one thing I am certain, however: without the influence my parents had upon our lives, as a family we would not have remained friends with Lowry to the end.

One sunny summer evening Lowry suggested that we might try out Newcastle's latest hotel for dinner, and we were delighted that he would consider a change of scene. In the new Swallow Hotel the restaurant is high up, and has a most magnificent panoramic view over the city. From the large windows can be seen the river Tyne, its various bridges, the shipping along the quayside and, over the breathtaking vista of great buildings, new tower blocks and old churches, Gateshead can be seen on the far side of the river.

As an industrial scene it out-Lowryed Lowry. We thought it would have great appeal for him and that this restaurant was a happy choice. It was also an agreeable surprise to find, in his new role of head waiter, a recently departed waiter from Tilley's who had been accustomed to looking after us there, and whose departure had been regretted by us all. Having been shown to the table with the finest view, Lowry promptly sat himself with his back to it. The head waiter presented us with impressive menus and, as he was more than familiar by the time with Lowry's personal likes and dislikes, he suggested Lowry might care for this and that. But indeed Lowry did not. He decided immediately that he no longer looked favourably upon *any* of the suggested dishes, cutting the poor fellow down to size in no uncertain manner.

As the restaurant began to fill up, a young pianist entered hesitantly and rather clumsily sat himself at the baby grand. I had heard him play before. He was an accomplished pianist. When the first gentle notes floated across the room, Lowry's old head lifted like an animal smelling danger. 'My God! What's that?' he bellowed.

Micky hastened to explain the boy's infirmity – he was blind. He might not only have been blind, but deaf and dumb as well, so far as Lowry was concerned – it made not the slightest difference.

'I'm not going to stand that,' he announced. 'Tell them to turn it down.' Few people had better hearing than Lowry, but my husband might just as well not have spoken.

Micky tried again. He explained that it was not the usual 'canned' music to which our friend objected so frequently, and to which he was subjected at the Seaburn Hotel, where he claimed he had to suffer it at breakfast.

'I don't care what it is or isn't, it's ludicrous. *Ludicrous*! Let's move our table.' Obviously we had trouble on our hands; heads were turning, and the head waiter moved swiftly in our direction to find out what it might be. A move would avail us nothing – the restaurant was fitted with a loudspeaker in every corner.

Starting his dinner, Lowry said his melon wasn't ripe. Nevertheless he managed to dribble the juice down his jacket. He continued to look thunderous, refused to speak, and his face was red with rage. 'Can't hear a word you're saying,' he would yell as we tried to converse with him. I wondered, as I often did, why we put up with his behaviour, but answered my own question, as ever, with the supposition that Lowry was almost certainly a man who had autistic symptoms. His family had 'found him good for nothing else', and so had given him the opportunity to become a painter, where maybe, some small condition of autism might go under cover of artistic temperament. There was his story of having wanted to join up during the First World War, but he had been turned down on grounds of health. He had been told to ask the consultant himself what grounds those might be. He failed to do so, he said, not wishing to learn bad news.

Dinner became an increasing embarrassment. Eventually Micky called the head waiter and, giving him a five-pound note, asked if he would give it to the young pianist and get him to take a supper break. The horror of the insensitive treatment of that blind boy haunts me yet. It did not haunt Lowry, however. The moment the music ceased he was once again all smiles, his blue eyes twinkled once more, and all sign of temper had gone as he launched into one of his eternal stories.

Much later, seeing the pianist re-emerge to take his seat again, I got quickly to my feet. 'Come along, Mr Lowry, time to go.'

'Time to go, Mrs Marshall – what are you talking about? It's only nine-thirty.'

'The music's starting again, Mr Lowry, we'd better be off.'

'Oh no, Mrs Marshall, I'm going to have another cup of this very good coffee,' he said as he filled his cup with cream while he put his other hand on my arm to prevent my departure. 'Ah, Mrs

Marshall,' he sighed contentedly, with reference to cream, 'good for young children and babies, you know.' His eternal small joke.

'Yes, well you can hear the music's started up again, Mr Lowry,' I replied firmly, 'and that evidently isn't good for young children and babies . . . come along, we're off.'

'No, Mr Marshall hasn't got the bill yet,' he smiled, and we had to remain another hour during which time he refused to leave, although he remembered to mutter occasionally, 'ridiculous – isn't it ridiculous – fancy having a noise like that going on while people eat!' In retrospect, it must be assumed that he enjoyed creating bizarre situations to sit back and observe how people coped with them.

Back in 1960 we put on our first exhibition of the forty-two-year-old painter Norman Cornish. Cornish had been working in the mines since the age of fifteen. He was still working at the coal face. He had also been painting since the age of fifteen. His work had previously been shown in travelling exhibitions along with that of Lowry and Henry Moore. Cornish still lives in the Durham village of Spennymoor where he was born. He has long since left the pit and become a professional painter. He has always painted the world about him – not for Cornish the pretty landscapes to which he might have turned in contrast to his life underground. His work was a response to the imponderables of water, weight, pressure, and contracting space – the result of years spent in three-foot-high seams. It was not pretty.

His exhibition sold out, caused a stir and Cornish never looked back.

Lowry bought several of Cornish's works in the years to come. Despite this, Cornish was the only painter of whom I ever saw Lowry show signs of jealousy, and once Lowry put me in an appalling position.

Lowry arrived in the gallery at his usual time of about eleven o'clock, for his morning coffee, and shortly afterwards Norman Cornish also put in an appearance. As midday approached I went out to the kitchen to tell Ella that Norman had accepted my invitation to join us for luncheon. I had left both painters chatting amicably with Micky, and was totally taken aback when after a few moments Lowry thundered out to the kitchen shouting, 'Either he goes or I go!'

'Good gracious, what on earth's the matter?' I inquired, always somewhat terrified of Lowry when he became violent.

'Now, just calm yourself there,' murmured Ella to him, 'I'll see about getting you a nice glass of orange – just you wait now till I get the ice.'

'I don't want any orange, and you can keep your ice, madam, and above all I don't want that man here. Either that fellow Cornish goes, or I go.' A little later in our acquaintance, I should certainly have told Lowry himself to go. As it was, I merely asked rather helplessly, 'But what on earth's the matter, Mr Lowry? You were getting along very well together just now.'

'The damned man will keep talking art – and you know very well I don't like talking art. Keeps saying he's got a painting problem and wants my advice. Thinks I might help him. I'm damned if I'll help him – why should I? Go and get rid of him, Mrs Marshall.' His face was red with rage. Lowry thundered out of the kitchen again, and I turned to Ella, asking, 'Well, what the hell do I do now?'

'I can't see you've any alternative,' she answered. 'You'll just have to go and explain to Mr Cornish.'

'Oh Ella, I can't – I've asked him to stay.' I was in despair. However, off I went to explain the situation to Norman as best I could. Cornish could not have been more understanding, told me not to give it another thought and very promptly took his departure.

But I was never more ashamed in my life. Had Lowry not taken the wind out of my sails with his unlooked-for rage, I am certain now that I would have found a happier way out of the situation, for as the years progressed I learned a thing or two in my dealings with him. As it was, I merely said to him with annoyance at luncheon, 'Well, I hope that chicken chokes you – and don't think you're going to eat all the bread sauce today!' But he was totally unrepentant, apparently enjoying himself more than usual.

There was another side to Lowry, however. There came the evening when we had occasion to be extremely grateful for his broadmindedness and his ability to remain unshockable, for no side of human nature shocked him.

Two clients and good friends of ours, aware that Lowry was constantly with us, asked him out to dinner one evening. It was kind and thoughtful of them. He had never previously accepted any invitation which did not include us, but he had met these people frequently in the gallery, and we were delighted, therefore, when quite happily he agreed to dine with them at the Station Hotel the following Saturday. He merely stipulated that there should be no one else present.

With tea over on Saturday and the gallery quiet at last, Lowry sat chatting with us in the office over a drink before it was time to take him to the hotel for his engagement. We noticed that he started to wander out to the loo rather frequently, and we recognized this habit of old. It did not augur well, for it was a sign of nerves.

At Lowry's fifth speedy disappearance Micky expressed his fears to me and, sure enough, as the car drew near the hotel Lowry fidgeted around, turned to me in the back (for he never sat anywhere but next to Micky in the front) and exclaimed, 'Now Mrs Marshall, I'm just thinking, you can't go all those miles home and start cooking dinner – it's not good for you.' (I wondered what he supposed I did when he was not with us.) 'You and Mr Marshall must come with me – I won't have you go home unfed.' After another great nervous heave, Micky relented. Lowry always had that power over us. Some quality in him could call out all our sympathy and he would get his own way.

Our friends were not expecting us, but Lowry insisted that did not matter, and Micky said that he would be host. Lowry laughed, once again completely at ease, and sighed, 'Aah, that's a good lad.'

The original host hurried down the hotel steps to greet Lowry and started to put me back into the car, when Lowry quickly announced, 'Mr and Mrs Marshall are coming with me.' I quietly explained the situation as the painter disappeared into the hotel. Only momentarily did I fancy our friend showed some hesitation, and shortly I was to understand the reason. When we joined his wife in the lounge she was not, after all, alone as had been agreed. Her daugher was there with a young man.

Drinks were ordered and conversation was remarkably stilted, but this would undoubtedly improve when the youngsters departed. Heads were turning constantly to look at them. They had only that day returned from a two-month hike around Italy. Both wore dirty raincoats and the boy's filthy shirt was open to his navel. His feet boasted a gigantic pair of ethnic boots into which he'd tucked his trousers – even Lowry had never painted so large a pair of feet. Long, straggling black hair hung down his back and even at a distance it smelled none too sweet. In comparison, Lowry appeared to be the height of sartorial elegance.

Hearing the girl's father tell Micky that we should now require a table for seven I felt a sense of abject terror . . . and, seeing Lowry's hefty wink in my direction, I felt no easier. Only a couple of weeks previously, when Lowry had been eating here with us, we had seen a man being asked to leave the restaurant for the simple reason that he wore a cravat in place of a tie, and a cardigan instead of a jacket.

I heard Micky say that he would arrange for a larger table, and as he had got his hands grubby parking the car he would have a wash at the same time. At the magic word 'wash', Lowry was on his feet in a flash and, with hands in pockets, trousers hitched, head close to Micky's, they disappeared in deep discussion.

When the menus were brought, I felt sick as I pictured our ordering, the food's being prepared, and then our ignominious dismissal. The two men returned and Lowry decided to enjoy life by asking for a second orange squash. The party chose what it would eat and the young man went relentlessly through the most expensive dishes. Lowry asked him whether he, like the girl, was an art student. No, the young man was a hotel kitchen hand but out of work for the moment. Lowry bestowed yet another wicked wink in my direction and I prayed he was not contemplating making this a habit throughout the evening.

The evil moment arrived – all was ready for us. Along an interminable corridor we trooped. For once Lowry did not mind in the least that heads were turning to look at others than himself. We reached the dining room, the double doors were flung wide to receive us, and Lowry picked that moment to visit the gents once more. With appalled and jaundiced eyes I watched helplessly as Micky chickened out as well, disappearing below with his friend. I turned quickly to the shepherd-of-the-hills-booted young man, and suggested that perhaps he also would care for a wash? Luck had deserted me – he would not.

With 'first-night' butterflies in the stomach, I stepped into the glare of the dining room. At that time, Saturday evenings there were something of a local occasion; at the far end of the enormous room, recently redecorated, with its blazing modern chandeliers, was a specially raised platform where a band played for dinner dances on winter evenings, and at other times a table was set for

VIPs.

'This way, Mrs Marshall,' I heard Tony, the head waiter, say as he led us the length of the room to the dramatic table with its spotlight above. I glanced neither to my left nor right as I led my strange assortment of guests through the thronged place, longing for the proverbial ground to open and swallow me up. Tony held out my chair and, not daring to look his way, I hastily seated the young man first – with his back to the room. Immediate company would have to suffer that navel, but at least others need not. The girl, still sporting her dirty mac, I placed next to him. So far so good, as I watched Lowry and Micky grinning their way down the long expanse of carpet. I sat Lowry to my right, facing the audience, to keep at least him happy.

As the girl put her shoulders back to shrug off the raincoat, I immediately became aware that she was about six months pregnant. Her mother was serene and apparently oblivious of her daughter's 'interesting condition'. As the girl stretched out her arm for some toast I noticed that she had an extraordinary rash on the underside of it and her eyes seemed strangely brilliant. Drugs as well as a baby. I looked quickly at the young man and saw the same brilliance in his eyes.

Lowry's performance that evening was superb; he exerted himself as never before and seldom afterwards. There were no scenes, he scintillated as we would not have supposed he would or could. He was happy, amusing, the life and soul of that ghastly dinner and had everyone constantly laughing, except for the two youngsters. But as everything was progressing well, thanks to Lowry, the young man rose to his feet without warning to depart for the gents'. He strolled down the room, raincoat still trailing from his shoulders; every eye followed his retreating form, then every head turned back to see whence he came. Bowing with a fixed smile to left and right, I only then became aware that apparently just about everyone we were acquainted with appeared to be eating there that evening. I heard Lowry saying, as he nudged me into attention, 'My word, you know a lot of people, Mrs Marshall.'

'Not really, it's just that they're all here tonight,' I moaned.

As the young man reappeared in the distant doorway I saw Lowry's old eagle eyes glinting behind his gold-rimmed specs – the situation was at least sufficiently bizarre even for him. This was the moment of trial. The hotel manager was now standing inside the doorway with Tony. Sure enough, the manager stepped forward and engaged the boy in conversation. I held my breath. Lowry gave me another great nudge. We both gave vent to sighs of relief as the youngster trailed his way back to us again and sat down. The girl's father asked what had been said to him.

'Oh, they just wanted to know whether I had got a tie to wear, and they suggested that I fasten up my shirt, but I told them I preferred it open.'

Lowry listened avidly to every word, then whispered: 'Bit of a triumph, that – eh, Mrs Marshall?'

Eventually, the agonizing meal came to an end, with Lowry still reminiscing as he poured jug after jug of cream into his cup, always with the words 'Good for young children and babies – eh, Mrs Marshall?' I averted my eyes and wished he would shut up about babies.

At home with us next day before a blazing log fire, despite the hot sun outside, Lowry was still chuckling. 'Oh my God, but they were a bonny pair. If I hadn't seen it for myself, I would never have believed it. I've never seen anything like it – I don't know how you got them into the dining room. My God, what would have happened if I'd been there with them on me own as we'd arranged? What would I have *done*?'

'Yes, and so were you and Micky a "bonny pair" leaving me to take them in. Oh, you really were a couple of rats!' After all, I hadn't a clue that Micky had had a word with Tony when he first went off on the pretext of having a wash.

'Well, you might have known Mr Marshall wouldn't leave you in the lurch altogether,' laughed the old man. 'Though I must say when we were downstairs Mr Marshall said, "I'd love to see Tilly's face now." '

This was the only occasion I can recall Lowry using my Christian name, albeit at second hand. Shortly after meeting him we had asked him to drop the Mr and Mrs Marshall, but he explained that, as he first addressed people, so he continued to address them, as that was the way he had come to think of them. Mr and Mrs, therefore, it remained, although after the painter's death we learned that he always referred to us in our absence as Micky and Tilly.

Nor did we take any familiarity of address with him, being aware of his intense dislike of being referred to as 'L.S.'. When he wanted to get his own way upon occasion, or was having some particular joke, he would refer to himself as 'Little Laurie', and when I used that name in fun he enjoyed it but, as a general rule, it was always 'Mr Lowry'.

Throughout that Sunday, as he continued to chortle over his post mortem on the previous evening and the 'bonny pair', he relived every detail. 'How d'you account for having got them into that dining room, Mrs Marshall?' he inquired.

'Oh, it wasn't my doing; it was Micky who managed it when he went along to ask for the larger table. He told Tony that he found himself in a very difficult position, and would be glad if he'd look after us as he always did, and help to see us through it. But, of course, I hadn't a clue. You know, if I'm not mistaken, the girl's six months pregnant.'

'*No*, Mrs Marshall, *never*! Oh, dear me – d'you think you're right?'

'Yes, I'm sure of it.'

'Well, does the mother know?'

'I don't think she does, or she wouldn't be so unconcerned. She's very intellectual, so I fancy she hasn't noticed.'

'Oh, my God! Surely you must be mistaken? But you're a very perceptive lady, I fancy. Bless me, I wish I weren't going home this week. I want to know if you're right.'

'Ooh, you're a dreadful man.'

'But Mrs Marshall, it's so interesting.'

'Then here's a bit more to interest you – those youngsters were on drugs.'

'Oh, Mrs Marshall – I can't stand it. You're making my day!'

'Well, you deserve a reward after last night. Seriously, you were marvellous. I've never seen you exert yourself like it.'

'D'you think so? But, you see, I found it all so interesting. I've been around quite a bit in m'day, but I've never seen anything like those young people looked. And I've seen some sordid things in m'time. Well, you know I've painted and drawn some strange characters and disreputables – but those two take the biscuit. That's a nice dining room, oh, it's very comfortable, and they can be very particular in those sort of places – well, bloody hell, we've seen them be particular, haven't we? Oh no, I'll never understand how Mr Marshall got them in.

'Reminds me – have I told you before?' (It didn't matter that he had, he was going to tell me again.) 'It reminds me of a very good restaurant I was in once in London, when an old tramp arrived and I thought to myself, "They won't serve you here." Well, I didn't think they would, not looking like he was. But to my astonishment the head waiter hurried forward and greeted him like a long-lost friend. "Good evening, sir. Nice to see you, sir. It's a long time since we had the pleasure, sir." And do you know that old fellow received far better attention than anyone else in the place. Never forgotten it. Oh, dear me, he was shabby – still he was *clean*. How d'you account for it? Personally I've always thought he must have been a duke . . . must have been. For when he was ushered to the door it was with, "Now *good* evening, sir, and I hope it will not be so long before we see you again." '

I had indeed heard this story often enough and it could vary. Sometimes the head waiter addressed the customer as merely 'sir', sometimes as 'M'Lord' and, on occasion, as 'Your Grace'. All depended upon the effect to be achieved. Lowry never recounted a story once, but would repeat it over and over again with ever more drama.

It appears remarkable to me now how we ran two shops and a gallery with the painter so constantly in our company. But we had a dear friend who worked part-time as secretary – Pru Morrison-Bell. We shall probably never have friends dearer to us than Pru and her husband, Sir Charles. They lived in a beautiful but extremely isolated home in north Northumberland. Pru was a delightful, thoughtful and charming hostess, always fashionably dressed, slim and attractive with small features, and a lovely sense of humour. Charles had never been a frequent visitor to Newcastle until he became intrigued with the gallery. He had previously been content with the paintings his father and grandfather had acquired, but gradually he began to buy contemporary work such as Picasso lithographs (seventy pounds in those days – heaven knows what they would be worth now). He was to add Lowry's works to his collection, making a present of them to Pru.

Lowry could be very awkward and more difficult than usual when being entertained in some of the homes to which we took him. He was such an ardent teetotaller; I used to think a drink might have helped him to relax. He would lounge back in ungainly fashion in a big chair, ignoring his hosts or newly introduced fellow guests, and, beckoning to Micky or me, would hold a whispered conversation about others present. 'D'you like her dress?' or maybe, 'That fellow over there fancies he's very knowledgeable!' It could be embarrassing. Or he would shift from foot to foot, hitching his trousers higher and higher until he looked as if he was contemplating going for a paddle. His hostess might inquire gently whether he would care for a wash, and receive a curt, 'No' but as soon as dinner or luncheon was ready, he would disappear for a wash and, judging from the time he took, he could have been bathing. The meal would be waiting long before he emerged.

On the first occasion we took him to High Green for luncheon with Charles and Pru, we were all nicely settled in the garden with our coffee when Lowry announced, 'Mrs Marshall and I are feeling cold, aren't we?'

Oh, sod him, I thought, but, raising my eyes to Pru, said, 'Yes, perhaps Mr Lowry and I had better pop inside – we don't want him getting a cold.'

In we trundled – after all, he was an elderly man, we had to make allowances. In the drawing room, to my annoyance, he began to chortle, saying, 'We weren't too cold, were we? But I don't want to be out there.'

'Well, you sit on the seafront sometimes.'

'Oh yes, but I don't want to be out there with those others.'

'Why not?'

'Well, they're all enjoying themselves.'

'Weren't you?'

'No – I'd rather be back in the gallery,' he answered.

'You wouldn't. Whatever for?'

'Oh, I like it there, you know.' Well, there were times he could have fooled me. But it seemed strange. Everyone that day had done their utmost to give him a pleasant time. He liked motoring; he had enjoyed the long drive to the border, but the moment he saw the house, when we were going through the entrance gates and up the drive, he had begun to hitch himself around in the car, saying: 'Oh, I didn't know they lived in a place like this – let's go back.'

When a little later Pru invited him for luncheon again on Sunday, she asked him, 'Do you care for salmon, Mr Lowry?' As well I knew, there was little he detested more. I never saw him eat salmon. But before I could reply for him, as I would have done, he answered quickly that he liked salmon.

'Oh good,' said Pru. 'That's fine – for Charles has been fishing.'

I was certain that we would not be going to High Green on Sunday. Sure enough, the following day he said to me, 'You don't want to go to that place for lunch tomorrow, do you, Mrs Marshall?'

'What you're really saying is, will I get you out of it.'

'Ah – that's a good Mrs Marshall.'

'All right – but why didn't you say you didn't like salmon? I knew the moment you said yes, and you knew that's what you were going to have, we wouldn't be going. I was going to tell Pru you couldn't stand it, but you went and said that you liked it.'

'Well, I knew I could trust you to get me out of it. And I didn't want to hurt the lady's feelings.' He always referred to Pru as 'the lady'.

'It'll hurt them a jolly sight more calling it off at this late hour.'

'Never mind, you go and ring up. I'll leave you to do it. And I'll come out and have lunch with you instead. It's a long drive right up past Otterburn.'

'It's a long drive out to us; and a double journey for whoever collects and delivers you back to Seaburn.'

'Ah yes,' he grinned and chuckled. 'But you're all very good to an old man – besides, now I can look forward to private-house chicken.'

'To what?'

'To private-house chicken.'

'What's that, for God's sake?'

'Oh, Mrs Marshall – chicken cooked in a private house and not in a restaurant. There's all the diference, you know. And, as I tell Carol's mother, yours is particularly good.'

'Oh heavens, you *don't*. Isn't Mrs Lowry a good cook then?'

'She thinks she is.'

'Well, it's more than I think I am. Though I tell you what I'd love to cook some time – your goose! All right, I'll go and tell Pru we're not going because you don't like salmon.'

'Oh no, Mrs Marshall – I trust you. Tell her I've got a cold.' I left him rocking himself to and fro in his chair, helpless with laughter, all tension released, and no longer worrying about having to do anything which might have put him under some strain.

'OK – that's all right,' I assured him on my return, 'but next time try and be bloody honest for a change.'

'I don't bloody well know how to be, Mrs Marshall,' roaring

again with mirth. 'I'm not a very nice man, you know.'

It has often been said that Lowry's friends never met, but that was not so. Certainly he kept a few of them in different compartments of his life, but we met a great number of them over the years.

Carol had been the first, of course, the next was the Reverend Geoffrey Bennett. He was a vicar in Carlisle, and he and his wife, both of whom hailed from Lancashire, had known Lowry for a long time. Mr Bennett had been a bank manager. A year before he was due to retire, he became an Anglican clergyman. He originally met Lowry when the painter's cousin Grace (sister of May) worked in the same bank. Geoffrey Bennett was an amateur painter, at times in the style of Lowry. He and his wife had been extremely kind to the artist, and they owned a splendid collection of his work – beautifully housed in the large Carlisle vicarage, which after his retirement Bennett was able to acquire and where he continued to live.

We would often take Lowry to call on his friends in Cumbria, and to hear the two men together was as good as any music-hall turn.

However, early in our acquaintance, Mr Bennett arrived in the gallery one day and I said, 'Oh, what a pity, you've just missed Mr Lowry – he's gone back home today.'

'Did he have that Carol Ann with him?' asked the reverend gentleman, as Lowry would sometimes refer to him.

'Oh yes, his niece was here also,' I answered.

'Calls this one his niece, does he? the last one was his goddaughter, the one before that his protégée. Five young girls I think he's been interested in. He has this thing about young girls, you know – and there's not a thing you can do about it! I'll not have him bring this so-called niece to see us – for I'll not have my wife work for a youngster.' He continued to be very forthright, until I recoiled at the outspokenness of this gaunt old man in clerical garb. However, as the years progressed the clergyman relented, and either Simon or we would take Lowry, with occasionally Carol Ann, to visit the Bennetts; making certain that we lunched first at the Crown and Mitre in Carlisle.

As we came to know her well, we dropped the 'Ann', addressing her only as 'Carol'; very soon Lowry did likewise. He had often talked of his so-called goddaughter, Ann. This was the girl he had told us drove him to Cheltenham and stayed with him there. He talked of her in detail; she was the daughter of a very wealthy man, and she had money in her own right. When the Second World War broke out, her parents immediately went missing. And Lowry would say, 'Now what d'you make of that, Mr Marshall?'

Micky seemed to know what was expected of him and would say, 'Were they secret agents?'

Lowry would say, 'Yes.'

There was never any suggestion that they had been interned, for Lowry would then describe their having left a very young daughter with a friend of his family. He saw a lot of the child as she grew up and when the war was over, the parents reappeared.

Ann trained in Italy as a ballet dancer, but did not care for the life and returned to her parents in the Cheshire stockbroker belt. Lowry became a great friend of the family, but his attachment to Ann caused her father to comment more than once.

Ann had a two-seater car. Once when she was driving Lowry through Devonshire lanes he complained that he would have seen more from the top of a bus. Upon her return home, she put her car in the garage and, taking him at his word, from then on they travelled by public transport. 'Haa! Diamond cut diamond!' he would laugh.

In 1959 he painted a portrait of Ann, which has since come to be considered his greatest portrait. He did others of her, but that one is outstanding. He told us Ann had visited the Stone Gallery. I expressed regret that she had not made herself known – he said she was shy and hadn't cared to.

After her father's death in 1965, Ann went to off to New York to work, and later she went on to Russia. After an absence of two years, she came back into Lowry's life, occasionally calling to take him out for lunch. I often talked to Lowry about Ann, and he would say she had not married because she wasn't the marrying kind. 'You know what I mean, Mrs Marshall?' One day his guard slipped, and he said, 'No, my goodness – no. She'll not try that again!' I asked what she wouldn't try again. His eyes suddenly hooded. 'I'm getting myself confused; what am I saying?' Then I heard him mutter to himself, 'Never liked the fellow. Told her she was a fool.'

In 1924 Lowry had made a straightforward academic drawing of a girl of indeterminate age. This, he always said, was Ann's mother. In 1976 this same woman walked into the Stone Gallery. She sat across Micky's desk from me, talking about Lowry. He had been dead for nine months. She opened the conversation bitterly with, 'I suppose you're just another woman who was in love with him?'

'Christ! In love with Lowry?' I exclaimed in total astonishment. 'He was a millstone round our necks!'

Closely I watched the miracle I was talking to. A woman who had not changed in appearance in fifty-odd years . . . until I remembered my Shakespeare:

> Thou art thy mother's glass, and she in thee
> Calls back the lovely April of her prime.

After Lowry's death, certain people started looking for his so-called goddaughter Ann. They were looking for a woman whose surname was Hilder. But Lowry's Ann was two girls – an amalgam of daughter and mother. For their own reasons, each wished to remain Lowry's *Dark Lady of the Sonnets*.

Lowry was a complex character. He was never, while he lived, publicly associated with any of the girls in whom he took an interest. He would cover his tracks by giving misleading information. How often he would say, 'As you know, I never have anything to do with married women, Mrs Marshall.' But he continued to write to several, and one girl and her family he would occasionally even visit when it was convenient for him. With Pat Cooke and her husband, he would visit Ireland for several days, or accompany them on some jaunt.

I can only write of the women in Lowry's life whom I met. Three I have no knowledge of.

Pat Gerrard came from Lowry's village of Mottram-in-Longdendale. Her father was the local builder who had undertaken certain alterations at The Elms before Lowry moved in when Pat was fourteen years of age. She was interested in painting and drawing, and when she left Hyde Grammar School she went on to Manchester School of Art for two years. Since her father had introduced her to Lowry she had become a great friend of the painter, and in some little fashion he assisted in getting her into the Slade in London where she continued her art studies. Lowry would visit Pat in London, taking her out and about. Her student days behind her,

Pat taught art in Altrincham; in 1957 she married a young scientist and became Pat Cooke.

One Saturday afternoon in summer Lowry brought them to the gallery to visit us. Pat was an extrovert, vivacious and great fun. She was tall and dark-haired, with strong features. Slim, elegant and perfectly groomed down to the last detail of her pretty gloves, she was very sophisticated and might well have been mistaken for an actress – she would have made a good one. She used a lot of make-up, and was the type of girl whom Lowry occasionally sighed over as being 'a gorgeous creature'.

Pat has always continued to paint, and has had several exhibitions in Manchester. Had Lowry brought her in the hope of interesting Micky in her work? I do not know but, while we were still having tea in Micky's office, the painter jumped to his feet, suddenly yelling, 'Let's be off!'

Poor Pat had just helped herself to a squelchy creamcake, but she shot to attention as her husband and Lowry went out of the room and suddenly looking totally terrified, grabbed her handbag and gloves. 'Oh God!' she said. 'He's got into one of his terrible rages,' and, with creamcake held aloft, she rushed to follow the master. We were to meet again – but that can wait for the present.

When we first met Lowry he talked a good deal of Sheila Fell. He never referred to her as Sheila – always Sheila Fell. She was a young painter whose parents lived in the Cumbrian village of Aspatria. Her father was a retired miner and a considerable character. His daughter had studied at the Carlisle School of Art, and went on to London's St Martin's School.

Lowry had become interested in the twenty-three-year-old painter when in 1955 he visited her first London exhibition at the now long-defunct Beaux Arts Gallery. Sheila was slim, more ethereal than Pat and, like Lowry's other girls, she had long dark hair – with a fringe across her brow. Her eyes always sported heavy mascara. Lowry promptly bought two paintings from that exhibition; he got to know the young artist well, escorting her out and about London. She took him home to meet her parents, and he arranged to make her an allowance of three pounds a week to assist her in her early struggle for recognition, and to enable her to continue living for the most part in London.

Sheila always kept in close touch with her parents, and Lowry would go each summer to spend a week with them in their Aspatria cottage when Sheila was staying there. He hired a car with driver, and they would travel around the countryside. Sheila was a landscape painter, and Lowry came to consider her to be the best one living. She would find the landscape which appealed to her and set busily to work. Lowry obviously made sacrifices for he never cared for landscape other than an industrial or sordid one. The beauties of the lakes were not in his line at all.

After we came to know Lowry, these visits to Aspatria only continued for about three more summers. Mrs Fell, so I heard, blamed us when Lowry's annual stays came to an end. We would have delighted in their continuation – respites from Lowry's company were becoming fewer. I am afraid he found it more congenial to his purse to spend time with the Marshalls, where a free car was always at his disposal. He was not able to take Carol to visit the Fells – and Carol was now his female motivation. Besides, something about Sheila had begun to puzzle Lowry and, if the painter decided that there was something he wanted to know about someone, he fast set about finding it out. What he discovered, he did not care for. He discovered that Sheila had married (so he said) and had one child – so out went Sheila.

Nevertheless, Lowry was a fair man – he still admired Sheila Fell's work. He continued to push her career, and persuaded Micky to see an exhibition she was having at Middlesbrough's public art gallery. Micky and I went together and liked the work up to a point. Micky suggested to Sheila that, if she cared to paint a new exhibition, he would show it. He went to London to see how her work was progressing, but suddenly she was unavailable. Time passed, and she said the show was ready. Arrangements were made, private-view invitations about to be sent out, but the catalogue remained to be printed, and Sheila delayed sending her list of paintings. At the eleventh hour it transpired that there was no new work, and the paintings Sheila proposed sending were those which had already been exhibited at Middlesbrough. The exhibition was immediately cancelled. Disappointed in Sheila though he was, Lowry persuaded my husband to give her another chance. She was to have her first exhibition with us in 1967, and two years after she had a second one. Lowry was extremely pleased with the result. While with us in June 1967 he wrote to a friend, 'Sheila Fell's show is on and doing very well, and up to now fifteen pictures have been sold – I am very glad and she must be very pleased about it.'

Shying away from public association with any girl, true to form, Lowry did not attend the private view of Sheila's exhibition. However, three consultant surgeons were among those present.

As she was getting ready in my office beforehand, Sheila pointed to a small patch on her face, and spreading yet more powder over it she complained of having been troubled with it for some weeks. Laughing, I told her not to worry – no one was going to notice it.

After she had returned home the following day, the three consultants arrived at different times in the gallery, each to inform me that Sheila had a virulent cancer on her face which must be treated immediately.

I felt I could not possibly tell the girl this, so I wrote at once to Lowry for his advice. He replied by return on 24 May 1967: 'I am very sorry to hear your news of Sheila Fell. With all the medical information you have received, if I were in your place I would tell Mrs Fell – and I think Sheila Fell ought to know too. But certainly Mrs Fell. She has a big influence over her daughter – tell her it is urgent and must be dealt with at once. All being well I shall be with you next Thursday – the 3.30 train. I look forward to seeing you. Hope you are well and working hard! Yours, L. S. Lowry.'

I rang up Mrs Fell who was at something of a loss to know what to do for the best but, discovering from her that Sheila was looking for a new London dentist, I arranged for her to consult a Harley Street friend of one of the anxious consultants. This man treated her free of charge, and in a casual manner he fixed for her to have the cancer removed – without Sheila knowing what it was.

In 1969 Sheila was made an Associate of the Royal Academy, and later was elected a Royal Academician. Perhaps the security of the knowledge that, whatever the quality of her work, from now on it would be shown to the public and would almost certainly sell, proved detrimental to the gift she had, for Lowry maintained that from this time Sheila's work deteriorated. She outlived him by four years. About twelve months before she died, Sheila was talking to me at great length about her daughter Anna, then twenty-one. 'Well,' she smiled, 'that was one little secret of mine that Mr Lowry knew nothing of!' I didn't disillusion her. He had known about her 'kid' for a very long time.

All in all, Lowry's private life remained very much his own – until after his death. And when his friend said of him, 'He has this thing about young girls . . .' perhaps it was a case of:

My glass shall not persuade me I am old,
So long as youth and thou are of one date;
But when in thee time's furrows I behold,
Then look I death my days should expiate.

(*From Shakespeare's Sonnet*)

3

There were times when we were more than a little fearful lest Lowry get himself locked up. He enjoyed taking a bus from outside his hotel which would bring him direct to Newcastle. It was then his pleasure to walk up Northumberland Street, the main shopping street of the city – once designated as the third busiest in Britain. Here are the many clothes shops whose custom it is to change their window displays often, and Lowry loved to walk up this street early in the mornings on his way to the gallery while this window dressing was in operation.

We were well aware that there is a type of man who enjoys staring at attractive female window dressers, and we were also aware that Lowry did not stop at this, for he would also stand for long minutes gazing at the disrobed models, and was intensely amused when the hair was removed. 'Oh, Mr Marshall,' he would laugh, 'the models in the life class couldn't achieve that feat!' Over his coffee he would relive his amusement until we, insisting that the walk was too much for him, begged and prayed that he would either let us collect him from his hotel or promise to get a taxi. Yes, he would promise, he would do either one or the other, having no intention whatsoever of keeping his promise. Hence we lived in constant fear of being called upon to bail out what anyone might reasonably suppose was yet another 'dirty old man'.

One day he was gazing at a young lovely who was dressing a nude model when the girl disappeared rapidly from the window. Almost immediately the manager came out of the shop to ask Lowry politely whether he could be of assistance. Lowry, resembling as usual some old unfortunate, replied why yes, a hundred thousand or so would be a help – times were very hard.

'Now be off at once, and don't let me find you hanging around here any more. Watch it – let me catch you again, and I'll send for the police.' Lowry came into the gallery hooting with mirth and, for once, instead of complaining of his imminent demise, related how he had come down with regard to the amount of assistance he was looking for – even a mere hundred or two would be welcome.

Another morning Micky received a phone call from our bank. Apparently an old man claiming to be the famous painter, L. S. Lowry, was trying to cash a cheque. According to the cashier this person was behaving in a mad manner and was putting on an act of being very angry at the refusal to cash it (it was before the day of bank cards), and had finally suggested that they ring up his friend Mr Marshall at the Stone Gallery. The cashier may have thought that no famous painter was likely to look like this old fellow, but before taking further action he decided to give Micky a ring. Micky urged the caller to hurry and cash the cheque for Britain's popular and famous painter before he found himself being sued in court: the anger was for real.

My husband recalls arguing Lowry's merits as a painter at a bankers' luncheon with a top executive from Manchester. Micky had suggested that it was time the banks hung some decent paintings in their offices and suggested that they might start with Lowry's. The official in question stated categorically that the old boy could not paint for nuts. After Lowry's death the bank decided to call their great new building in Manchester 'Lowry House'.

In Newcastle, at the corner of Northumberland Street and Northumberland Road, a short distance from Tilley's restaurant, there was, and still is, a shop specializing in fine fur coats. At one stage it became a sheer impossibility to get Lowry past these windows as we walked with him to and from the restaurant. As a rule these window models were clad, but on occasion they were not – which made peeping toms of us all. I have known quite a little crowd to gather behind us as we gazed, while I would be urging our party on its way, horror-sticken at the spectacle we were making of ourselves.

Alas, there was nothing one could do about it. Micky played Lowry's little game: he was the only one of us who could enter into this surrealist situation. 'Just look, Mr Marshall, isn't she beautiful? What's she thinking, d'you suppose?' Lowry would ask as he gazed at a tall model in fine mink, a supercilious tilt to her head, one arm at her hip and the other oustretched with a beckoning come-hither invitation. 'She seems to be taken with us, Mr Marshall. I wonder if it's you or me she fancies?'

Or, 'Oh look, she's sad today, Mr Marshall – her friend there has a better coat. . . . Po'r thing, she's upset about it. She's been up-staged as you might say, Mrs Marshall.'

His imagination would weave endless stories around these damned dummies. 'Oh – Mr Marshall, we must stay with her a while, you can see she was jilted last night, and all she's got to show for it is a fur coat – she thought he was serious. Fancy him jilting the poor lady like that – I wonder what she's thinking? Mrs Marshall come back – you're really most unsympathetic. . . .' I was. 'Mr Marshall and I are trying to cheer her up. . . . You mustn't walk on like that or she'll think you're looking down on her.'

He never tired of it. 'Look Mr Marshall – aah, that's better, the lady's happy today, got another fellow in tow, I fancy. At any rate she's got another coat. Oh, that's good, she's not doing too badly after all. Collected quite a few coats she has now. Look how she's carrying her head today. But, oh dear, she doesn't seem to learn – she should learn that pride comes before a fall. Shouldn't like to see her fall – d'you think she's fallen, Mr Marshall?' Micky was certain that she'd fallen.

'Well, she's bonny,' sighed the old man. 'I wish I'd a nice lady like that – oh no, perhaps better not; she'd expect a fur coat and times are hard.'

One day Pru had been with us for luncheon, and on our return to the gallery Lowry, as ever, stopped in front of the furriers to treat us to his usual routine, when he suddenly became aware that Pru was wearing a coat remarkably like the one on the particular model he had picked out for scrutiny. Realizing that he would be running into deep water were he not careful, he turned to her with a rather embarrassed air; Pru simply laughed his embarrassment away by giving him a kiss. I had never previously seen anyone kiss Lowry and wondered how he would react. He smiled with complete delight, and after that Pru always greeted him or bade him farewell with a social kiss on the cheek. Having seen Pru greet him so, the wife of the then northern art critic for *The Times* followed suit and would usually give him a kiss upon meeting him. He loved it. I know of no others who kissed him – even two women friends of many years standing (they are now dead) confessed to me that they never dared.

Unfortunately, when Lowry and Micky entered into these theatrical conspiracies, they became so involved with the intricacies of their plot that they would appear to forget that they were in contact with the real world. In a restaurant they would suddenly decide that some quiet, inoffensive, domesticated man was a murderer, or an embezzler, or some such villain, weaving out of his eating gestures, the colour of his tie, or even the parting of his hair, a complete character of evil and sinister intent. They would stare at the poor man, whisper together, or decide to go to the lavatory for no other purpose than to get a closer look at their victim. They would quiz perplexed waiters about the man's order, whether he were in a hurry or not, and would discuss endlessly which of them should go to the police to prevent some imminent crime.

My husband was always able to enter the painter's world of fantasy. Micky, although so much younger than Lowry, had seen many of the artist's favourite music-hall turns. They would ramble on about the merits of Dick Tubb and Billy Bennett, or Ernie Lotinga and Harry Tate, Rob Wilton, George Formby, Albert Whelan and Stainless Stephen. The name of Nosmo King never failed to amuse – the comedian had chosen it one day as he had walked down Charing Cross Road and seen a 'No Smoking' sign somewhere.

Left to themselves, Lowry and Micky virtually did their own music-hall turn, each seeming to anticipate how the other was going to react to a situation – one playing stooge to the other. No one else I ever saw had this relationship with Lowry.

I remember an occasion when a gossip columnist from the Newcastle *Evening Chronicle* came to the office to interview Lowry. He was rather a serious young man, and can be heard nowadays reporting for the BBC on affairs in Ulster or some other trouble spot. As he introduced the young man to the painter, Micky said, 'This gentleman writes "Eldon Notes", Mr Lowry,' whereupon the artist replied at once, 'Oh yes, I know your cousin very well.' The young reporter looked surprised and asked who that might be?

'Eldon Square – I know Eldon Square very well,' laughed Lowry. (Eldon Square, now demolished, was once the pride and joy of Newcastle, a square of lovely late Georgian houses.)

Our visitor looked a tiny bit peeved, so Lowry promptly pulled himself together – although he could find it difficult with his partner in crime present. Lowry began to trot out his usual old 'gubbins', while the journalist sat down to make notes and sip his coffee. Eventually he decided to pry a little deeper and to dig into Lowry's cultural interests but at that Lowry curled up, feeling it was a little near the bone for a gossip column – maybe for any column. So Micky intervened with the information that Lowry was very fond of good poetry.

The young man brightened considerably, 'What sort of verse do you like, sir?'

Lowry looked over towards Micky and said, 'Well, Mr Marshall and I read an awful lot of poetry together, you know. Now Mr Marshall, what was that favourite poem of mine we read the other day that we greatly enjoyed – very moving thing – very moving indeed?'

Micky, immediately picking up his train of thought answered, 'Oh, you mean the one about young Billy?'

'Yes, that's the one, such a moving poem.' The young reporter looked terribly keen at this progress and asked Lowry to quote the verse.

Lowry replied, 'Oh, Mr Marshall has a much better memory than mine – I'll leave it to him,' and Micky, encouraged at this confidence shown by his friend, agreed that it was indeed a fine thing . . . surely you must know it?

> 'Billy in one of his bright new sashes,
> Fell in the fire and was burnt to ashes.
> Now, though the room grows chilly,
> I haven't the heart to poke poor Billy.'

Looking extraordinarily serious, Lowry said, 'There, you see? Moving, you must agree, sir?' The journalist looked truly appalled, as well he might. He was not pleased at all, and neither was Lowry when he read the report in the next evening's paper.

Early in November 1963, Micky and I went to meet Henry Moore at his home to see the work he was then engaged on, hoping to choose some more pieces for the gallery.

The morning sun was just coming through the autumn mist as we arrived. In his home we chatted to Moore and his wife and saw the works of various painters that he had collected – not many. Then it came time to walk across a field to one of his work sheds. I was wearing boots, but Micky was not. There was nothing for it:

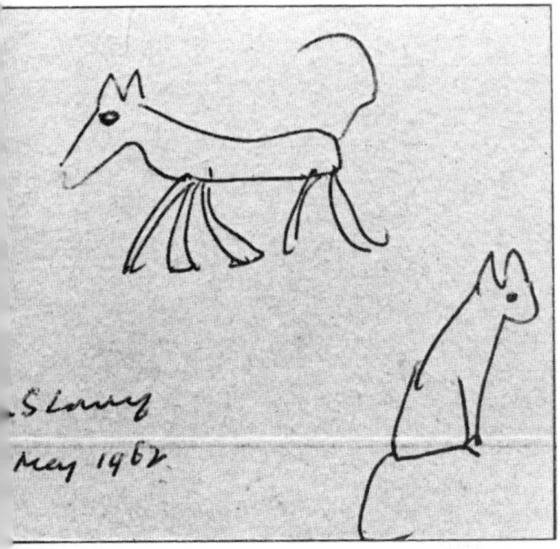

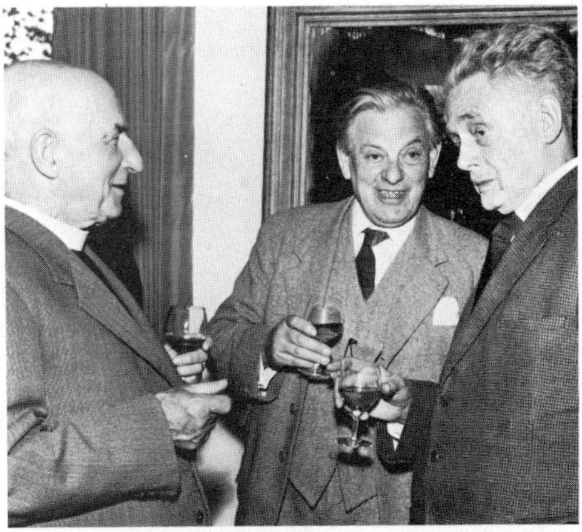

Five-legged dog. Drawing on the back of a cigarette packet.
'Why shouldn't a dog have five legs?'
Signed L. S. Lowry and dated 3 May 1962

The author's father, William Johnstone and Hugh McDiarmid
during a Stone Gallery private view.
Hugh McDiarmid had written the foreword to the catalogue
for Johnstone's exhibition in August 1963

Lowry in front of his painting *Family Group*,
photographed in the Stone Gallery at the time of his
1964 exhibition

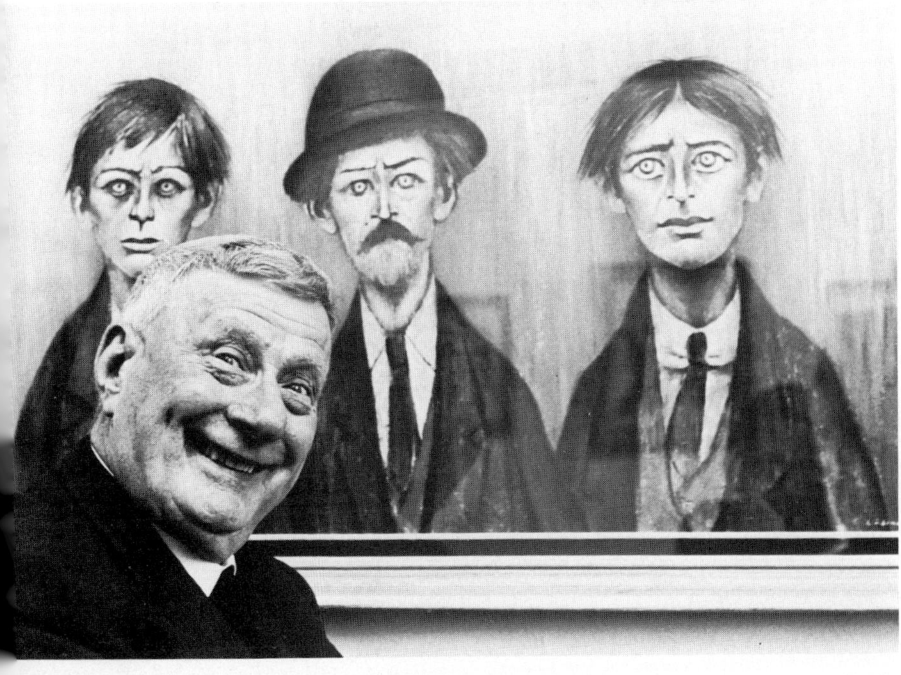

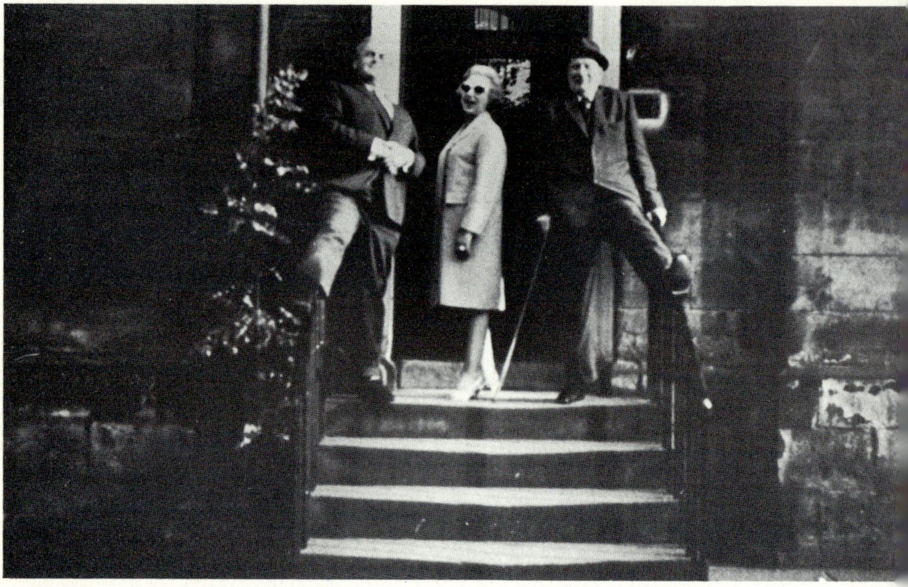

Micky and Lowry acting the fool with author, centre,
outside the Stone Gallery one evening, May 1965

The Stone Gallery, Newcastle-upon-Tyne.
Drawing by L. S. Lowry, October 1965

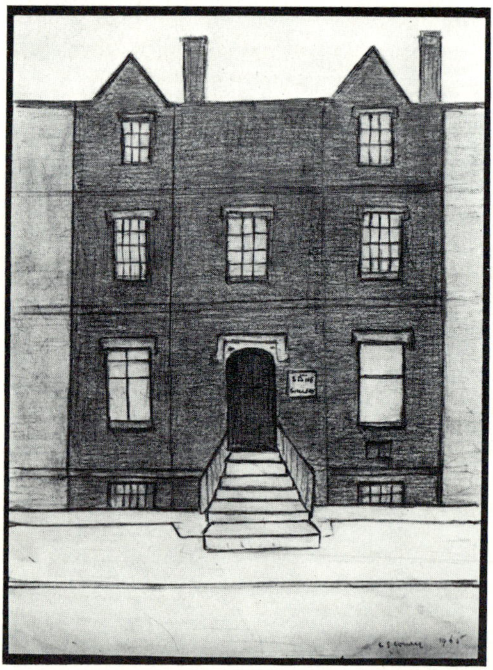

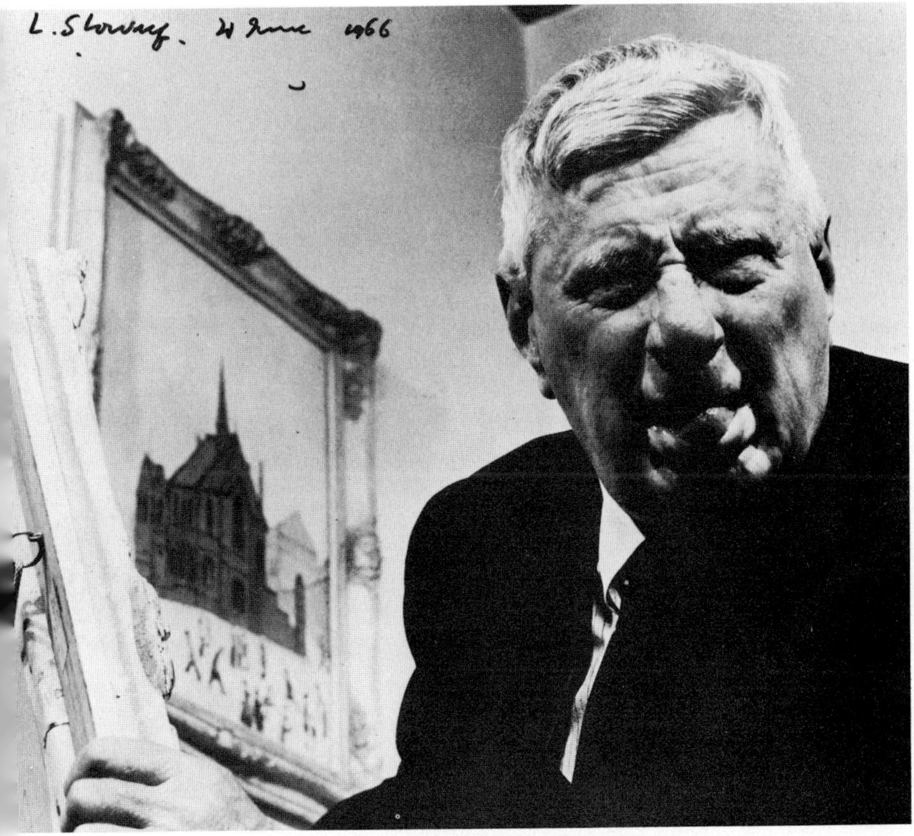

Lowry's favourite photograph of himself –
'But don't show it to anyone until I'm dead!'
Signed L.S.Lowry, 4 June 1966

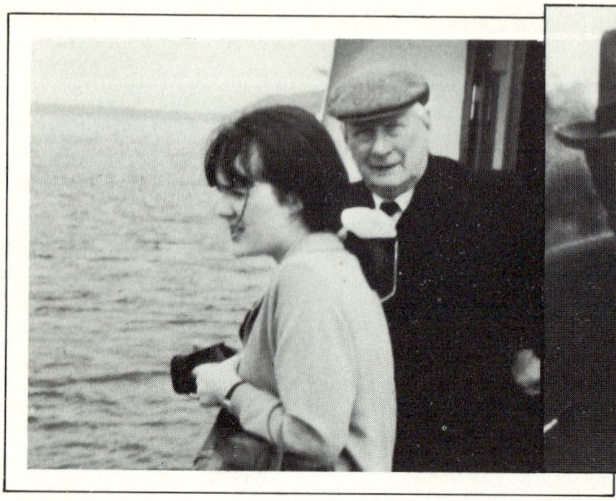

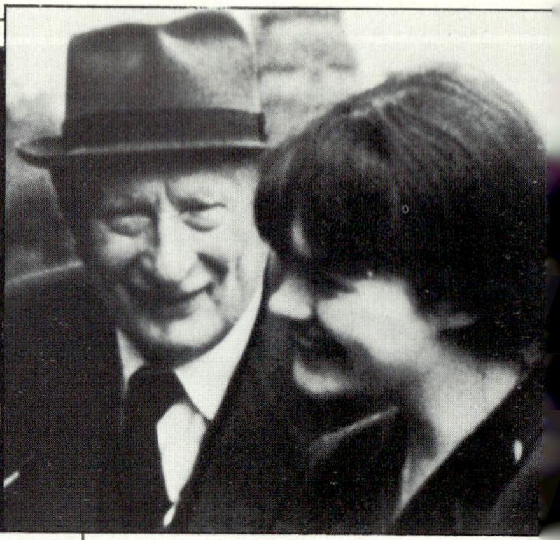

Lowry and Carol en route for Northern Ireland with Simon. June 1968

Lowry with Carol in the park at Bolton – from the Tyne Tees Television film *Mr Lowry*, August 1968

Carol Spiers, Lowry's heiress. Photograph taken by Simon at Carol's request for the purpose of Lowry's painting her portrait, which he declined to undertake. Summer 1968

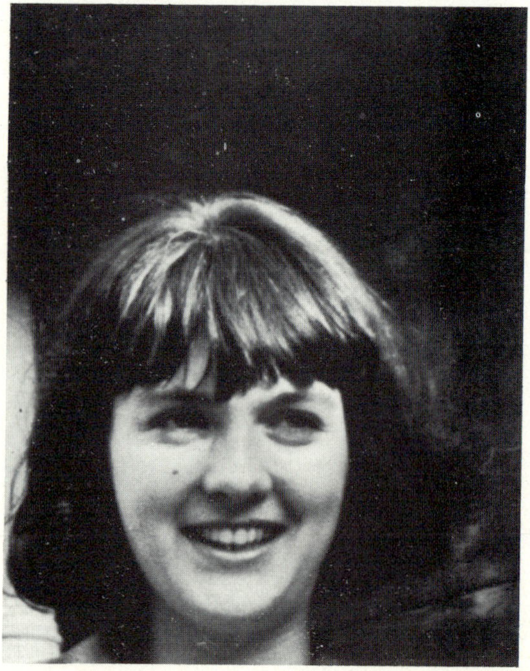

Micky had to borrow a pair of 'wellies'. He couldn't have cared less if he got his feet wet in a good cause – Moore, however, would have none of it. Very thoughtful – quite unlike Lowry. Micky admired a lovely sculpture, out in the open where Moore prefers to see his work, and asked Henry Moore if when he was a youngster he had ever supposed he would be so great a sculptor.

'Oh,' replied Moore, without a second's hesitation, 'I thought I would be much better!'

Moore and Lowry had only one thing in common to my mind – both were remarkably clever businessmen.

This is intended to be an account of how we spent the years with Lowry even if the Stone Gallery comes across as an institution for looking after one particular painter. Although it felt like that at times, in reality it was not so. Despite all the time the old boy, Carol, and Lowry's other friends spent with us, normal business proceeded on its way and the exhibitions rolled on.

There was always a private view before opening an exhibition to the public, and after the private view we gave a dinner party for the artist where he or she had the opportunity to meet good clients and certain critics. Some of those dinner parties were memorable. Two given for Anne Redpath spring to mind. She was the most wonderfully amusing guest and raconteur, and so was an American painter, Joe Downing. A thirty-eight-year-old from the blue-grass state of Kentucky, Joe grew up in the small village of Horse Cave. After wartime service he spent four years at the Art Institute of Chicago, returning to Europe in 1950 to spend three months in Paris. He has remained there ever since. He received a 'well-done' pat on the back from Picasso, which set him on his way. His only British exhibitions have been with us. He was a magical character and his paintings reflected that magic. His friend Roger Berthoud came over for the private view and dinner. At Joe's party he told dreamy stories in his Southern drawl until our hard-headed tycoons rocked with laughter, remained sober, and refused to call it a day at midnight. At two in the morning we all ended up in one of their boardrooms, hung with modern paintings from the gallery, and then breakfasted together in an all-night café near the station at five o'clock.

Another private view was the cause of Simon going down with a heavy cold. The painter we were showing was the mercurial William Johnstone; the foreword to his catalogue was written by Hugh McDiarmid, the Scottish Communist poet. That evening the local paper announced in headlines that, 'The Stone Gallery catalogue will set the City buzzing,' which set the gallery buzzing too . . . for that evening apparently the entire university gatecrashed the private view. (McDiarmid's foreword was later published as a chapter in his next book.) Simon found himself constantly tearing round the corner to a little pub to haul out this controversial character. As he disappeared for the third time, Simon shouted 'I'll bring beer back for the boozy bard!' The penny had at last dropped: McDiarmind didn't care for champagne. Although I certainly saw him drinking plenty.

McDiarmid later found a boon companion in Lenny Jacobson, chairman of Montague Burton's, and the biggest individual employer of labour in the country. But at those private views one never knew who was going to hit it off with whom.

I found that the dinner parties were becoming larger and more unwieldy, and changed the routine. In two rooms on the gallery's top floor we could give a buffet supper available to all.

In the summer of 1964 we became aware that, when Lowry had said he had no work available for an exhibition, he had not been speaking the truth. The Lefevre Gallery showed an exhibition of his recent paintings, a number of which Lowry had commenced as drawings while Simon was driving him around the north-east. They were still the kind of works that London welcomed. We had not shown any interest in his own painting – so one could not really blame Lowry.

By now, he was hinting that he hankered after an exhibition with us. Still maintaining that he did not have enough work for a selling one, he put forward the idea that his friend and client Mr Monty Bloom, who in those days had a large collection, might be willing to let us put on a loan show from it.

On 18 September 1964, Micky and I motored over to Southport to see this Mr Bloom, whom we had not previously met. Lowry remained behind with Simon in Newcastle. We found Mr Bloom to be an extremely handsome, young-looking, middle-aged man. His house groaned with Lowry's works. Every wall appeared to be covered, and the pictures were beautifully hung. Mr Bloom also showed us wardrobes and cupboards stuffed full of drawings. His main collection was Lowry's so-called later work, but he had some examples of the middle and earlier periods also. Mr Bloom explained at length to us that years previously he had realized that art might be a good investment and, after seeing the 1956 John Read film about Lowry, he had decided there and then that here was the painter for him to collect. A local public gallery director had advised him most strongly against collecting Lowry's work – the man couldn't paint. Nothing daunted, Mr Bloom began his collection, concentrating on the single figures and groups of larger figures which the painter always maintained London did not care for. London still wanted only the mill scenes.

Micky made his selection for our exhibition. These later drawings and paintings of Lowry's were something new to Micky – a Lowry unknown either to himself or the public. No beautiful industrial landscapes. Uncompromising painting. 'The Later Paintings of L. S. Lowry' was the title of the show when it opened on 23 October 1964. From my diaries of this period I see that either Micky or Simon took Lowry out for some jaunt every day, and there was no time when he was not in and out of the gallery during the week, or at home with us on Sundays.

Shortly before the Lowry loan exhibition it was necessary for Micky and I to go to Paris on business. It was an interesting time, and included a fascinating luncheon when the Duchess of Windsor was present. I had often wondered what qualities she possessed that a king should give up his throne for her. After two hours I was none the wiser – although Micky confessed later that he had found her utterly captivating.

It was rather a dreary prospect to return to the gallery office, where we found Lowry sitting waiting for us, nervous and uptight at the coming interview with T. S. Ferguson, art editor of The *Sunday Telegraph*. Micky had arranged for Ferguson to meet the artist, and he would then decide whether or not to send his then art critic, Edwin Mullins, to review the exhibition. Neither of these men had met the painter previously. Lowry was heavily on his guard with Ferguson, as he never failed to be with the press. It was decided over luncheon that Mullins would arrive early the following week.

We were already acquainted with Edwin, as his first commission to write on art for the *Sunday Telegraph* had been an article on 'Who Buys Modern Art?' Two years before he had visited the Stone Gallery one Saturday morning and had interviewed a number of enthusiastic collectors, who were treating the gallery, he was to write, 'rather like a club or café'. Before this second visit he asked that Lowry should not be present the first day. He wished to view the works without him there, and they would meet the following morning. We decided to take critic and painter to lunch at Tilley's, where interruptions would be fewer.

How well I recall Lowry's dreary po-face as he answered questions up to a point, or avoided them nimbly if he saw fit. I could have screamed, as over luncheon he would mutter, 'Um . . . urr . . . ahh . . . yes': his constant refrain when he was ill at ease. I longed to urge him to be himself, and to show some sign of the more interesting man with whom we were familiar. This critic had travelled the length of England to interview him, and all he was getting was the same old stuff Lowry churned out for all the press.

Suddenly I had what I thought was a bright idea. . . . 'How is Carol, Mr Lowry?' I asked.

Instantly he changed – he was off and away into the land of dreams. Inwardly I congratulated myself for presenting the real man for the first time to any journalist. Here was the intensely excited spirit of the painter; the uncontrollable emotion of the artist as he talked on. No more umming and aahing and glum muttering. I had managed to present an unusual side of the real Lowry to Edwin, who was a serious young man, extremely kind, but with somewhat preconceived ideas. I glanced across to see his reaction to Lowry, who was behaving as a human being for the first time that day, as totally off-guard as he was when he talked endlessly to me of Carol. I swore inwardly. Mullins was engrossed in discussion with Micky, and no word of Lowry's discourse reached him.

His review in the following Sunday's paper was good, saying that the exhibition 'concentrated not on the industrial landscapes swarming with tiny pipe-cleaner figures . . . but on the pictures which Lowry himself values most'. Had Edwin Mullins – the only journalist ever to be given the opportunity – only listened to what I had handed him upon a platter, I wonder whether he would still have headed his review with the cliché 'The Loneliness of L. S. Lowry', or written, 'Lowry has been amongst the loneliest of men.' The painter was happy, however. He maintained with a very astute smile that the image of 'lonely old man' could always be relied upon to get splendid reviews.

The private view of Lowry's first exhibition with us was held the evening following Mullins's visit. I decided that a buffet supper was not Lowry's line at all. Mr Bloom was to stay overnight at the

Seaburn Hotel with the painter, and Lowry, to my relief, decided that he and Mr Bloom would have a quiet dinner together before arriving. There was no need for them to be in the gallery early, as there was for us. Lowry said he would stay until ten o'clock, but not a moment longer. This suited us perfectly, as none of us could imagine Lowry helping himself to the buffet supper, or standing around while others did.

There were no Lowry works for sale, but there was a wonderful stock of other artists' work for clients to buy. The building was packed and all was proceeding according to plan when Simon rushed up to me where I was talking with a group of people and said breathlessly, 'For God's sake, come quickly – Mr Lowry's simply doing his nut!'

'Oh, for heaven's sake, what's the matter with the old devil now?' I asked.

'He's bawling around in a murderous state on the top floor, saying there's nothing there he likes to eat, and he wants his dinner. I've never seen him like it – he's truly throwing a tantrum, and we don't want everyone to see him like that; it spoils his image.'

'But I knew he wouldn't eat anything up there – he promised to have dinner with Mr Bloom before they arrived. It was all arranged.' Looking at my watch, I saw that it was almost ten o'clock. I said to Simon, 'Get your father at once – whatever he's doing, and never mind who's with him, then get Bloom – and hurry.' He departed with speed and I turned to be confronted with a purple-faced Mr Lowry. My son was right, I had never seen him look so obstreperous as this. What could be the cause? The need for sustenance could hardly be responsible for such a reaction. Had he overhead some derogatory comment on his work?

Heedless of those standing near, he shouted at me, 'I want my dinner – what d'you call that on the top floor?'

'I thought it was arranged that you had dinner before you arrived,' I answered him as gently as I knew how.

'Well, you can start to think again, because I didn't. But I want it now. I want to sit at a table with a white cloth on it and order myself. I'll give you till ten-thirty, but not a moment longer . . . if you're not ready yet.'

'Oh, *I'm* not coming with you, and you won't wait till ten-thirty either. Waiters have to get home, you know.'

'Well, I'll have Mr Marshall and Mr Bloom come with me.'

'Yes, I've sent for them already,' I said. Suddenly I espied coming down the stairs a young friend, James Cropper – a diffident, charming and delightful man. Quickly moving over to him I said, 'James, do me a favour – ask Lowry for his autograph will you?'

I had never expected to see the boy's face other than controlled, but his expression at that moment became a study as he gasped, 'Tilly, I've never asked anyone for an autograph in my life!'

'No, but there's a first time for everything, James,' I answered firmly. 'And you're going to now.' He did.

The situation was saved for the moment, for Lowry turned to him with his most angelic smile, all temper gone, blue eyes sparkling. 'Why certainly, sir. Did you enjoy the exhibition?' James murmured something appropriate, looked slightly sick, and made his getaway. My moment of agonizing fear was over. Turning to Lowry, I told him I would ask Pru to ring through to Tilley's for a table, and she might just as well order at the same time – it would save half an hour.

'Oh, now then, let me see, I'll have a little plaice and chips tonight.'

Micky's reaction at having to leave a crowded building of interesting and interested men and women to eat fish and chips with Lowry is unprintable.

By midnight they had returned, and it was well after 1.30 before Lowry and Mr Bloom were to take their leave – many thought the private view only started after this. Lowry never mixed well with numbers of people present, and his tall, slouching, ungracious personality could certainly put a damper on these occasions.

It was that night we came to terms with the fact that Lowry was the most difficult and eccentric painter for whom we had ever worked. And it must be accepted that private gallery directors do work very hard for their artists.

On the following Sunday, Simon collected Lowry from the Seaburn Hotel and drove him home to have luncheon with us. This meant tea and dinner as well . . . he would not leave before midnight.

It was the most perfect October day; when we get a fine autumn day in our part of the world it can be very lovely indeed. The north-east is not subject to the fogs and mists that gather in the west, and Lowry maintained that our dry, clear air suited him better than the damper atmosphere of his native county. I was certain that, for once, even Lowry must comment on the beauties of the day. But, looking with unseeing eyes, he sighed, 'Aah, God give me strength, I think I'm at the end you know – yes, it won't be long now.'

As I stood there in the sunlight, in a garden designed by the last Duchess of Cleveland, I gazed at the huge trees, every shade of gold and copper, interlaced with variegated hollies and pines. I looked at the beck far below, meandering round three sides of the garden, and then across to the stark grey cliffs beyond the water, and turned to gaze up at the ancient crenellated keep, and it occurred to me that this was a strange man indeed who could feel no inner stirring at the beauty around him. All I heard was, 'Oh dear me, I'm dying y'know – lead me to a chair,' as, turning quickly, Lowry vigorously climbed the stairs to the tower room. This room occupies almost the entire upper half of the building. Immensely high, it has a double row of windows, set into four-foot-thick walls, and from the lower ones there is a view over the tops of the trees to the hills beyond, or over the chase to the great castle of Raby. There are various stories and traditions attached to the place we live in, and Lowry is the only person who never remarked in any way upon it, having no more sense of history than he had sense of beauty – beauty as the world accepts the term. Lowry's idea of beauty was always the industrial scene, or the sea. It was his love of the latter which drew him to stay as a rule at the Seaburn Hotel, for he considered Seaburn unspoilt, while at the same time it was near to industrial towns and therefore combined both his loves.

Comfortably settled in a huge wing-back chair, waiting for his coffee to cool, Lowry was asked what he thought of Edwin Mullins's review in that morning's paper. He replied that he never bothered to read such things. (He subscribed to two press-cutting agencies.) 'Well, there it is,' said Micky, handing it to him. He did not trouble to glance at it and merely commented complacently, 'I told him what he wanted to hear, I think,' thereby confirming that he had indeed already seen it at his hotel.

The *Observer* sent Helen Dawson to see the show and talk to him on the following Tuesday. He told her what he usually told the press, but as she was young and female he preferred her to Mullins, although he considered she would do the job less well. *The Times* covered the exhibition, and there were other reviews, but for the first time since our early struggle we experienced difficulty in getting the press to send their critics, and over the years Lowry was the only painter whose work proved difficult to get reviews for, particularly in the Manchester area.

When Lowry discovered that we were prepared to exhibit his later work, we became his second commercial gallery. 'Recent Paintings and Drawings by L. S. Lowry' was the title of his next show with us. There were twenty-seven oils and thirty-nine drawings, and this time all the work was for sale. It took place from 11 March to 8 April 1967. In June Lowry wrote to Mr Bloom, 'Mr Marshall is a very imaginative and very good dealer. The success of the show was due to the cleverness and the personality of the promoters. They are marvellous people, you know. Remarkable.' And he added, 'That shook the great Gerald, didn't it?' as he cogitated on the interest the exhibition had attracted, taking a sly dig at the senior director of his London gallery. But to our faces Lowry gave no inkling of his satisfaction.

It is our experience that, if one is working to promote a painter or sculptor, the gallery's interests come second to those of the artist. Over the years many journalists attached to the popular press with whom we were acquainted expressed a wish to interview Lowry. For a day and sometimes a couple of days at a time, Micky would put his office at their disposal for this purpose. Neither the gallery nor the company Lowry met at the gallery over the years featured in such interviews. It was to be supposed that the painter was forever gazing out to sea at Seaburn . . . always the lonely recluse. There was not the slightest hint that most of his days and nights in the north-east were spent in the company of some one or other of us, being fed and cared for.

However, the day before his second exhibition with us, the local daily paper, the Newcastle *Journal*, sent a young man round to the gallery to interview the painter, and on this occasion of course the gallery was mentioned in the interview.

I can see Lowry in my mind's eye now, sitting in a window seat of the main exhibition rooms that sunny morning. He was in remarkably good humour in anticipation of his private view that evening.

'Now, tell me something about these works, Mr Lowry,' invited the young reporter.

The old blue eyes glittered and with a smile the painter answered, 'Well now – I'm afraid I don't know anything about them! These paintings and drawings, sir? No, I know nothing about them – nothing at all.' I remember smiling at him affectionately, appreciating his little joke. It did not appear quite so amusing, however, the following morning, when I read that L. S. Lowry knew nothing of the works on exhibition at the Stone Gallery. (I could have wrung my brother's neck when he rang me up to congratulate us upon our exhibition of what might be considered fakes.)

I wanted no repetition of the painter's behaviour at his first private view, so this time I arranged a dinner party at Tilley's for about twenty after the opening. But, as he sat on the banquette at the top of the long table specially arranged, Lowry glowered now and again at the chatter emanating from the rest of us. I think he quite enjoyed it in his own way but he undoubtedly preferred smaller parties.

He contrived to complain with some bitterness of the extremely poor tea I'd given him and his friend at the Station Hotel in the afternoon. For once Micky and I were staying there overnight: there was a good deal of organizing to be done in the gallery for any private view. Monty Bloom was arriving by the afternoon train so Micky and I gave Lowry luncheon at the hotel, after which he was able to sit on in the lounge over his coffee until he and Micky were joined by his friend. It was then necessary for my husband to hurry back to the gallery and I had a cup of tea in my room upstairs while I changed.

This did not please Lowry. As a working woman I could by no means always be on hand and, as our dear friend was more often than not self-invited, we did not look upon him as a guest in the normal way. But it would take all the charm it was possible for me to muster and more tact than is mine by nature to bring a smile to Lowry's face when he took it into his head that his hostess ought not to have gone missing. Hence, during the evening, whenever I came within earshot, I would hear his refrain that I'd given him the worst tea of his life . . . 'fiendishly bad!'

The morning following the private view the television cameras were clicking away in the main gallery, and when they had finished with Lowry he came happily downstairs to have his coffee with me. He was beaming away and pouring the usual dollop of cream into the strong black liquid. I put the local newspaper before him with, 'Well, a nice exhibition of fakes we've got!'

He had obviously seen the article at his hotel, as he answered straight away, 'Well, the damn fool should have known I was joking.

How could I start telling him about the paintings? What was there to say about them? They were there for him to see. Press men! They're all the same – damn fools.' He tossed back his coffee like a much-needed double whisky, and we exploded in laughter together.

Few of Lowry's television interviews went well, and unfortunately it was always I who came in for the full brunt of Lowry's fulminating anger afterwards. He would usually contrive to keep his mood cool before others, but I was forever the target once we were alone. 'What the devil did he expect me to answer when he asked, 'Do you consider yourself a good painter?' One saw Lowry's point. After innumerable near-disasters, he eventually insisted that he would only be interviewed by Micky. Lowry's innate shyness, plus his obdurate perversity, undoubtedly made him a difficult subject. Harold Williamson was Lowry's *bête noire* in this respect. Harold is now very well known for his interviewing of children – had he only sensed the eternal child in Lowry!

The artist would often relate to us how he had once been chosen for John Freeman's *Frankly Speaking* programme. A less happy choice under that title it would be difficult to imagine. Fortunately for all concerned, the programme was pre-recorded and, as it transpired, it was a non-starter. When the painter was faced with the first question, he announced that it was too personal and refused to answer it. Freeman tried a second, but was informed that it was worse. There was a third and fourth, but Lowry's reaction was the same. 'Oh, let's call it off, shall we?' Lowry had fumed – and caught his train home.

Taking coffee into the office during one of our friend's many interviews there, I heard him being asked, 'Why do you come to the north-east so much?' and his reply, 'Well, I like the sea, you know. . . .' None would have supposed that Lowry spent his time otherwise than looking lonelily out to sea at Sunderland, whereas the reality was very different. The company Lowry kept in the north-east was extensive, and highly entertaining to him.

He told us as far back as 1962 that he considered he was saying more in his later work than he ever did with his 'prettier' industrial landscapes. We accepted the painter's honest assessment of his vision and this, I think, is what bound him to us for the remainder of his days. As it happened, Carol also never deviated from her preference for his 'single figures'.

Over the years we had a lot of fun together, but there is little doubt that our liking for his paintings of down-and-outs and seascapes, and the fact that we were prepared to publicize and show them, gave an added meaning to his life. He had hit the jackpot with his industrial scenes, but when we came to know him we found he resented most fearfully that his later work was unacceptable in London and virtually unknown to the public at the time. When we first exhibited the later Lowry work it was almost like starting from scratch with an unknown painter.

We never found Lowry's work particularly easy to sell. It was not a question of our public finding his prices beyond its reach, but more a plain dislike of his fame, and failure to have bought Lowry's works when they cost next to nothing . . . for originally it was almost impossible for us to sell his paintings when they were as little as a hundred pounds each. The north-easterner is forever on the hunt for bargains and fails to understand that there is hardly such a thing in the art world today. At a period when investors' publications constantly supply information on what and what not to buy, it is now necessary to pay a market price, and then one will have a bargain tomorrow. Our particular public indulges in the idea of finding its own great painter of the future, little realizing, or maybe refusing to accept, that a dealer's job is to be a talent spotter and that he has to promote a painter's work at great cost to himself. Without this support the artist will remain obscure and his work will not increase in value.

Having made these statements, I can hear 'Van Gogh' being yelled on all sides. Neither public nor media allow for the fact that times do change. As Lowry was never tired of stressing, 'Van Gogh? I've no use for *him*. An impatient man. He couldn't wait for the success that was to be his.' And one must concede Lowry the point, for if anyone understood better than Lowry the necessity for patience I have yet to meet him. Lowry continued to paint in spite of his inability to sell his work or to find success until he was well into his fifties. Not for Lowry to cut off his ear, or to take himself into the next world before his appointed hour.

From mid-July to mid-August 1968 we gave Lowry the last exhibition of new paintings he was to have. This was indeed his last statement in paint to the world. After that he ceased painting to all intents and purposes. '*Nine New Paintings by L.S. Lowry*' as the show was entitled, was an exhibition in which every work was a major one of considerable size. Perhaps one of the most interesting things about it was that he had decided to cover every aspect of his painting . . . mill scene, crowd scene, seascape, groups of larger figures – the lot. He said he wished to paint the mill scenes and crowds to see whether his talent had diminished. It had not. Lowry did not want to part with any of these paintings – so a note in the catalogue announced that no work was for sale.

When we were next to see those nine major oils it was after his death, in the Retrospective Exhibition at the Royal Academy in September 1976. They hung in the frames for which we had paid, and nowhere in that catalogue's biographical chronology of the artist was there to be found any mention of the exhibition in which they had first been shown. Indeed, there was no mention of any exhibition Lowry had with us – and yet we had in the end achieved the largest coverage in the national press for this painter.

The 1968 show was widely reviewed with photographs in *The Times*, *Daily Telegraph*, and *Guardian*; it also received good national TV film coverage. But, of course, Lowry himself was a devil in his day for disparaging the image of the commercial gallery. At the precise moment of the exhibition he saw fit to give an interview to the *Weekend Scotsman*, in which he said, 'I can well understand what that French painter meant when discussing the middleman's profit; he felt like the horse on hearing that the jockey had won a large prize.'

Both Degas and Lowry were in error in their simile; very seldom is a jockey awarded a prize, and it would be a remarkable horse capable of keeping a straight course to win his race without the assistance of its jockey – and then it would be disqualified!

Possibly Lowry had supposed his quote would never come to our attention – but he reckoned without Dr Chalmers Burns, who took considerable umbrage at this implied criticism of us. When I pointed out to Lowry that in his current exhibition there was no work for sale and the expense to the gallery was extremely high, he laughed it off by saying that he had been referring to the art world in general. 'As you yourself always say, Mrs Marshall, when we're discussing art together – "present company excepted". '

That was just splendid – our discussions were private but his comment had been public. At that moment we felt like the jockey whose horse has bolted.

Lowry had some remarkable qualities and there were times when his modesty, for instance, was something to marvel at.

A lovely small oil painting of his was hanging in the gallery office, when one day a certain judge wandered in. The man was something of a dealer-cum-collector, for many of the works he acquired he promptly sold at a profit, announcing that he had become tired of them. He thought he might like the Lowry oil and wondered whether he could try it in a particular place in his home. If it failed to meet with approval, he would return it the following day. We did not make a habit of this kind of thing, but it was nevertheless difficult to refuse his request as we had known him over a great number of years – indeed he once confessed that a cousin of mine had emptied a bucket of water over him when they were at school. I was not very surprised.

Off went the judge with the painting and back he brought it the following afternoon when Lowry was sitting in his usual chair in the office. Handing us the painting the man turned abruptly to the artist with, 'You know, Mr Lowry, eighteen hundred pounds for that is ridiculous – now don't you honestly think so?'

Lowry rose from his chair, put his hands in his pockets, gave his trousers a mighty hitch with his usual side-to-side movement, went very pink in the face and answered, 'Well, it's considerably less than it would fetch in the sale rooms, sir.'

'Oh, I'm not arguing that – but your prices are mad, they're absolutely mad for your work. Now don't you agree?' Poor Mr Lowry might well have been a prisoner in the dock. 'I mean, I know and you know your work is just one great big lark. Your work's a joke! Why, that painting's not worth more than thirty pounds . . . and that would be too much for it, in my opinion.'

Lowry murmured quietly, 'Well, whatever you say, sir,' and returned to sit in his chair again.

The man took his departure, and we tried to give the artist a little comfort. 'My goodness, Mr Lowry, you were patient with him. Why didn't you tear a strip off him? I don't know how you remained so calm.'

'Oh, you get used to it, you know, Mr Marshall,' was all he said, and one might have supposed the incident had gone from his mind. Some time later, we were discussing details before his 1967 exhibition and he said, 'There's just one request I would make if you don't object. I should prefer that you didn't invite that judge –

whatever his name is – to the private view; the one who said my work was just a big joke.' Looking at Lowry's face, we could see that the quiet hurt remained.

One afternoon, Lowry was sitting in his chair alongside Micky's desk. The office door was open and a lady who was on her way to the exhibition gallery upstairs suddenly dived into the room, saying, 'Oh, you've got some of those awful things! I can't stand that man Lowry's work. Dreadful, colourless, dreary paintings. Why on earth is he so popular?'

'You possibly prefer a pretty Mediterranean scene?' asked Micky sarcastically.

'Well, I don't care what it is so long as it isn't a Lowry!' She laughed rudely.

'Oh, I'm sorry you don't like my work, madam,' said the painter quietly, from his corner.

The woman turned as though she had been shot. 'Oh, my goodness, I'd *no* idea you were there. Good gracious, I never thought of seeing you here. I'm from Manchester like you. Oh, how dreadful of me.'

'Not to worry,' murmured Lowry, 'you've every right to your opinion. Just as I've every right to paint what I please as I please. I'm not asking you to like my work.'

'Oh, but I'd never have said what I did if I'd known you were here. I'm afraid I just saw the door open – it never occurred to me that I might see you in *Newcastle*.'

'I'm seldom to be found anywhere else these days, madam. But, if there were more people like yourself about, I shouldn't have to run away from my own home to escape all m'callers. Always knockers on m'door. Always someone wanting something for nothing.' The painter was on his feet by this time, and his blue eyes suddenly twinkled mischievously; he could be extraordinarily engaging at such times. He leaned slightly back with hands in pockets, and smiled. 'Well, it's a pity you don't like my work, or perhaps I might have been persuaded to make you a present of one.' He had an ability to make a person feel that they had made an immediate conquest. For a moment the lady looked rather hopeful until suddenly Lowry threw back his head to rock with mirth. The woman flounced hurriedly from the room.

Once again we commented on Lowry's forbearance.

'Oh, Mr Marshall, it takes all sorts to make a world, don't forget.

She looked a bit hopeful though, didn't she? Thought I'd have a bit of fun. Aye, they can change their minds when they think they're going to get something for nothing.'

Once a young man brought some work in for us to see in the hope that we might approve and give him an exhibition. The works were very erotic and, looking at them with Micky, Lowry was torn between examining the drawings and the young man's wife sitting on a stool opposite him. She was extremely attractive, and wearing a very see-through crocheted dress, mini-skirted. The girl sensed that she was making something of a hit, crossed her legs, leaving little to the imagination, and began to discuss Lowry's own paintings hanging in the room. Getting thoroughly into her stride as she observed the painter's amused gaze and gleaming eyes, she informed him that she considered his works quite disgusting. Not letting him off lightly, she demanded that he look at all those pillars, figures and chimneys – nothing more than phallic symbols. His work was simply full of them.

Lowry twinkled and smiled and still led her on. He even went so far as to clean his spectacles the better to see her, admitting quite blatantly afterwards, 'Oh what a pair of tits, Mr Marshall – can't forget them. Aye, I think I'll have a go at drawing those. And how I longed to tell her that, if I were painting phallic symbols, I could do much better and more realistic ones than what she was looking at.'

In February 1965, Gabriel White, Director of Art for the Arts Council, came to visit us at the gallery. We were about to open the first British exhibition of K.R.H. Sonderborg. Born in Denmark in 1923, this artist, like Lowry, was fascinated by all aspects of people: the pace and gestures of people in the street, women's swaying hips, men in bowler hats, Chaplinesque twirls of an umbrella, an advancing crowd turning a corner and disappearing, leaving nothing but the traces of their soles; he depicted the bustle of a city, the activities of business quarters, distant views of miles of docks, airport scenes. Except that Lowry and Sonderborg both worked very much with black on white, there was no other similarity in the expression of their interest in crowds, people and movement. Sonderborg's work was full of sensitive complexity during his Paris era, and finally his New York era produced a rhythmic constructivism. For my husband, his work had a much greater appeal than ever Lowry's had.

Gabriel White was favourably impressed by what he saw of Sonderborg's work. White was a comfortable, rather untidy man, with long greying hair. He seemed pleasant, gentle and perhaps just a mite ineffectual. Glancing bird-like over his half-moon spectacles, as he munched a cucumber sandwich and drank tea with us and Pru in the office, he mentioned in passing the Lowry Retrospective Exhibition which the Arts Council was contemplating holding in eighteen months' time. It was due to open at Sunderland in the autumn of 1966 and, after visiting Manchester and Bristol, would go on to the Tate Gallery in London. We were aware Lowry was looking forward to the exhibition as Micky had already drafted his letter of acceptance.

Mr White went on to tell us that the Lowry show would not, of course, be in the Tate Gallery's main rooms but would be mounted in the basement, as the Arts Council intended to run it concurrently with a Dubuffet exhibition which would have pride of place.

'Oh, well then – you can forget the Lowry show,' announced my husband without hesitation. 'Lowry's under the impression it is to be in the main galleries but, if he supposes it is to be an also-ran, he won't play.'

Micky was fully aware that Lowry would agree to an exhibition more or less at any time, anywhere (so long as he didn't have to paint new work for it), and would certainly not have put his foot down at the thought of the Tate Gallery basement. But Micky never missed an opportunity to work for the painters he handled, and had decided to push Lowry upstairs.

'Do you think Lowry's work would be equal to the Tate's main gallery?' asked Gabriel White. Micky assured him that he certainly thought so and, what was more, it would be extremely popular with the public. He added that a good man to write the foreword to a Lowry catalogue would undoubtedly be Edwin Mullins, who was already acquainted with the painter.

'Well, after seeing your Sonderborg exhibition and other things here, I've got to admit that I trust your judgement. We shall consider very seriously what you say.'

Micky immediately warned Lowry of what the Arts Council plans had been and, for all he knew, still were.

Lowry inquired, 'D'you think they'll play?' Micky assured him that he thought his exhibition would now go into the main gallery – so long as he threatened to call it off should the plan still be otherwise.

The Tate's main gallery it proved to be (the Dubuffet exhibition was cancelled, which caused Micky some regrets), and Mullins did indeed write the foreword to Lowry's catalogue. But after this the artist was never overfond of Gabriel White. 'How's old Gabriel Grubb going on?' he would ask Micky from time to time. Later, when Mr White's death was announced, 'See old Gabriel Grubb's left us – pity – poor old Grubb.'

In the very early autumn of 1966, on the Saturday when Lowry's Arts Council Retrospective Exhibition first opened in Sunderland, he brought Carol to have lunch with us in the gallery before we took them on to the exhibition. He was naturally excited at the prospect and during luncheon was in very good spirits, wondering whether Gabriel Grubb had done the job well. Wasn't it good of the Arts Council, he asked with heavy irony, to give an exhibition to a man always described as a recluse who wore big boots (in the years we knew Lowry he invariably wore fine leather slippers in and outdoors) and who used to be regarded only as a primitive painter? And for once he remembered a small word of thanks to Micky for shoving him upstairs.

We set off for Sunderland. Micky was driving – Lowry in the front as ever – Carol and I in the back. As she and I chatted away, I became aware of a strangely unpleasant odour in the car. Lowry's nervousness that day was of a different order from the kind he suffered if we were merely going to visit people with whom he feared he might not be at ease. He was quietly apprehensive by this time, not in the least tetchy, appearing relieved to have about him those he felt close to. But the dreadful smell was there. I'd noticed previously that if he became unduly excited he exuded this terrible smell. As we travelled it became almost overpowering. It may be distasteful to mention this, but it was a fact which had to be coped with over the years and it was not funny.

Lowry talked away, ironically regretting that he did not look like a proper artist for such an occasion. He wondered whether his battered trilby was at the right angle? Then he brightened, recalling his favourite photograph of a group of European painters exiled in New York in the forties. From time to time he would ask us to get this photograph out of the files for him to laugh over yet again.

There was Mondrian looking like a school teacher; André Masson looked the very double of an insurance agent once known to Lowry; Lipchitz could so easily have been a tram driver; and Zadkine, Tanguy, Ernst and Chagall all looked like business men; Léger could be mistaken for a farmer.

'My word, they knew how to do it, and they didn't have to dress up – look, not a beard in sight. I always say, "The longer the hair – the shorter the art." '

We all knew the road to Sunderland well by this time but we awaited the inevitable Lowry commentary. He regretted the lack of shipping on the river and considered that our shipbuilders were more interested in putting their money into Japanese yards than wasting it in their own strike-torn British ones. The earth-scrapers working on a new stretch of road reminded him of prehistoric monsters. We passed a favourite cemetery, his pride and joy. It was a singularly unattractive place, dotted with uniform tombstones. Lowry thought the Co-op had supplied them all, and wondered how many stamps to a stone. The graveyard reminded him of a giant wartime tank trap. The very plain entrance gates bore a similarity to those at the entrance to a certain Scottish estate. The gates had once so taken his fancy that he had painted them. It was a singularly bad picture which could have cost him little effort in either work or time or imagination. Few cared for it but he eventually sold it when he had become better known. As he said, 'You always get a better price, of course, the better known you are – no matter how bad the picture. It's the way of life.'

The cemetery provoked him into discussing his funeral again. His solicitor would be there, and the undertaker of course (he always overlooked any bearers), and after the interment the solicitor would look at his watch, see that it was later than he had supposed, and ask the undertaker whether he would give him a lift back to town. It never varied. As ever, the three of us told him not to be daft – we would be present as well to see him safely into the ground. And, as ever, he gave it a little thought and then agreed, yes, we would be there too. He sighed, 'He died with his family about him – and they didn't even ask him to sign his last pictures.'

At the Sunderland Art Gallery we made our entrance like a posse looking for outlaws, headed, of course, by Sheriff Lowry. Then he began to savour the moment. The entrance hall was an ideal place for reflection and he began to recall an earlier visit when he and

Micky had asked to be shown two studies for Rosetti's *Astarte Syriaca* in the gallery's possession. To Lowry's disgust they were in a store room. As the librarian, who was also in charge of the art gallery, led them into his office, Lowry hissed at Micky, 'See if he'll do a swop!'

'What for? One of yours? You haven't a hope, chum.'

'Do have a go, Mr Marshall – for Little Laurie's sake.' In all reason both men were aware that the museum official could not possibly oblige even had he wanted to and it was evident he did not. So on this Saturday afternoon here was Lowry again urging my husband to have another 'go'. We passed a few extremely nondescript works but no cajoling would hurry the painter. Sucking his teeth with approval, he drew in his breath to expel it again as he extolled the merits of this mediocre work or that. Then he suggested a cup of tea but as promptly discounted the notion. Suddenly with no warning he was gone.

In the main gallery I found Lowry standing alone in the centre of the room, leaning slightly sideways and backwards upon his walking-stick, his isolation immediate and total. There was no one present for him. There was only himself and his work. When he wished, he always had this ability to put a wall round himself.

The impressive exhibition was superbly hung. The paintings were spread around the walls in such a way that they gave authority to the condemnation of what man had done, not only to the landscape, but to his fellow creatures in their degradation. Of course, we had been prepared to be impressed, prepared to pay homage to the painter. It could have stopped there, but the works in that particular setting were awesome. It was only at Sunderland that Lowry's work had such an impact upon us. The same exhibition, with additions, failed to produce the same element of wonder at the Tate. For one thing the impact had already been made. For another, it was less well hung in London. Screens had been used to form cubicles and, because of the number of spectators standing in these tiny three-sided rooms, it was impossible to see the exhibition as a whole – it became fragmented. The emphasis at the Tate was put upon the industrial scenes with their anonymous puppets scuttling through mazes of domineering rectangular buildings. London, to Lowry's eternal disgust, always put the emphasis upon this side of his work.

There was no official opening of his exhibition, and there were very few people in the Sunderland Art Gallery that Saturday afternoon. I looked again at Lowry, now totally relaxed, still leaning upon his walking-stick, serious, satisfied – as well he deserved to be.

A man in a trilby hat approached him and they exchanged a word or two. Lowry called my husband over and the three of them talked together for a few moments. Lowry and Micky were later amused to relate that this had been the Mayor of Sunderland, who had asked, 'Oh, you're the painter, are you?' And when Lowry admitted such was the case, the gentleman shortly took his departure, his duty done. The exhibition was on its way.

The northern art correspondent for *The Times* arrived with his wife, and she and I went slowly around the pictures together.

'God, the drains here need seeing to!' she said.

'Shut up,' I replied, 'it's Lowry!'

I always enjoyed viewing an exhibition with Margo Gow; she teaches art, and I remember her saying, 'Tilly, isn't it extraordinary, Lowry breaks every rule, but in the finished work he gets away with it.'

A lady of about my own age was talking to the painter and a little later Lowry introduced her as an old friend of his, Mrs Margo Ingham. She had loaned an early oil painting to the show, and we all went over to look at it. It was already arranged that Micky and I, with Simon, who had arrived under his own steam, should join Lowry and Carol for a cup of tea at the Seaburn Hotel, and the artist asked Mrs Ingham to join us. I have said that Lowry on no occasion paid for anything when he was in our company. That afternoon tea at the Seaburn Hotel was the exception – that he did put on his account.

In the upstairs lounge, Lowry complained bitterly at the lack of butter on the toasted tea cakes. He always enjoyed masses of running butter on such favourite items as toasted tea cakes or hot potato scones. He dearly wanted to make his displeasure felt that day but was restrained by Carol, who calmed him down and acted charmingly as hostess, until a fellow resident came into the room and promptly turned on the television. In a flash Lowry leaped to his feet, gave the man a dirty look and said that we would return to the Stone Gallery, where we might find a little peace.

The painter maintained that he loathed television and never looked at it, but occasionally he was caught out when it became clear that he had enjoyed some play on the small screen in one or other of the hotels in which he stayed. He did not have a television at his home.

At his insistence we all got quickly to our feet and left the Seaburn lounge to the painter's loud refrain of, 'Ridiculous, isn't it? Simply ridiculous,' with Lowry still casting resentful glances in the direction of the stranger. We took the cars across the ferry, which Lowry wanted to show to Margo Ingham, and we arrived back at the closed gallery in the early evening. Carol looked around the current exhibition and admired some work or other, which 'Uncle' immediately bought for her. Over a drink in the office we discovered that Lowry's friend was not due to return to the south until later, so I invited her to join us at the Station Hotel for dinner.

It made a jolly change from the meals Micky and I so often ate alone with the artist, night after night. Mrs Ingham was delightfully knowledgeable on matters of art. She was at one time married to Ned Owens and they had given Lowry an exhibition at their gallery in Manchester, the Mid-day Studios, as far back as 1948.

About ten o'clock it was time for her to catch her southbound train and Micky offered to see her into it. As they moved across the dining room I announced to my three companions that Margo Ingham had remarkably beautiful legs.

'Maybe,' said Lowry. 'But, my God! fancy a woman of that age wearing a skirt as short as that! Ridiculous – silly fool.' With legs as good as hers, I said, I too might have been so tempted. Lowry noticed some small displeasure on Carol's part at this discussion – for the departed legs were truly superb, and neither Carol's nor mine were in the same class. The painter always enjoyed a sadistic technique of working upon another's small jealousy and he suddenly decided to agree with me. 'You're right Mrs Marshall – Mrs Ingham has remarkably fine legs – oh yes, simply splendid.' But then, to make amends to Carol, 'Oh, but at her age that skirt's bloody mad!'

Simon jumped to his feet saying that he was off.

'You're off, sir?' asked Lowry. 'Where are you off to? It's early yet.'

'A party. Friend at Darlington – it'll be a good do. It's a twenty-first – in a bedding factory!'

The painter snorted. 'What, at this time of night?'

'You've just said it was early,' teased Simon, then turning to Carol he suggested she might like to go along.

For a moment the girl hesitated, but Lowry interposed at once with, 'Good heavens, you don't want to go to a party, do you Carol?' Poor Carol looked as though she would dearly enjoy a little change of scene and company, but shook her head.

'Well, I'm picking you both up in the morning,' said Simon. 'I can easily come back with you tonight, Carol, if you like – I'll stay with the Grans.' Again Carol declined.

'Right, 'cuse me, I must rush. Ta-ta,' and Simon gave a particular lilt to his farewell in imitation of Lowry's occasional valediction. I glanced at the girl beside me and noticed a sad little droop to her mouth as she continued to sit listening to 'Uncle's' chuntering – everything he had to say we'd all heard so often before.

Upon reflection, it is strange that the Arts Council chose Sunderland rather than Manchester as the provincial city in which to open Lowry's Retrospective Exhibition before it went on to the Tate. Perhaps it is proof in some small measure of the painter's little-known affiliation with the north-east of England. This affiliation has been increasingly overlooked since the artist's death, especially by many who had no part in Lowry's last years – and some, indeed, who had no part in his life at any time but were to cash in on his fame after his death. I can hear him sighing again, 'It's the way of the world, Mrs Marshall – it's the way of the world.'

In an article in the *Sunday Telegraph* on 20 November 1966, just prior to the opening at the Tate Gallery, Edwin Mullins quotes Lowry as saying:

> It was suggested that I went in for art as I was fit for nothing else. . . . At school I had few friends, and I never passed any exams. Time went on and on and on, until finally an aunt remembered that I'd drawn little ships when I was eight years of age. So that was that. It was any port in a storm. As we lived in Manchester I went to Manchester School of Art in 1905 and stayed there a great many years – I suppose about ten in all. Between 1909 and 1939, when I had my first exhibition, there's really nothing to tell. There's nothing in my life except what I've said. I've never robbed a bank, or shot someone, or married. . . . I often think I should have been a stockbroker and not an artist. . . . For a great many years, when I was very active, I used to visit all the industrial towns and stop a couple of nights in each . . . and I always gravitated to the poorer areas. It wasn't that I felt sorry for those people: they were just as happy as anyone else, and certainly as happy as I was. . . . Of course I often used to wonder if I'd make any money. I was living at home so it wasn't urgent, but every now and then I felt thoroughly fed up and I'd say, 'This is ridiculous; I'll

take a job.' But I didn't like the thought of going to the office with a bag in my hand at half past nine every morning. And then some little sale would come along – there were always a few private buyers in Manchester and Salford – and that was enough to keep me going for another year.

Often Lowry would say to me that I was the only person who had found it incomprehensible that he should have had the guts to continue painting when his works hardly ever sold until he was fifty-two. He had sold the odd one here and there for a few pounds, but not until he was into his fifties had he made a small profit. He would describe how as a younger man he used to visit London regularly once a month, always staying with an aunt, and would frequent the art galleries and see current exhibitions.

His mother had been very musical and might have been a concert pianist had she wished. His father remained a much dimmer figure, but Lowry had one or two stories to relate about him. He was particularly fond of telling how he and his father were once invited for a meal at the home of an acquaintance where there had not been enough to eat. Discussing it afterwards, as Lowry complained of pangs of hunger, his father had said, 'But surely you had something to eat beforehand? You should always have a good meal before partaking of anyone's hospitality with which you're unfamiliar.' He would then describe how his father had been acquainted with several wealthy Manchester men who enjoyed giving musical evenings in their homes and how, sparing no expense, they would employ the services of the top musicians of the day. Lowry's father had apparently enjoyed these occasions.

After his father's death Lowry was left to look after his mother for the following seven years. He would tell us in detail how he had nursed her night and day – for upon the death of her husband she immediately took to her bed, becoming a helpless invalid. Once, as a consequence of all his nursing, Lowry came close to a nervous breakdown and his friends suggested that he take a job simply to get out of the house. He had tried one for a week, but it brought him even closer to a breakdown, so he promptly left it.

No article we read about Lowry during his lifetime told us anything new. He always churned out the same stuff to the press. I often used to urge him to give this critic or that interviewer something a bit different. He said he couldn't, as nothing different had ever happened to him. As Lowry was never publicly associated with any female, every new young journalist obviously supposed him to be a homosexual – and hoped to get the inside story where others had failed. But they got the same old stuff each time. Whenever any member of the press met Lowry, the artist would hood his eyes, adopt his hostile guard and often put on an act of going to sleep. No man could go to sleep more hastily.

Eventually he urged me to write a book about him. But somewhere within the complex character I felt there was a secret man of whom even we were not permitted knowledge. So I stalled. How, I would ask, can I write a book about a man to whom so little had ever happened?

'Well,' he would say, 'you'll have to accept it, Mrs Marshall – it's only the work that matters.' And I would argue, saying that he was interested in every detail of Rossetti's life.

'Oh yes, Mrs Marshall, but Rossetti was a rum bird. You couldn't call me a rum bird, now could you?'

'Well, what about all your "totties"?'

'I tell you you've got it wrong, Mrs Marshall – no lovely ladies in my life.'

'I didn't say "lovely ladies", I said "totties" – there's a difference.'

'Mr Marshall knows, don't you, Mr Marshall?'

'Knows what?' Micky would bring his mind down from the clouds, for if someone else was amusing Lowry he would take the opportunity to think of other things.

'Well, I've told you, haven't I? I've never had sexual intercourse.'

'Oh yes, certainly that's what you've told me.'

'Well, maybe Rossetti didn't have all that you give him credit for!' And at that Lowry would rock with laughter, and continue to tease me through half the day and all the evening.

I would become more and more annoyed, announcing at last, 'Well, you're just proving my point – it's no use eternally saying, "It's only the work that matters, if one's researching a painter a hundred years hence. . . ." '

'Well, even you won't be researching a hundred years hence, Mrs Marshall!'

'Oh shut up, you know what I mean – whenever one's researching one wants to know more than just what a man painted, one wants to know what made him tick. Well, at any rate *I* do. And why give any interviews to the press as you do, if you don't believe the public is interested to know about you as a man? It's so often the small things that are important. What was it Shaw had Mr Bohun say in

You Never Can Tell? You p'raps don't remember but I do: "It's the trifles that can wreck you at the harbour mouth." '

'I never cared for Shaw m'self,' Lowry grumbled, and I remember pushing the point once with; 'Wasn't it Aldous Huxley? – anyway I think it was one of the Huxleys who claimed it's the little things, like a man being constipated, that can prevent his becoming Prime Minister.'

'Well, I'm not going to tell the world when I'm constipated! Why *don't* you write a book about me, Mrs Marshall? I'd give you all the help I can.'

'Like hell you would,' I'd laugh. 'No, you're a bit too like Ruskin – I think I'd better leave my book about you till you've gone hence.'

'You'll have to accept it, Mrs Marshall, it's only the work that matters,' he would reply crossly. One did not have just one conversation with Lowry about something, one had the same conversation a hundred times.

'When I write my book about you, I know how I'll start.'

'And how will you finish, Mrs Marshall?'

'Oh hell, I can't tell you that – you'll have to be finished first!'

'Ah well – you won't have long to wait now.' With a great sigh he put out his hand for another hot sausage roll. He loved these hot, but his tea was always left until it was cold before he would drink it, with the inevitable comment, 'It'll soon be warmed up once it gets inside.'

'Now tell me again how you'll start, Mrs Marshall.' And we would laugh while I recited, 'Getting off Lowry's bed, and pushing my feet into my shoes. . . .'

The day following the Sunderland opening of Lowry's Retrospective Exhibition, after luncheon at our home we were sitting over coffee with the painter and Carol when a crowd of Simon's friends arrived. Obviously the painter was not thrilled at this invasion, and there was general relief when the young people decided to go for a walk. 'Splendid, off you go,' I urged them on their way, 'and I'll have some tea ready when you get back.' Without hesitation this time, Carol opted for a walk and amid a good deal of noisy chatter and juvenile wise-cracking the party trooped off to the delights of Langley Dale. All but one, Netty, who announced that she was not going for a walk, not with the opportunity to stay and talk with Mr

Lowry.

Netty was not unlike Carol in appearance, perhaps a couple of years younger, with dark hair worn rather long, and small attractive features. Her father had been killed by hooligans during his work as steward of a young people's club, and this gave the girl something of a bizarre attraction in Lowry's eyes. Netty had also at one time spent a year at art school.

When the walkers returned Netty was sitting, wide-eyed, on the floor at 'the Master's' feet, leaning against his chair before the blazing log fire. Not once during Carol's absence had Lowry thought to ask where she was and what she was doing, as was his wont if she was out of sight. Netty's conquest had been instantaneous. Already it was arranged that on the coming Wednesday we would collect her and take her to Sunderland where she would meet Lowry and spend the day with him. He wanted to show her his exhibition, which she was longing to see. They were chuckling and laughing together as Carol came into the tower room. Netty was still sitting on the floor and gazing up at Lowry with intelligence, interested in all he had to say, amused and amusing, and his hand rested in fatherly fashion upon her shoulder.

As I prepared supper much later, Carol came to talk with me and said she felt rather awful – she really shouldn't have left 'Uncle' to go on the walk. I reassured her that he hadn't missed her and she really couldn't be forever at his beck and call. But she was due to return home the next day and she considered she had made an error.

Talking the events of the day over with Micky later we both agreed that the old boy didn't need any more 'nieces' and we decided that for him to become involved with yet another was rather more than we cared to cope with. Very naughty of us, perhaps, but we told Lowry that Netty could not keep the appointment, and Netty that Lowry could not. Carol had put in a long stint with the artist by this time and we felt that some sort of loyalty was her due as a consequence. I have no idea whether we were right to act as we did, but that was the way of it.

Because Carol had been such a big influence in his life, Lowry had discussed her endlessly over the years, asking our advice about this or that with regard to her. At home he loved to lean around the kitchen while I prepared meals; he would ask again and again, how did I think Carol was developing? Did I like her current boyfriend

David? And later, what did I think of another – Sam? On and on the questions would go. Did I suppose that if he ailed in his last years Carol would push him out in a wheelchair? 'Oh, come off it,' I'd laugh, 'you'd be a hell of a weight!' But many times as the years passed I suggested that he ought to organize his life rather better; he was always moaning about his awful little house and how he offended people by leaving letters unanswered, so why not move to a more suitable abode and let Carol act as his companion–secretary? He announced in the press that he was coming to live in the north-east. But eventually he dismissed all such ideas, going hopefully on his way, gambling that his end would come suddenly as, fortunately, it did.

After Lowry first brought Carol to meet us he never made any bones about the fact that she was his heiress. This was discussed frequently in front of Carol – she was fully aware of it. And as he continued to heap luxury holidays, clothes, and you name it upon her, so he began to buy works of art for her. Indeed, it became a joke – I only had to admire a painting and he promptly bought it for Carol.

Now my maternal grandmother instructed me that there were three subjects of conversation which were to be avoided during dinner: food, money and politics. But I was to discover that they were three of Lowry's favourites. Sitting with Micky and me in Tilley's one evening, Lowry decided that it was time he got down to making his will. He had been talking of it for long enough.

He was certainly never going to leave any of his own work nor any of his collection of Pre-Raphaelite paintings and drawings to a public gallery. From the earliest days of our friendship he would rage against the public gallery practice of showing certain works with regularity while others of great interest never saw the light of day, being stored in the cellars. He was not going to have his works buried in public gallery basements.

On the evening in question, he started to get down to the business of disposing of his estate, stating for the umpteenth time that Carol was to be left everything.

'Oh, but surely you'll still leave Mr Bennett his favourite clock?' I queried. He and the 'reverend gentleman' had recently had a small tiff.

'Oh yes – he can have that. I never go back on my word. He's hankered after it for long enough, can't disappoint him. Though he's been very unkind to "Little Laurie".'

'Right, then he gets the Tompion.' We were all certain that the tall grandfather clock in question was not a Tompion, but it pleased Lowry to think it was.

'And, of course, I'll see Mrs Swindles is all right.' Mrs Swindles was his aged housekeeper or, rather, daily help. In the circumstances he was extremely fortunate in having her services; it is hardly possible that anyone else would have put up with the conditions in his house. (She was only a year younger than Lowry – and outlived him by one year.)

'But everything else will go to Carol,' Lowry was repeating.

'What about the large Rossetti chalk drawing to the left of your fireplace in the sitting room? You've always said it was to go to your solicitor.'

'Why, you know m'own will better than I know it myself, Mrs Marshall. I'd forgotten that,' he laughed. 'But everything else will go to Carol – po'r little wretch.'

'Oh God, you do annoy me when you call her that,' I exclaimed. 'You know what people will think when you die? They're bound to suppose that Carol was either your mistress or your illegitimate daughter.'

'Ha, ha, Mrs Marshall, and I'll be up there laughing my head off!'

'Oh no, you won't – you'll be down below. Laughing your head off maybe, but maybe not. It could be a bit too hot even for your liking.' Then, more seriously, 'But surely you're going to leave Ann something?'

'Oh, indeed no – she's got more money than is good for her already. I'll maybe leave her the paintings of herself – but she didn't care for them much.'

'Certainly the large '59 portrait is a masterpiece,' said Micky. 'It should be in the Tate.'

'That man Rothenstein never liked my portraits – self-opinionated man!' (Sir John Rothenstein was an ex-Director of the Tate – and had been responsible for its first Lowry acquisitions).

'Well,' I said, 'what about Sheila?'

'Sheila Fell? Good God, no!'

'I thought you'd have remembered her.'

'No, Mrs Marshall – I've done enough for Sheila Fell. I've put her on the right road. My word, yes. But Sheila Fell has a life of her own now – well that's all right with me – but I shan't do anything more for her. Too fond of the bottle, I'm afraid. Well, you saw it yourselves at that John Moores exhibition and dinner, didn't you?'

'Well, you've forgotten Cousin May. . . .'

'No, I haven't – I'm not leaving her anything either. Lost her own money – she needn't set about losing mine. Anyway, she's too old – might go before me.'

'Come off it – she's younger than you are.'

'Not all that much – anyway, she's not having anything, so that's that.'

'Then there's Mr Robertson – he's very ill – maybe he won't be able to work again.'

Lowry suddenly banged his fist upon the table, glasses rattled and heads turned. '*Mr Robertson*? What are you talking about, Mrs Marshall? He's a mere casual acquaintance! Met him in a café over lunch.'

'I don't care how you met him – he's surely more than *that*?'

'He's certainly not – a mere casual acquaintance.' This hard comment surprised me, for Philip Robertson was another of Lowry's friends. The artist had first brought him and his wife Margaret to the Stone Gallery on the last day of his 1964 exhibition. Micky and I had promised to go to a party at the home of Harold Williamson, Lowry's *bête noire* TV interviewer. But Lowry and his friends sat on and on in the gallery office, and it appeared impolite to chuck them out suddenly at seven o'clock as I hadn't mentioned that we had an engagement. So I went off to telephone Harold and tell him we couldn't make it, which was really much more impolite. Instead, we took Lowry and his friends round to Tilley's. Margaret asked me whether we'd met his so-called niece, and was surprised to learn we had – no one else had, but Lowry talked of her a great deal.

The Robertsons live in Glossop, a small town not far from Lowry's village of Mottram. Philip is another amateur painter, and enjoyed coming to stay at Seaburn with Lowry for a week or so each summer – when they would spend most of their time in the gallery. We had entertained Philip a great deal over the years and now to hear Lowry refer to him as a casual acquaintance was astounding.

'Well, anyhow,' I continued, 'you've always said that the taxman has taken all your money, so I really don't know what you're nattering about.' I had done my best for a few people whom I had supposed Lowry might have remembered in his will – aware, however, that I was up against a stone wall. Once Lowry decided upon a course, that was that.

Lowry continued to tie up all the loose ends with regard to his will, and announced that his executors would be his solicitor and his bank. 'Good God! Surely that would be unwise,' exclaimed my husband. 'I mean, such executors would not be a first choice in the normal way – and you're not a normal man!'

'And what d'you mean by that, sir,' smiled Lowry.

'Well, you're absolutely crazy to consider appointing a bank to deal with your affairs after your death – as a painter, you must have someone with a knowledge of the visual arts.'

'No, Mr Marshall, it'll be all businesslike, m'solicitor and m'bank; that'll be the best.'

Micky was still trying to persuade him to think again, when I heard Lowry muttering, 'I don't really care much about posterity so long as I can make the odd penny or two while I live. Let the rest take care of itself. I shan't be here to enjoy "posterity".'

'What? You don't care whether your work will live after your death or not?' I looked sideways at him in surprise.

'No, Mrs Marshall, why should I? After all, the work will speak for itself. Nothing anyone says, does, or writes will make the ha'p'orth of difference.'

'Oh, dear me, you and I have argued along these lines so often. And I'm sure you're only right up to a point. You've achieved stature in your lifetime – but seldom a day goes by when you don't complain bitterly that when you leave the north-east and go home you're surrounded by hangers-on and speculators whom you promptly have to flee, and return to us. After you're gone that kind of people aren't half going to move in on your reputation.'

'Yes, I dare say you're right, they will. A lot of people will claim to have known me who never did. But that's not going to worry me when I've gone. I'm leaving m'solicitor that Rossetti so he'll not charge my estate.'

'Well, the bank'll certainly charge your blooming estate,' I laughed.

We were aware of our friend's enormous obsession with money. Once I accused him of mixing with the wrong kind of people when he returned to his native city because he would come back to us with his miserly instincts even more pronounced. There were occasions when he quite sickened me, and I made no secret of the fact. I recall his once looking at me very sharply indeed after being tackled on the point and thenceforth he mended his ways a little, at least in front of me, but certainly not altogether.

We had a client and acquaintance, Ben Worthington, a young stockbroker who in his spare time worked ceaselessly to raise money for a new Cheshire Home. Incidentally, he and his wife had acquired two nice small Lowry oils from us.

One day, Ben, having met Lowry several times in the gallery, took Micky aside to ask him if he would approach Lowry with a request to give a drawing for a forthcoming fund-raising auction in aid of the charity. Lowry turned down the request in no uncertain terms. We had a National Health Service to which his taxation inevitably contributed – let that suffice.

The Worthingtons' two Lowry oils went into Christie's sale room without delay.

At coffee time one morning the artist plonked a letter down on Micky's desk as was his habit; it was a suggestion that perhaps he could see his way to donating a work which would be auctioned in aid of the restoration fund for York Minster. Well-known artists were listed as already having promised works – amongst them Henry Moore. Again Lowry refused. He considered that in view of the wealth of the Church Commissioners they could afford to look after their own minster and need not turn to him for assistance.

4

In July 1964 a cold 'wind of change' blew over the Stone Gallery; starting as a small breeze, it ended as a hurricane which blew away Micky's original policy for the gallery.

During that month we showed an exhibition of modern sculpture, which had been particularly expensive to put on. At the private view things were going with the usual swing; those present were admiring or otherwise the many works, meeting new acquaintances, arguing with old ones, discussing everything under the sun. But nothing was selling.

There was much talk of a coming general election. The Conservatives had been in power for a considerable number of years, and it was now fully expected that Labour would be the newly elected government. One of our biggest collectors informed me that, should Labour get in the following October he would no longer be in a position to buy works of art. His taxes would be too high. There was sculpture on view that night which normally he would have bought. His boardroom groaned with paintings and sculpture he and his family directors had purchased from us. They were a self-made family providing a great deal of employment on Tyneside. His home was also by this time full of works of art. He often came in for criticism from his friends who could not appreciate these things – when he had acquired a large piece by Henry Moore, he was laughed to scorn.

Among the tycoons present it appeared to be the general consensus of opinion that they were about to face taxation which would put an end to art collecting. We had not originally opened the gallery with the primary idea of making money, but selling to the rich enabled us to present important exhibitions of modern art to the poorer. Many thousands of people passed through the gallery

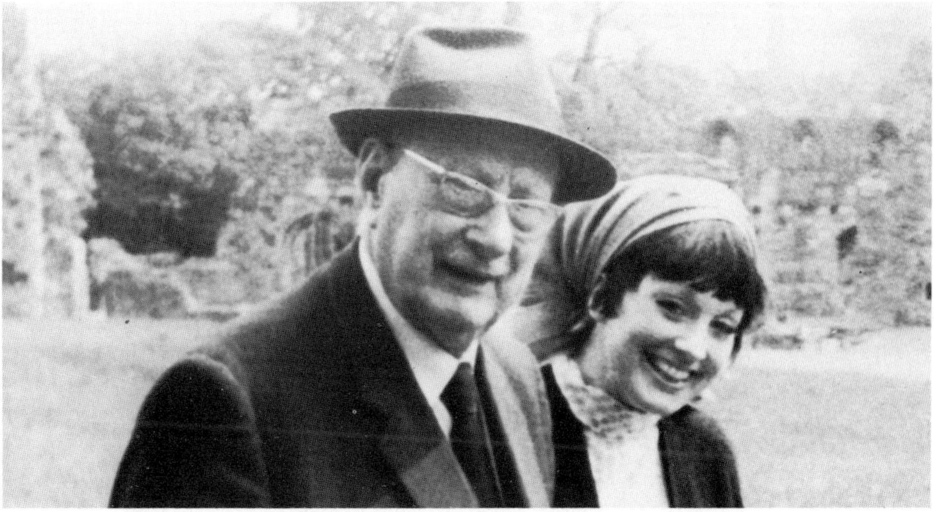

Lowry with Pat Cooke, May 1973.
Photograph taken by Pat's husband
when they were visiting the Rhyl area so that Lowry
might find again the old castles that he
had sketched in the 1920s

Sheila Fell in the Stone Gallery at the time
of her exhibition in June 1969

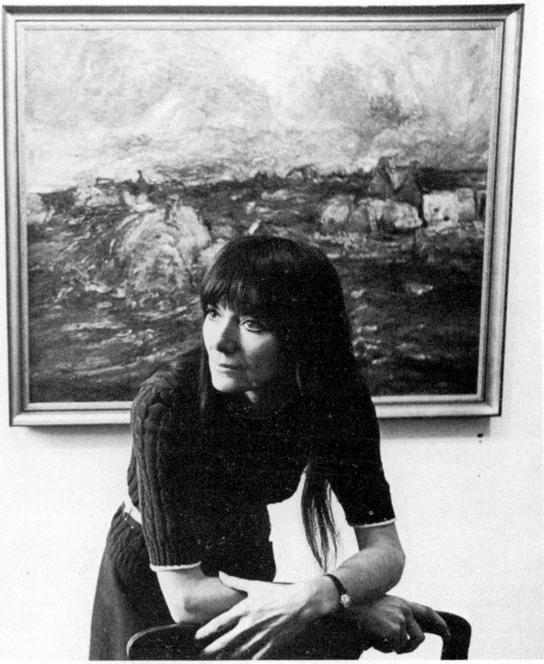

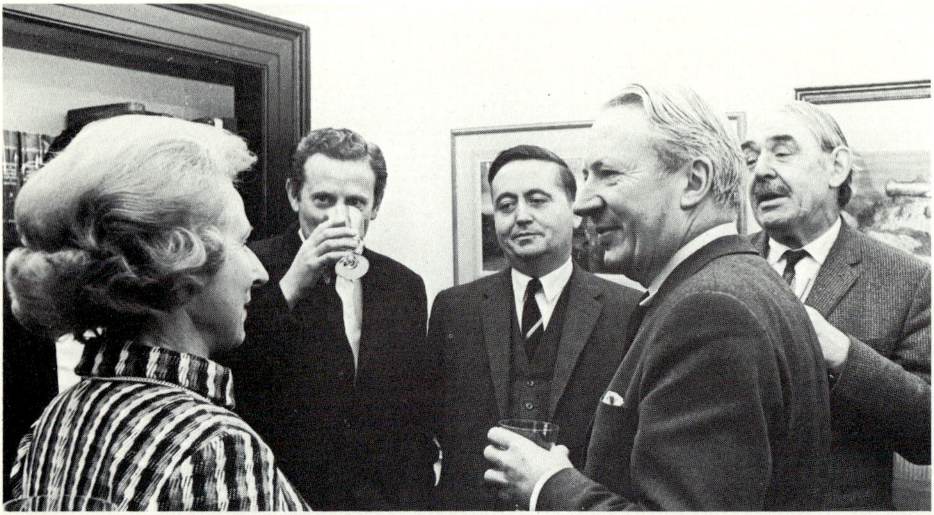

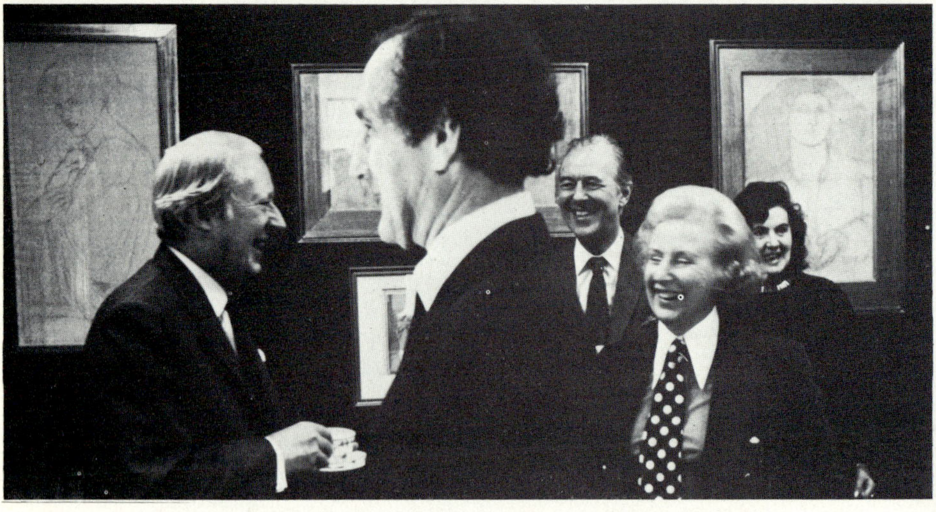

Top: The author, Donald Gow (*The Times* correspondent), Ian, Edward Heath and Chalmers Burns gathered in Micky's office in the Stone Gallery. January 1969

Edward Heath, Michael Clark (the Rossetti Society's Master of the Horse), Michael Denison, the author and Veral during a Saturday morning gathering in Micky's office. 1972

Opposite page: Lowry celebrating his eighty-fourth birthday party in the Stone Gallery, 1 November 1971, with (*in the top picture*) Micky, Ian, Lenny Jacobson (Chairman of Montague Burton) and Simon

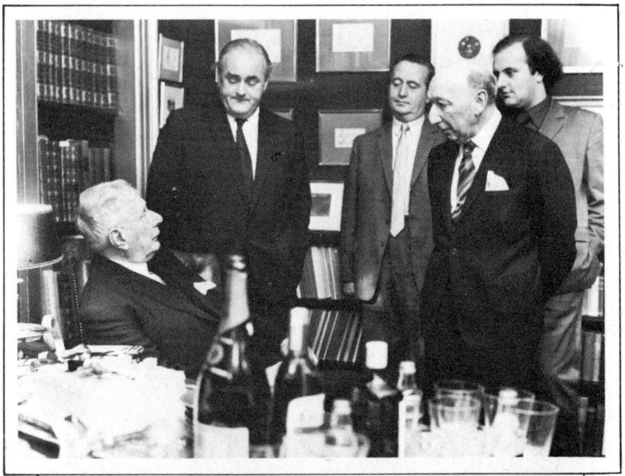

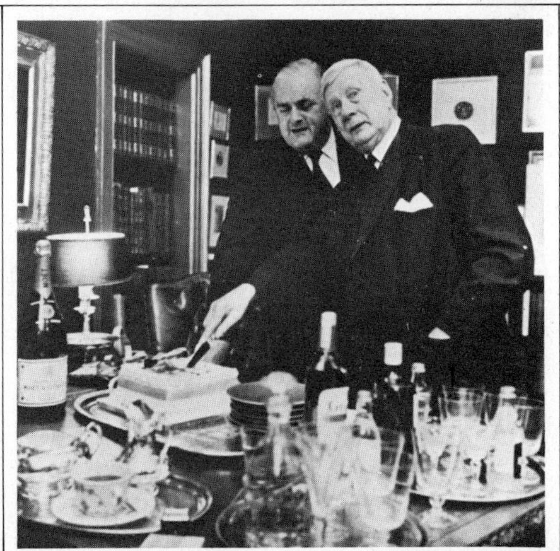

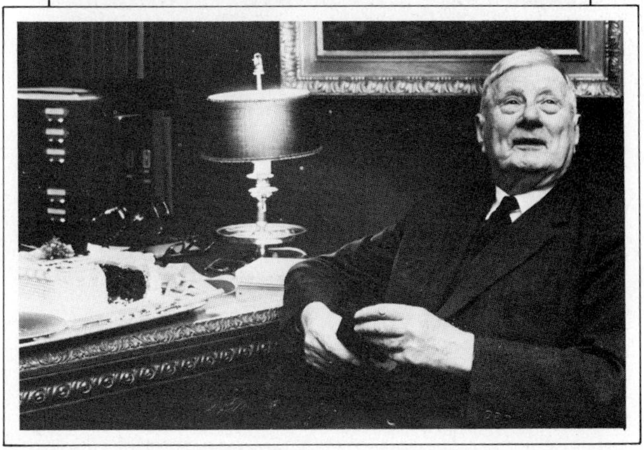

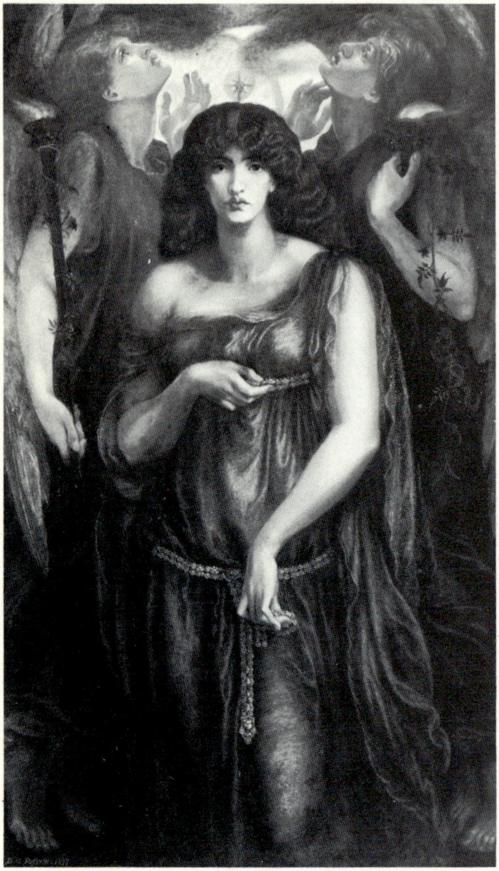

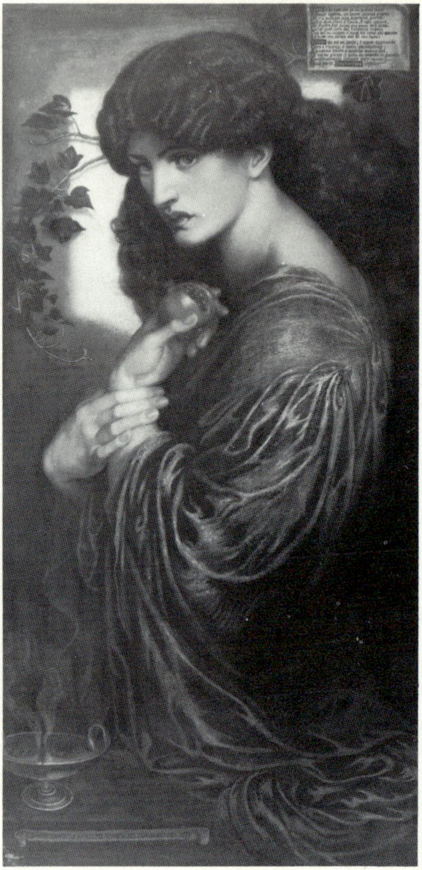

Left: *Astarte Syriaca* (Oil painting 72 × 42 ins.)
Dante Gabriel Rossetti.
Signed and dated 1877 lower left.
Collection Manchester City Art Galleries.
Lowry valued this Rossetti above all others

Right: *Proserpine* (Oil painting 46 × 22 ins.)
Inscribed, signed and dated lower left:
Dante Gabriel Rossetti ritrasse nel capo d'anno del 1877.
This, the major Rossetti work acquired
by Lowry, was specifically bequeathed to Carol in his will
quite separately from the remainder of his estate

doors who would never be in a position to buy a work of art, but they would linger to talk over the things they were seeing, and argue about subjects other than painting and sculpture. The local press had already written that the gallery had 'shown many world-class works before they were shown in London, a reversal of the time-honoured trend'.

Micky's wide vision for gallery policy had worked to the advantage of the area. When he and I were horrified to learn that a great firm of shipowners were about to give an order for a new ship to Sweden, it was explained to us that the price could not be equalled in this country. We had a good client who bought very modern works and happened to be a director of a family shipbuilding firm on the Wear. We considered that this enlightened fellow would see the importance of keeping the order in the north-east. We got the two together at a private view, and the local yard got the work.

Our economic situation deteriorated. Labour got in. The wealthy had not waited for that, however – since midsummer they had clung fast to their money. The north-east, owing to its hard experience during the depression, is a nervous area.

The Regional Arts Association and the city council, when applied to, both promised long-term assistance to the gallery, upon the condition that we set up a non-profit distributing trust to run it. As a family we would still be required to find the major finance, and we would be in a position to be outvoted on any matter by five votes to two. Nevertheless, we were ready for such a trust so long as others serving on it had a knowledge of the visual arts. We suggested willing men with experience in such matters but every suggestion was turned down in favour of city councillors. One of them was the man who had laughed at our friend's Henry Moore, and another name we had to accept was T. Dan Smith.

At this point Jennie Lee had just been made the first Minister with Special Responsibility for the Arts. She spent an hour and a half in the gallery, but, as she explained, her responsibility was to get as much money as possible from the government for the Arts. It then went to the Arts Council, who in turn had to give grants to the Regional Arts Associations – and it was those associations which were in future to be responsible for how the money was spent in the provinces. We were back with the NEAA – the first director of which was a 'resting' Labour MP, Arthur Blenkinsopp, a left-wing socialist of outdated Fabian principles.

The future of the Stone Gallery was argued in the correspondence columns of *The Times*, in leaders and articles in the national press; we gave interviews to art critics and journalists, but it was a losing fight. Throughout this time Lowry remained at our side. He would doze off in his chair in the office with one pressman present, and awaken to see another in his place. He was quoted in our local press as saying, 'Newcastle should be as proud of the Stone Gallery as Manchester is of the Hallé Orchestra.'

In July 1965, a year after our first fears, Lowry advised us to close, and we did. His firm opinion was that the north-east found the gallery undesirable. 'You must understand,' he said, 'some people do not want the answer to problems. They prefer the problems – for on those they can rise to political power.' He smiled sardonically at the Arts Council's rebuke that no one had *asked* us to work for a cultured citizenry of tomorrow. It was a self-imposed task.

'We should have been content to leave the public to its booze and bingo and football,' sighed Micky. Lowry concurred that in a welfare state it must obviously be accepted that the idea of personal service to a community was a thing of the past.

'It's very, very sad,' sighed Lowry. 'No wonder the country's plagued with violence. Where will it all end, I wonder. Man's inhumanity to man – but what about bureaucracy's inhumanity, eh? Now there's a nightmare!'

'But surely, Mr Lowry, it was all predicted in the 1940s and 1950s when we had "Action Painting". That was a breakdown in values . . . all the visual values as we knew them. And visual values are related to spiritual ones – so here we have the whole breakdown of the values of ordered society as we have known it,' said Micky. 'But I think the terrifying factor for which we have to allow is that other part of modern painting, the very severely classical abstraction – very, very cold, such as Ben Nicholson's. . . .'

'D'you like his work, Mr Marshall?'

'Well, never mind for the moment whether I like it personally or not – that's not the point. The point is, it exists. And it's very organized – down to the last detail; ordered and mathematical: predicting what is in front of us. We're going to have, indeed have got, this bureaucratic, cold, inhuman approach to the world and humanity in general. Our society is going to find itself under computer control – and, as you say, Mr Lowry, God help us. The violence will increase, but that will be as nothing compared to the organization under which we shall have to live – or perhaps I should say, exist.'

'Ah, dear me – it's just as well I'm an old man. I'll not be here much longer to have to put up with it. And where do you think I fit in, Mr Marshall? As a painter – d'you think I'd ever have been heard of, if I hadn't lived through the time, as you might say, of social awareness?'

'I think that it's more than possible you might not have been.'

'Aye – you're an honest man. I appreciate your opinion. I've sometimes wondered m'self. I fancy you could be right. Social awareness – aye, but for that I'd possibly have gone to the grave unsung.'

How little Lowry suspected that once in the grave he would be sung to the 'Top of the Pops'.

With the gallery closed it was very strange that friends and clients continued to arrive, knock on the inner glass door, and once inside behave as though we were still open. Only the general public was no longer going in and out.

Lowry continued to show up at coffee time as before, bringing Carol if she happened to be spending a few days with him at the Seaburn Hotel. One day the northern art critic of the *Daily Telegraph*, F. W. Fenton, looked in. There was nothing for him to review, of course, but he was used to a free meal and we could not disappoint him, so he joined Lowry, Carol and us at luncheon. I was chattering away when I saw Lowry at the other end of the table bestowing one of his huge winks in my direction. Deciding he wanted me to shut up, I did. Shortly the conversation turned upon Lowry and the critic asked him whether he was doing much work?

The usual ton of bricks fell. 'Good heavens, no! Why should I? What age d'you think I am?' The critic knew full well Lowry's age, for he had already written the painter's obituary, as we were aware; it was being held in readiness for Lowry's decease. What the critic could not know was that Lowry would long outlive him.

Suddenly a new thought struck the elderly painter. 'My eyes are giving me a great deal of trouble, aren't they, Carol?' he inquired, waiting for her confirmation to give added weight to his impromptu excuse. She gave it. Lowry was encouraged to warm to his subject and began to overplay his part. 'Oh yes, m'eyes are very bad now. Very, very bad. I really don't know how much longer they'll hold out even for normal use. Of course I'd hoped they'd see me through to the end.' Now he was complely carried away by his role of 'po'r blind critter'. 'Me specialist says he hasn't much hope, and Carol here will probably have to lead me around. You'll lead me around, won't you, Carol?' Carol obliged with another affirmative.

Lowry's eyesight was in fact remarkably good, although we wondered how he managed to see anything at all through his spectacles, as he very seldom cleaned them. He was constantly taking them off and putting them on so the lenses became extremely greasy and cloudy. We did not know why he wore them in the first instance. True, he usually read with them on, but they were not bi-focal and, as he often forgot to take them off to see at a distance, his sight must have been truly exceptional. Many a time I wrested his spectacles from him with, 'Gosh, those are awful,' and gave them a good polish.

He would sigh, 'Oh, you're very kind to an old fellow.' He would lose them constantly down the side of a chair or the banquette at Tilley's, and we became weary of returning to restaurants to retrieve Lowry's specs, searching around under tables, tickling some poor woman's legs. At last I went off and bought him a chain, so that he might hang them around his neck. I never really supposed that he would use it but after the first self-conscious five minutes he became remarkably attached to it.

When the critic departed, Lowry informed me I had been casting my pearls.

'Well, a big help you were, winking away there. I'm sure he saw you. You're always doing it, and why you should suppose I'm the only one to notice I can't imagine. I hope you weren't casting *your* pearls.' No, Lowry had certainly not cast his, he'd really done his stuff, for on the Monday the newspaper came out with a headline 'Lowry Going Blind'. He was inundated with other pressmen wanting to know details. Was it cataract? Would it entail an operation? It took all Lowry's ingenuity to talk himself out of that one.

Week after week went by, but still Lowry stayed on. He would arrive and, after his usual 'dying' act, would inquire with eyes glinting, 'Well, any news?'

A little surprised we would answer, 'No – what news could there be?' Ella and I wanted to proceed with dismantling the gallery, and we always intended to start the next day, but after dinner in the evening Lowry would announce, 'I'll be in at the usual time tomorrow.' So the day of dismantling never dawned.

It was necessary for us to go to Edinburgh on business and, sure enough, Lowry said he would like to come with us. We gave him lunch at The Cally, and during the course of the afternoon we looked in at the Royal Scottish Academy to see the Summer Exhibition. 'D'you know what I like about you, Mrs Marshall?' Lowry asked, as we strolled around it together.

'No? I wasn't sure there was anything – tell me?'

'Well, to start with, I like that joomper you're wearing, and I don't often comment on a lady's appearance.'

'Well, not unless they're "totties",' I laughed.

'What colour would you call it?'

'This sweater? Well, I suppose it's a sort of scarlet – or is it rose?'

'Aye, well it's very nice.' This was praise indeed. 'But another thing I like about you is that you're the only person who can look at an exhibition as quickly as I can m'self.'

'Come on, let's go,' I laughed.

Charles had asked us to look in at High Green and have supper with him on the way home. Pru was away with the children. It was a heavenly summer evening as we drove out of Edinburgh and, leaning back comfortably in his seat, Lowry relaxed. He told us that at one time he had been a constant visitor to the Edinburgh Festival with his friend Ann.

'Ah,' he sighed, 'those were the days. We fell out about Carol, you know. But I always promised her I'd see Carol all right.' We were surprised how familiar these roads were to Lowry – he knew what was around every corner. And now the journey across the hills brought back his memories of Ann. Becoming unusually expansive, he talked of Pat Cooke, Sheila Fell, Carol and then, turning suddenly to Micky, he announced, 'Of course there was only one whom I would ever have married – that was Ann.'

At Otterburn we turned off the main road and took the quiet byroads over the desolate moors to High Green. Golden pheasants strutted over the lawns, and the evening sun was still warm as Charles came to the open door to greet us.

Lowry was suddenly a different man. Gone was the charmer of a short time ago: here was a man of ill-mannered mood – bored and boring. There was Lowry's orange squash, but the painter barked, '*no*', as his host proffered a small dish of radishes; and again '*no*', to a little bowl of onions. A gentle man, Charles resembled one who had received a mortal wound, but nothing daunted he held out a jorum of nuts. Lowry demolished the lot without so much as a thank-you. He was passionately fond of nuts.

Lowry looked with great displeasure at the various paintings on the walls: a new glowing MacTaggart, a dramatic Benrath, William Thomson's portrait of Pru in the style of Kokoschka. He then denounced a small collection of Brabazons, pretty and innocuous. 'What on earth made you buy those?'

'Oh, er – I didn't. I'm afraid my father rather cared for them.'

We found ourselves searching uncomfortably around and outside ourselves for conversation to interest Lowry. Charles eventually suggested that we might have bacon and eggs in the kitchen. At the magic word 'kitchen', Lowry was on his feet in an instant. 'Oh, come along now, sir, and we'll all help. Now tell me, why does one never get a *lightly* fried egg in a restaurant? Oh, the fried eggs at the Seaburn are shocking. And there's nothing I like better than a lightly fried egg.'

Thanks to our host's happy thought to eat in the kitchen, the remainder of the evening passed as pleasantly as had the day. Sitting cosily at the table in a corner of the large and efficiently pleasant room, Lowry enjoyed himself enormously, once again talking emotionally of his memories of Ann. His pleasure in being the centre of the picture was obvious as, totally relaxed, he related his feelings for his 'goddaughter'. It was the only time I remember him showing us this side of his character. As he lighted one of his Gauloise cigarettes, Charles was watching the painter closely. 'You know,' he said after a while, 'I'm rather relieved to see that you know what love is all about. You're always maintaining you're a cold fish, and you've never been in love.'

'Oh, well, sir, I shall probably maintain that again tomorrow! But yes, I know what love's about – yes, I admit that, at any rate for tonight.'

'Good. I'd begun to think you were only a voyeur – or maybe a paedophile.'

'What's that, sir?'

'Never mind, something not very nice.'

'Oh well, you must realize I'm not at all a nice man, sir.'

It was after midnight as we drove away over the moors. Lowry humped himself round in his seat, made himself comfortable and said, 'I enjoyed that, but I'm rather sorry for that gentleman.'

'Sorry for Charles?' I exclaimed.

'Yes. You see, Mrs Marshall,' the painter hitched himself around the better to talk to me, 'that gentleman's a romantic. Romantics can be very lonely people.'

'You're speaking from experience, I presume?'

'Bloody hell no, as you yourself would say, Mrs Marshall.'

When we reached the Seaburn Hotel he got out of the car like a two-year-old. 'Come across and look at the sea,' he commanded. Lowry leaned on the wall looking over the still expanse of cold water, shining silver-grey. 'Ah,' he murmured. 'Now there's something for you. What would happen if the tide didn't turn next time, what if it just came on and on? I often wonder that. And one day the tide of life will come on and on and I shall be gone.'

'Now, Mr Lowry, if you're turning melancholy, we're off.'

'No, Mr Marshall, you must understand – one day it'll happen to me. It happens to us all in the end, doesn't it? I think one day I'll paint a self-portrait; I've an idea. A tall straight pillar standing up in the middle of the sea, waiting for the sea of life to finish it off. I must try and get what I have in mind.'

He worked for some time on this new idea, and eventually completed four such 'self-portraits', of which Carol has one, and we have the other three. None has been shown in any exhibition, but one at least should have been included in his Retrospective at the Royal Academy. It was Lowry's last idea for a new painting subject.

About ten persons along with the Marshall family – which held majority shares – decided to form a private company to reopen the gallery. Some amusing meetings took place – Lowry attended them all, and became a shareholder. He would sit silent, but fascinated, while we discussed whether the gallery should reopen as a non-profit distributing trust, or a commercial concern. In my mind's eye I can see him again, nodding appreciatively when one rich businessman confessed that he had never been connected with an uncommercial concern. All agreed that to show only modern painters was a charitable activity in itself, and the majority voted to reopen as a commercial gallery, so exhibitions must in future cover good painting of all periods. For Micky there remains some sense of defeat in that he no longer works only for living artists. The gallery reopened after having been closed for three months. But for Lowry's friendship, curiosity, and continual presence with us, it would almost certainly have stayed closed.

To celebrate the reopening Lowry made a drawing of the gallery exterior. One bright autumn day, I turned into the road with Simon and exclaimed, 'Look – there's a young man drawing the gallery.' A tall figure with cap pulled well down over his eyes, long legs crossed, leaned nonchalantly against the low railings on the opposite side of the road, totally engrossed with pencil and sketching pad. It was Lowry . . . and the years appeared to have dropped away from him as he worked with a happy preoccupied sense of involvement. It was perhaps sad that Lowry allowed his resentment against current Chancellors of the Exchequer to get the better of him – he might have been happier if he could have seen his way to painting until the end.

His drawing of the gallery was used for the cover of the catalogue of the reopening exhibition, and was used constantly thereafter.

About a week after the reopening Mr Edward Heath visited the gallery one Saturday morning, having sent word in advance. Lowry decided that he could not be present, although, contrary to the generally held belief, Lowry was a staunch Conservative. Originally of Liberal persuasion, he felt that party had gone into decline, and became Conservative. He would bellow with mirth when it was assumed that because of the type of subject he painted he must of necessity be Labour. Lowry's loathing for the Labour Party was deep and bitter. Nevertheless he was sufficiently astute to suppose that it might be detrimental to his reputation if it were generally known that he was a Conservative, and he was determined to run no risk of being seen consorting with the leader of the party. Not that Lowry considered his politics were the concern of anyone but himself. He never believed in an artist of any description using art as a political platform.

Lowry was by no means the only one of our shareholders to fight shy of appearing in the Stone Gallery during Mr Heath's visit. Usually we might expect our tycoon collectors to foregather every Saturday morning, but we suddenly became aware that it was no use hoping for building contracts from Labour-controlled councils, if one was seen in opposing party company. Heath's visit also failed to attract local Conservatives to the gallery's cause. One cannot win.

Mr Heath had apparently altered a tight two-day schedule, and on the following Monday when a photograph of him in the gallery appeared in the *Guardian* the local Conservatives were not too pleased, as his visit to us took precedence over politics. Like Miss Jennie Lee (as she was then), Heath had a good knowledge of painting. He was extremely courteous to press and photographers, and expressed the hope that the next time he found himself in Newcastle he would have a chance to look in to the gallery again. The kind and polite words of a good politician, we assumed.

The following summer, after a busy day in our shops, I returned to the gallery a little exhausted. Lowry was not ready for his tea, and wanted to have a run down to the coast with Micky first. On their return we had tea and finished rather later than usual. I took out the tray and debris to the kitchen while Lowry still hugged his last cold cup. I came back to sit with him – he hated to be left alone for a moment – while Micky went upstairs to switch off lights.

The office door was pushed open, and a handsome man in pale grey suit, poised and elegant, courteously asked whether he might come in. 'Oh Christ,' I thought, 'another blasted sales rep – why has he decided to call here?' Then I saw that it was Edward Heath. Rising to greet him, I said, 'Yes, of course, do come in – I'll just call my husband. This is Mr Lowry.' Lowry propelled himself out of his chair and put on his attractive public face with the blue sparkling eyes – all was well.

Only a few days previously Lowry had stumped into the office one morning at the usual coffee time, thumped a letter down on Micky's desk and asked, 'Now, what d'you think of that, sir?'

Micky had read the letter and said, 'Well, that's very nice, when will you go?'

'I shan't, sir!'

'You won't? What excuse are you going to give then?'

'I shan't give any excuse, Mr Marshall. Masterly inactivity, that's the answer – I shan't reply.' The letter was from the Prime Minister, Mr Harold Wilson, asking Lowry to visit him at 10 Downing Street. Wilson had long been an admirer of Lowry's work apparently, and wished to meet him.

'You don't fancy going, then?' queried my husband.

'I do *not*, sir,' barked Lowry, 'After all, he knows where I live – if he wants to see me, he knows where to find me.'

'Oh, come off it,' laughed Micky. 'How often are you there?

We'll compose a reply while you have your coffee.'

'Aaah – no! Masterly inactivity – that's the answer. I'm not going to reply or be polite to *that* fellow.'

Remembering this incident as we strolled around the gallery with Mr Heath, I turned to him with some amusement, 'By the way, you're one up on Mr Wilson now.'

Because of his political standing at that moment, Mr Heath looked a little surprised, until I explained that the Prime Minister had expressed a desire to meet Lowry, only to be foiled as the old boy wasn't having any. Heath asked Lowry whether he ever went to London and received the reply, 'Oh *no*, I never go there now.'

'Oh, you do lie!' Breezily I took him to task. 'Why, you were there with us only recently.'

Lowry looked bad-tempered for a moment, then relented and twinkled, 'Oh, was I? Yes, that's right, I'd forgotten. But I don't go as often as I used to.' Mr Heath said he would be delighted if Lowry would visit him sometime in Albany. The painter agreed that something might be arranged. And so it was.

Lowry enjoyed his morning with Heath in London. It happened to be the day when Enoch Powell's first open opposition to the leader of the Conservative Party broke upon the public consciousness, the press doing its utmost to create some sort of crisis. Lowry was full of appreciation for Heath's handling of the matter, and for his unperturbable temperament that morning as he entertained him, when it might have been supposed the leader of the Opposition would have other matters on his mind. The artist never forgot it and would constantly express his admiration for Edward Heath.

One young Conservative MP made something of a hit with Lowry. This was Geoffrey Pattie, who had been up at Cambridge at the same time as our honorary company secretary, Bill Taylor. One Saturday evening we gave a small dinner party at the Station Hotel, which included these two young men and Bill's beautiful wife, Valenda. I was a little anxious, expecting Lowry to be rather uptight, as he invariably was when meeting someone for the first time, but Mr Pattie was a great success with the artist. It so often happened that when people met Lowry and found they could not get behind his apparently dull and po-faced exterior they gave up the effort. This certainly was not the case with Geoffrey Pattie. He put himself and his own interests entirely to one side and set about discovering the painter's enthusiasms, listened to his experiences, and immediately put this essentially shy old man at ease. In no time, he had him smiling, relaxing and laughing as Lowry would normally have done only in entirely familiar company.

One other politician for whom Lowry expressed a regard was Lord Glenamara – Mr Ted Short as he was known to Lowry – who as Postmaster General chose one of the painter's works to be reproduced on a postage stamp, in July 1967. Our friend was truly delighted at the honour that, along with George Stubbs and Sir Thomas Lawrence, he was the third painter chosen . . . and he would recount to us how he had been entertained for luncheon by Mr Short in the restaurant at the top of the Post Office Tower. He described in detail the splendid view, and how the restaurant very gently revolved. At the same time, Lowry expressed no little resentment toward a fellow Royal Academician, James Fitton, who, while serving on the committee responsible for the choice of stamps, had voted against a work by Lowry.

The painter had reason to be grateful to Ted Short – but, alas, would not go to the length of putting himself out. On Saturday, 6 April 1974, Lowry was drinking his morning coffee in the gallery office in the company of Simon who, to interest him, was reading an article on Sotheby's from that morning's *Times*. Becoming a little bored with this, Lowry interrupted with complaints in his usual strain about his taxes. Just then Ted Short arrived at the gallery, and Simon fancied this to be a most welcome interlude for Lowry. At any rate if would be a more worthwhile pair of ears than his own to harken to Lowry's tale of woe. He put his head around the office door to tell the painter that he would bring in the then deputy leader of the Labour Party – but Lowry met the suggestion as bad news, commanding Simon to go and look after the politician, and make sure he closed the door behind him, and on no account say Lowry was in the vicinity.

After our friend's death, when Lord and Lady Glenamara were in the gallery one day, I happened to mention the Lowry postage stamp – to learn that the luncheon had been at the House of Commons. Lord Glenamara was amused to recall that art was the one subject Lowry had refused to discuss. This was entirely in character. In retrospect it must be admitted that it was also in character for the painter to indulge in – to put it mildly – some small inaccuracy. One can only suppose his motive in hiding the fact of his visit to the House of Commons to have been a wish to dissociate himself, as ever, from all matters political.

Lord Glenamara was unaware of Lowry's knowledge of Fitton's opposition. He then told us that not only James Fitton RA, but the entire committee had been opposed to the choice of a Lowry work, at which point he, as Postmaster General, disbanded the committee, and for eighteen months made himself responsible for the selection of postage stamps.

In December 1968 Mr Heath sent word that he would like to visit the gallery early in the New Year, and if it were convenient he would like to meet some of the painters working in the north-east. There were not many good painters, but my husband suggested that he would gather together painters, writers, architects, musicians, and one or two patrons of the arts. This suggestion was approved and the gathering was arranged for 17 January 1969.

Two days before, a short, precise, pleasant man called into the gallery to see my husband. It was Bryan Forbes, actor, film director and writer. He wished to film Edward Heath's visit and, on the understanding that it had no political significance, we agreed. Mr Forbes said he gathered that Lowry was going to be present, which I confirmed, but I had to add that the painter was unaware that any filming would be taking place. If we had not informed Lowry he would, of course, have been there as planned, but what his behaviour might have been was quite another matter. We should have to warn him in advance.

In his house Lowry had a telephone which was so adjusted that he was able to ring out, but no one could ring in. With 'everyone wanting something for nothing' he maintained, his life would not have been worth living. If we wished to get in touch with him speedily, we would send a telegram asking him to ring us. After talking to Bryan Forbes, Micky followed this procedure and Lowry was on the phone within half an hour.

'L. S. Lowry here – are y'there?' I told him we were confirming the arrangements for the following afternoon, but thought that we should let him know that on the day of Heath's visit there would be some filming in the gallery. I was delighted to hear him reply, 'Well, that's very nice – very nice indeed.'

'Oh, that's fine then,' I answered, 'we just wanted to make sure it was OK with you. The film isn't being used for political purposes.'

'No? Now it's a funny thing Mr Marshall should have asked me to get in touch, for I was just going to ring you up to say I shan't be able to get over after all.'

'Oh heavens! Why not?'

'It's m'bronchitis, Mrs Marshall – it's quite shocking.'

'Oh, come off it now, your voice is as clear as a bell. I know when you've got bronchitis – you're not coughing or anything.'

'No, but I'm just going to have a bout of coughing, Mrs Marshall,' and down the line came a fiendish noise, the best he could achieve in the circumstances.

'Now stop it,' I could not help laughing. 'You've got to do better than that.' So he tried again with worse effect.

'Hell, don't play that old excuse with me of all people. How many times have I heard you fob off the reverend gentleman with that one? Come along now, no more excuses. Come and lend us your support. Please, Mr Lowry. You needn't go near the blasted cameras.'

'Aah – but, Mrs Marshall, I fancy those blasted cameras might come near me!'

'No, honestly, if you don't want to be filmed, we'll see to it that you're not.' We argued on but he remained adamant. 'Oh! then I'll tell Mr Heath that you refuse to play second lead to him.'

'Ah, that's right – I'll play second lead to no man,' he chortled. 'Aye, that's very well put; you tell him that. But now I promise you one thing, on 17 February I'll be with you all, never mind m'bronchitis; I'll be with you if I'm dying. It's Carol's half-term and she wants to come over. I fancy she's very fond of that car of Simon's. So we'll be with you then.'

'Bugger him!' I thought as I replaced the receiver, two large tears of self-pity rolling slowly down my cheeks. Could he never do anything for anyone but Carol? I was feeling ill; indeed, my doctor supposed me to be in bed, and there was that bloody-minded old man making up imaginary ailments.

Being entirely familiar with the ways of the world, Lowry expressed no surprise when he saw shots of the gallery film used in a party political broadcast before the next election, which was to make Heath Prime Minister, nor did he leave us in any doubt that he hoped to be remembered long after Prime Ministers might be forgotten.

I must add in passing that, when in the north country, Mr Heath never fails to look into the gallery; he collects works of Norman Cornish – indeed, when Peter Walker arrived one day, also to buy some Cornishes, he told us with amusement that Heath was our best salesman. And there is the story of some man being shown a Cornish by the then Prime Minister, who said to him, 'Can you do anything for men like this?' It was a painting of a miner – the man in question fancied he could, and got a ministerial job. But, as the years went by, it never became any easier for us to persuade our tycoon shareholders to meet Heath. A pity, for some went into Europe for business long before Britain became a member of the Common Market, and Heath would have enjoyed meeting them. And Cornish, meeting Heath in the gallery, did not dare be photographed with him. 'Never get another man to speak to me in Spennymoor – and then what would I do – it would be an end to painting!' said Cornish.

One morning Lowry decided to stroll along the seafront at Seaburn. Returning to his hotel for luncheon, he discovered that a heavy security guard was mounted at the door because the Prime Minister, Mr Wilson, was the guest of honour at some function. Lowry, looking to any one unfamiliar with his appearance like a down-at-heel, failed to gain permission to re-enter his hotel. Argue as he might, it was not credited that he was a guest there. Insisting that the doorman be sent for, Lowry heard one security man call to another, 'This old fellow says he's staying here in room four! Who does he think he's kidding?'

Lowry continued to fret and fume, but in those circumstances his demeanour could become even less credible. Eventually someone was found to identify him.

'Well, you daft thing,' I laughed as he related this for the umpteenth time during the afternoon. 'Why on earth didn't you tell them that Mr Wilson had long been wanting to meet you? After all, you might have got a free lunch.'

'Good God, no! I wasn't giving him that pleasure – rather pay for m'own lunch than that!' For Lowry this was some sacrifice. But his laughter rang out constantly during the remainder of that day as he thought again of Mr Wilson, unaware that the man whose painting so often appeared behind him during television broadcasts (borrowed, Lowry said, from the Ministry of Works) was eating alone nearby.

Lowry affirmed that he had been offered a title twice by Mr

Wilson, and a CH from Mr Heath. Over a number of years he would maintain that he would have liked and accepted an OM – 'Suitable for an old man . . . eh?' Then with chuckles he would say that if only they cared to make him a duke, that would be a bit of all right, and he wouldn't say no to that!

We had not foreseen that when Lowry became a shareholder in the Stone Gallery company he would take up semi-permanent residence in the office, although some warning might have been taken from a splendid story he never tired of telling. He would relate how an elderly Mancunian friend of his, having retired from business, found time hanging heavily on his hands. He lived with his sister and she, to get him from under her feet, suggested that he rent a nice office in the city, employ a secretary, and go along there every day.

The old gentleman decided to follow this advice. He would arrive in time for his morning coffee at about eleven; at twelve o'clock Lowry or another friend would call to go out for luncheon with him; at three o'clock they would return to the office, and at about 3.30 the man would say to his secretary, 'Now, Miss . . . ' whatever her name was, 'isn't it time you got ready to make a move? Traffic gets bad later on, and you don't want to get held up in it, so I should get yourself off now.'

The routine was followed for many years, and Lowry delighted to relate how in his opinion it kept the old boy going, and he lived longer as a consequence. When first employed, the secretary had arrived with excellent shorthand and typing speeds, but after some months of virtually no work she confessed to Lowry one day that her skills were becoming rusty and at this rate she would shortly be good for nothing; she fancied therefore that she ought to leave. Lowry's firm advice was to put such an idea out of her head. 'You look after him, and, take my word for it, he'll look after you.' So she remained in her strange job. Many were the 'joompers' she knitted, and the trousseau she stitched was magnificent. Sure enough, when the old gentleman departed this life the lady was left a very large sum of money. 'She would certainly never want again,' Lowry would add. 'And didn't she deserve it? She kept up the façade of a busy office existence – oh, my word, yes.' He would sigh over the reminiscence.

Whether memories of his old chum gave him the idea or not, for many months of many years Lowry followed this pattern himself. He bettered his old friend's example, however, in as much as no expenditure fell upon him. The office was provided, the coffee, the luncheon, tea and dinner: nor did he have to find a secretary's salary or budget for her future, and because these facilities cost him nothing they were undoubtedly the sweeter. When he left his hotel in the morning early and he was asked what he was going to do that day, his reply would be, 'Oh, I'm off to the office.'

Such a situation as this had been foreseen by no one except the painter. On more than one occasion, therefore, we had to remonstrate with him. I well remember February 1968 when our family accountant advised me that we were spending far too much of our personal money on the elderly painter. We agreed that Lowry must be tackled on the subject at an auspicious moment.

This appeared to present itself one evening as he, my husband and I sat at the usual table in Tilley's restaurant. Screwing up courage, and looking Lowry gently in the eyes, I said, 'Mr Lowry, I don't really think that this year we can afford to entertain you as we have in the past. Of course, we shall love to see as much of you as possible, but I don't think there can be any question of entertaining either you, Carol, Mr Robertson, or other friends of yours or Carol's, as we have in the past.'

Lowry's eyes flashed, he banged his fist on the table, heads turned, waiters and manager came running to see what was the trouble. Smiling them away, while inwardly quailing, I heard the painter demand, 'What about that picture of mine you've just sold, eh?'

'Well, what about it? You got two thousand pounds for it, the gallery one thousand – but that's nothing to do with us personally.' Suddenly my quaking spirit was moved to anger, and I said, 'Right, if that's the way you think, we'll get the picture back from our client; you return the two thousand, and the gallery will return the third, and take your picture home and yourself with it!' I wondered inwardly whether indeed the client in question could possibly be prevailed upon to render up the recently purchased little oil – but I'd meet that situation in due course.

Lowry dismissed the suggestion, and with an angelic smile he said, 'No, no, we can't possibly do that. Now, never mind, Mrs Marshall, let's forget it.' Which is precisely what he did. He behaved as though the subject had never been raised, and he was with us more than ever that year, as were his friends.

It was a long while before we became aware that sitting in the office he was gently picking off certain of our clients as he saw fit. Should someone express interest in Lowry's work, we never gave a second thought to introducing the painter, when maybe he would receive an invitation to look over a rope works, attend a launch, or visit a factory . . . We did not usually see that particular client again.

Once a Lancashire manufacturer bought three Lowry works from the gallery and asked to be introduced to the artist when the 1967 private view took place. This man said that he wished to build up a Lowry collection; so we were surprised that, when faced for the first time with a considerable number of new and excellent works, he left without buying, and never returned to the gallery.

About a year later my husband was due to drive Lowry back to Mottram, when Lowry said that, after all, Micky need not bother – he would go by train. 'Are you sure?' asked Micky, a bit surprised.

'Oh yes, it'll suit me better, as it happens, on this occasion. A good friend is going to meet me at the station; I'll be having some tea with him, then he'll take me home for we've a bit of business to discuss. He's a good client.'

'Fine then, if that's OK with you,' sighed my surprised but rather relieved husband, for Lowry dearly loved a lift home.

'Aye, this is a nice young chap. Likes my work and buys well. So that'll be all right, Mr Marshall; I heard from Mr Satinoff this morning confirming the arrangement.'

'Mr Satinoff?' I queried gently, looking at Lowry over the top of my teacup.

'That's right, have I told you about him? Nice fellow – very well off too,' ruminated the artist.

'Oh yes, I remember Mr Satinoff,' I murmured. 'He particularly asked to be introduced to you at your last private view here. We'd sold him two or three of your things previously – you must remember, *Girl with Dog and a Half* . . . I've forgotten for the moment what the others were. We were disappointed that after meeting you he showed no more interest in your work, for he'd said he intended making a good collection. Oh yes – I remember Mr Satinoff very well.'

Lowry had turned a mild scarlet hue; he seldom let his guard slip. Being of a devious nature, his right hand mistrusting his left, it was not often he gave any but the most carefully thought-out and rehearsed information.

Lowry was the most obstinate of men, and I can recall no instance when he was prepared to do anything which did not suit his purpose or advance his own interests. The only other human being I saw him consider was Carol. For instance, when tea was served he would look to see what there was, asking, 'Now will that be all right Carol?' Naturally the girl always replied pleasantly that yes, it was very nice. But I wondered what he supposed I was going to do about it had she said otherwise. Or he would turn and say, 'Now Carol, if you're not tired, would you like Simon to take you for a run in his car somewhere?' As she had often just returned from a two-week holiday in Ireland, Cornwall or some other spot with her mother and was now having a week with 'Uncle' at Seaburn before going with a friend into the Yorkshire dales, or perhaps Gloucestershire, ere she departed with her school to Switzerland for a week, while the rest of us went without a holiday of any description, it was sometimes hard to take.

One August day, tea over, I left Lowry, Carol, my husband and Simon happily chatting away, but when I returned to the gallery some little time later the painter was sitting bolt upright in a leather chair facing the huge desk in the office – a chair I had never previously seen Lowry occupy. I looked at him a little more closely and saw that he was busily reading *The Times* upside down, his face red and angry, while Micky was engrossed with some papers on his desk. There was no sign of 'the children'.

'Anything wrong?' I asked. Lowry flung the paper to the floor where it lay in a mangled heap. 'Anything wrong? I should bloody well think there is!'

'What on earth's the matter?' My stomach turned over, as usual when our friend treated us to one of his unexpected rages. All had been most peacefully happy only a short time ago, but here he was doing his nut.

'That damned Carol!' he yelled at me, turning his scarlet face in my direction, then suddenly pounced on Micky with, 'Oh, do stop whatever that is you're doing, Mr Marshall, and listen.'

My husband looked up, unperturbed. 'I heard it all – you don't have to tell me anything.'

'No, but I'm telling Mrs Marshall – and I want you to listen.' Lowry got to his feet, wildly hitching his trousers. 'Now, Mrs Marshall, I noticed this morning at breakfast that Carol got a letter from someone, and when I asked who it was from she just said, "a friend", and put it away in her bag. Now, if you please, she's just announced that it was from a friend of hers who's been working during the holiday at Butlin's and has saved four hundred pounds, and that if only she'd been free to work during her vacation she'd now have four hundred pounds saved. And I don't think Carol would, you know, because she couldn't save if she tried. At the beginning of the summer she thought she might take a vacational job, so I said, "No, I don't want you to do that – I'll give you whatever you'd earn," and I gave her four hundred pounds.'

'I heard it all,' said Micky trying to pour water on the fire, 'but Carol says you forgot to give it to her – you promised, but you forgot.'

'Forgot? *Forgot*? I never forget anything to do with Carol. Of course I gave it to her. What does she mean by saying I didn't?'

'Oh, dear me,' I muttered, not knowing what to say. 'Well, where is she now?'

'Flounced off to the coast with Simon in his car!'

'Well, I'm sure you'll sort it out all right. And youngsters do have better memories than us older folk, Mr Lowry.'

'Yes, but I can see the way the wind blows – it's going to cost me another four hundred pounds to sort out, as you say, Mrs Marshall. I can see that – another four hundred pounds, dammit.'

'It seems a lot.' I had no clue as to whether Lowry was well-off or otherwise, so I really did not feel there was very much I could say; the matter was entirely between him and Carol.

'Well, that's the end – I've finished with her. My God – the little liar!'

'Of course you haven't finished with her – you'll sort it out,' I remonstrated, for I had never seen him react in this fashion before. Eventually we persuaded him to change the subject and tried to interest him in something else, but he still appeared out of sorts and rather preoccupied. He announced that he would have a wash, and then, 'Let's be off round to Tilley's. We won't wait for them.'

'Well,' murmured Micky unenthusiastically, 'I suppose they'll know where we've gone.'

'Doesn't bloody well matter if they don't!' We had never seen

Lowry take this attitude previously, and I never saw him angry with Carol again.

Simon and Carol never had much use for one another. Possibly they were too alike, being born on the same day with about two hours between them, but at any rate there was never any rapport. In the early days Simon could be pretty awkward. When Lowry obviously expected that with Carol present he would stay and eat with us, Simon would announce, 'Oh no! I've got a date with a gorgeous bird. Not the common or garden sort you see around here!' or some such crack, and give Carol a mischievous glance. I must say she always took it very well; it was the way he might have treated a sister.

On this particular evening, when Simon and Carol joined us for dinner, his behaviour was entirely sympathetic towards her, as she was obviously very upset at the scene Lowry had created. During their run out in the car, Carol had had a good sisterly weep on Simon's shoulder, and our son was entirely of the opinion that 'Uncle' had indeed forgotten his promise – but, whatever the way of it, by the following day all was well again, as indeed we had known it would be.

Lowry was very possessive in his relationship with his 'niece'. We had sensed this for the first time one Sunday when they were spending the day with us. We had decided to visit Harrogate to see an exhibition of Victorian paintings at the art gallery there and we called in for luncheon at the Red Lion at South Stainley. Towards the end of the meal Simon and Carol decided they would go to York instead, a favourite haunt of Carol's at the time, and away they dashed in the little red sports car.

We enjoyed viewing the Harrogate exhibition in the company of Lowry; it was always a rewarding experience to see any art show with him. As he looked at works with his painter's eye, he would point out where this painting failed and that drawing fell apart. Sometimes we would bypass something which we thought of little account, when Lowry would pull us back for a second look and explain how and why, in his opinion, we were seeing a little masterpiece.

He never cared greatly for nineteenth-century painting as a whole, usually discounting all pictures which carried a message or a sermon. His passion was for the work of Dante Gabriel Rossetti – but never his early work; it had to be the later. He had little or no regard for what he termed Rossetti's 'subject' pictures, preferring the painter's poetically imaginative works which are entirely free from Victorian sentimentality. He loved the paintings of what he called 'Rossetti's women'; these made their appeal to him through the basic theme of romantic love. Although this theme is undoubtedly to be found in some of Rossetti's early work, Lowry felt that Rossetti only achieved what he was looking for in the late works. His view would not meet with general support in the art world – Rossetti scholars for the most part prefer the early work, and Lowry, fully aware of this, despised that view accordingly. The increasingly erotic element to be found in Rossetti's late paintings, induced in some measure by his addiction to chloral in 1870, found some echo within Lowry's own nature and proved irresistible to him.

It is well known that our friend was a great admirer of the Pre-Raphaelites, but it must not be supposed that he cared for the work of either Millais or Holman Hunt to the extent of wishing to own any. He approved of early Millais paintings and drawings but considered that after the artist's marriage to Effie Ruskin his work went into total decline. Holman Hunt he thought something of a fool, disliking his harsh, realistic painting and the heavy religious principles which pervade many of his works. He had a fondness for Burne-Jones's melancholy ladies and considered him at times to be a very great painter. Ford Madox Brown, in Lowry's mind, was the greatest craftsman of them all. Brown's subjects, however, did not appeal to Lowry in the manner that Rossetti's did.

We arrived back home that particular Sunday evening and, as we sat before the fire awaiting the return of Carol and Simon, our friend began to give a very good imitation of a cat on hot bricks. 'Why aren't they back yet? They said they'd be back for supper at eight – where are they?'

'Oh, they won't be long,' Micky consoled. 'Well, *where are they*?' Lowry kept demanding. 'They should have gone to Harrogate with us – what did they want to go to York for instead?' At last the phone rang, and Simon informed his father that they had been delayed but would be home in about an hour.

Micky told him to get a move on as the old boy was getting very het up. 'Oh, sod him – whatever for? We've just looked in at the Black Bull, and Carol's enjoying herself!'

We had no doubts that Simon was also enjoying himself. Carol always got along very well with Simon's friends. She fitted in extremely easily and appeared to revel in young company. It must have been a sacrifice on both their parts to have to return for supper with us. When they did Lowy was once again all smiles. He wanted to know where they had been, what they had seen – everything, down to the last detail.

The painter met many of Simon's friends over the years, as they would call in at home when he was with us. I recall him once admonishing us to warn one attractive blonde damsel not to marry the foolish young man to whom she had just become engaged. Foolish, that was, in Lowry's eyes. We looked at the painter in amazement, as we thought the pair were very happy together. Needless to say, we omitted to pass on his advice. But he was an extraordinary judge of human nature, sometimes uncannily so. A few months later Simon was dressed in his finery, about to set off for this young couple's wedding, when his car refused to start. He was cussing like blazes as he cleaned a plug at this unpropitious moment, yelling at me that he was going to be late. I consoled him with, 'Oh, don't worry, Mr Lowry vows they'll be separated before you get there!' And he was almost proved right – they parted after nine months.

One day there was a large gathering of friends in the gallery. It was too large for the painter's liking but Carol was visiting during a half-term holiday and, as she talked happily away, laughing spontaneously with Sherree Bell, a very beautiful golden-haired millionairess, tanned, tiny and dressed in tailored navy shirt and slacks, Lowry began to cheer up. Looking at the two girls together on a window seat, the painter sighed with pleasure and murmured to me, 'Ah, Mrs Marshall, that's what I want for her. I want her to mix with people like that when I've gone. You'll see to it, won't you?'

What an extraordinary thought, but I passed it off with, 'When you're gone? Go along with you – we'll probably all go first!' Such was his incredible energy that I sometimes half believed this would be the case.

That same evening our friends Russell and Nola Bell asked us to bring Lowry and Carol for drinks. They lived in a very beautiful house, Callerton Hall, set in lovely gardens not far from Newcastle. As I watched Lowry that evening glance distastefully at a small reclining figure by Henry Moore and poke a forefinger through a Hepworth hole, I was certain that only his interest in Carol's future persuaded him to be passably pleasant.

'Yes, yes,' he muttered to me later, 'those are the sort of people I want her to mix with.'

I have heard it said, and seen it written since his death, that the women in Lowry's life were 'dream women'. This presumption was perhaps made in view of the fact that the paintings of Rossetti's which Lowry preferred and wished to own above all others were 'the women with the dreamy look in the eye'. By this Lowry was in no way referring to dream women. He was more aware than most people that Rossetti's women were anything but 'dream women'; they were all painted or drawn from ladies who were part of Rossetti's everyday life at some time or another. Having plenty of female company himself, Lowry had no need of dream women. He did not leave his estate to a dream girl, but to someone who had for many years been very much a reality in his life. Nor did Lowry ever associate Rossetti's women with himself, as has been suggested.

It was Dante Gabriel Rossetti's ability to produce paintings of women who looked 'out-of-this-world' which Lowry so admired. 'They were queer birds were Rossetti's women, Mrs Marshall,' he would say constantly. 'But Rossetti turned them into mythological women,' and Lowry always maintained that even the Old Masters could not get that expression in the eyes which Rossetti achieved time and again. The Dutch Old Masters turned the Virgin Mary into a peasant girl holding a baby, but Rossetti could paint a woman as an ethereal being, and it was this unmatched technique which our friend so admired. Lowry taught us to recognize an authentic Rossetti by looking at the eyes; much else of Rossetti's women may not be so difficult to fake – but it is never possible to fake the expression in the eyes.

The women with whom Lowry was friendly were usually quite worldly women, and they treated him in a worldly way. Lowry's concentration was always upon worldly things, and dreams did not interest him.

Once a policeman was relating to us how he had recently taken a man in charge who had been following a girl crossing a pedestrian bridge. The steps were steep, and the girl was sporting a mini-skirt, so the man had an extremely revealing view of the girl. He found the urge to pinch her posterior irresistible and he was promptly had up for indecent behaviour. Lowry's reaction to this story was a raucous peal of mirth. 'Well, what the devil did she expect? What did she wear a skirt that length for?'

He was remarkably earthy in his attitude to young women, and he would stand at one of the gallery windows watching them pass by. His ribald comments would have shocked many. 'Oh my God, I'd like to slap that one,' he'd exclaim, as some girl bent down to adjust a shoe perhaps, or retrieve something she had dropped.

Simon and Lowry tended to lead each other on. 'Hi, Mr Lowry – quick, come and see this one!'

And like a flash the artist was out of his chair to gaze from the window with eyes aglint behind those spectacles. 'Oh yes, Simon – a good totty that one. Tell me when another pretty one comes in sight – don't bother me with the ordinary ones.'

Perhaps the painter's attitude to women was a shade odd. On one occasion my husband was reading the sordid details of an enticement case to him and Lowry could see nothing wrong in it at all, commenting fiercely, 'Well – the fellow bought her, and why shouldn't he? If you've got the money you can get what you want and, if the girl preferred the rich fellow to her husband, what was wrong with that? Po'r little wretch, she didn't deserve to be murdered by her husband.'

Simon was about nineteen, and the law had not yet been amended, when Lowry advised him that the Piccadilly end of the Burlington Arcade was the best 'picking-up' place. The National Gallery wasn't bad either, but at the Tate you got a rather less experienced type of girl. The fact that Simon was not in the habit of looking for 'pick-ups' mattered not a whit to Lowry; he was bent on giving his advice, and had us in fits of laughter – which might have been his sole intent.

During my Pre-Raphaelite researches I happened to be studying *The Life and Letters of Frederic Shields*; Shields was a nineteenth-century painter associated with D. G. Rossetti, Ford Madox Brown, William Bell Scott and Arthur Hughes, amongst others. Shields spent his early years in Manchester and lived for some time at Ordsall Old Hall with an old daily woman as his sole attendant until he married Cissy, a girl who had been his model since she was a small child. I was recounting the peculiar story of Frederic Shields and his marriage to Lowry one day. He became riveted by it and demanded that I read extracts to him. These so took his fancy that nothing would content him until we promised to find him a copy of the book; when we did, he was wholly delighted with his present. Lowry had no use for Shields as a painter but he revelled in his extraordinary behaviour. The early chapters of this book make distressing reading for, as a direct result of the appalling social conditions of the hungry forties, every member of Shields's family starved to death. Lowry was not in the least interested in those chapters, however.

Dante Gabriel Rossetti had married a young and virtually uneducated girl of the lower classes, as had Ford Madox Brown when he married for a second time. According to the marriage certificate, Cissy was sixteen when Frederic Shields married her, and he was forty. The diary continues on the day after the wedding. 'August 16th – Blackpool. Good sermon. Monday 17th – Alone in Blackpool. Walked much. Fine weather. August 20th – No letter from Cissy since I left home. Could rest no longer. Back by 4 train.'

I can see Lowry's face again, with the tears of mirth pouring down it, as he rocked himself back and forth in his chair in the gallery office, shouting, 'Oh – Mrs Marshall, "No letter from Cissy since I left home." Could the fool really have expected one after leaving the child on their wedding day? Oh, dear God, it's the most splendid thing I ever heard of – read it to me again, Mrs Marshall.' And so I would.

It was all very well for Lowry to laugh outrageously at Frederic Shields's peculiarities, but I could not help seeing a slightly parallel case with his own. Each even had the same abhorrence of noise. Once, when Shields had been searching for a new home in London, he had great difficulty in finding a house where he could not hear barrel organs, pianos, railways, traffic, parrots, canaries, German bands, babies, dogs, cats, horses moving restlessly in stables and clanking their chains, pigs being killed, or anything else likely to disturb his sensitive ears. His greatest loathing was for the background music of German bands and barrel organs in the streets.

Lowry did, however, differ from Shields in that, although he adored being teased by Ella and me about 'popping the question' to Carol, he never seriously considered marriage with anyone so much younger than himself. 'It would be worse than Frederic Shields's state, Mrs Marshall,' he would laugh. 'Why, there's fifty-five years between Carol and me.'

One day he, Carol and Simon had taken a trip down the Tyne

and had arrived back in the gallery for tea. Lowry proved to be in great form, saying that they had held a contest for the choicest smell on the river. Agreement had been reached that the prize must go to the bone works at Gateshead – the glue produced a smell second to none. It was a close thing, however, as the Jarrow plastic smell got high marks for depth of purpose, but failed because it tended to confuse the senses. Someone had thought it might be candy floss; Simon had thought it was liquorice; while Carol assumed it to be beer or rum. The Hebburn gas works' smell came high on the list but lack of originality spoiled its boldness. However, all were agreed that the attractive domesticity of Howdon's fried onions was meritorious. Lowry had enjoyed himself enormously on this river trip, telling me upon his return how he had introduced Carol as his wife to someone on board. I glanced at the girl to see her reaction – there was none.

5

I do not want to give the impression that it was all give on our side and take upon Lowry's. As a family we learned much of importance from him and he doubtless saved us from making errors when, after the reopening of the gallery, we started to show nineteenth-century works. Dealing in this earlier period entailed considerable research. Sometimes very reputable dealers would show too great an optimism in their attributions, and in our opinion some with unlimited money were short on homework. Nineteenth-century painting is reasonably well documented and so this meant seeking out many rare volumes, hence Lowry's constant teasing: 'Oh, you need more books, Mrs Marshall.'

It was from Lowry we learned that it would be wise to forget the great mass of nineteenth-century *genre* painting and under his guidance we specialized in the Pre-Raphaelites as the only important movement in art to come out of Victorian England. The emphasis was centred upon the works of Dante Gabriel Rossetti, William Holman Hunt, John Everett Millais (but only his early work), Ford Madox Brown and some of their associates such as W. J. Webbe, Arthur Hughes and Charles Fairfax Murray. Lowry had a great admiration for Murray because he was not only a painter but also an extraordinarily successful dealer.

But even before we specialized in the Pre-Raphaelites, my husband was able to guide Lowry on the price he would have to pay at auction for Rossetti's great painting *Proserpine*. On 14 November 1964, having set his heart on acquiring this, the finest of Rossetti's works Lowry was to own, Lowry happened to mention that he was prepared to go to three thousand guineas for it.

'Oh, you won't get it for that,' exclaimed Micky. 'I think I will, you know,' replied Lowry. 'A few years ago no one would have given five pounds for it.'

'A few years ago no one would have given much more than five pounds for one of yours, chum, and you ain't dead yet!'

'What d'you think it'll fetch then?'

'Well, let's see – you'll have to go to five thousand, I should think.' I recall Lowry turning back as he got to the office door to pull a face and, with a snort, discount Micky's judgement.

Shortly afterwards it was reported in the press that Lowry had bought the painting for exactly five thousand guineas and his greeting of Micky when he next came visiting was, 'My God! You were right – five thousand!' His London gallery had bid at auction for him and he told us that he would then exchange one or two of his own paintings with them for the Rossetti. He added that, unknown to anyone but himself, Ann's father had been at the sale lest the painting went higher, when he would have carried on bidding after the gallery dropped out. 'Wasn't it good of him?' Lowry asked. 'But I was determined to have it, and he was determined that I should, and was going to make quite sure of it for me.'

I would date the revival of interest in the Pre-Raphaelite painters in this country from 20 November 1964 – the day of Lowry's purchase of Rossetti's *Proserpine*. It is very seldom that a painter collects other painters' work, hence this acquisition was highly publicized and interest reawakened in this nineteenth-century school of art.

Lowry had been amused to have a caller at his home two days after the sale. A director of an American gallery who had mistaken the day of the sale had come to find out whether Lowry would part with the work at a handsome profit. Lowry would not. He was quietly delighted and proud of his new possession and he looked forward to showing it to us after it had been professionally cleaned. Sure enough, it was not long before we were to see *Proserpine* for the first time.

Lowry's house seldom failed to give me the creeps. It stood on the outskirts of the village of Mottram-in-Longdendale, facing the Staleybridge Road. It was a small, gloomy house, of grey stone, probably built about the turn of the century. It gave the impression of having been designed as semi-detached, but either finance had run out or the builder had become disheartened and given up.

The tiny front garden was surrounded by a hedge; a short path led to the front door; there were two steps up into the hall. It all appeared dilapidated and run down, and badly in need of attention. The tall narrow window of the sitting room was to the right of the front door, with two more windows of the same proportions above. The whole was strangely angular and uncompromisingly uncomfortable to look at. At the rear was a neglected piece of land, and to the right a small private road where we would park the car.

Inside the house one would meet a stack of for the most part unframed canvases propped against the right-hand wall of the passage – works Lowry had brought at various exhibitions over the years, usually only as a form of encouragement to painters who were little known and likely to remain so. These were never hung and he gave a few away occasionally if he was fortunate enough to find someone to give them house room.

There was a collection of walking sticks in a peculiar stand resembling a half-open umbrella complete with long handle; a coat rail on the wall held his assortment of raincoats, aged overcoat and battered trilbies, all looking identical. He liked to give the impression that he only ever owned a single hat at a time but this was not so. They merely appeared to be one and the same so long as they were not seen *en masse*. There was sometimes a dreadful old overcoat thrown over a chair of strange construction, possibly dating from his eldest cousin Ruth's years in Hong Kong. Against the sandy-coloured wall stood three grandfather clocks in assorted sizes: a modern miniature, one of normal height and then the gigantic, supposed Tompion.

His living room opened off the right of the passage and, like the hall, was full to overflowing. In the middle stood a dining table covered with whatever Lowry might put on it, including opened and unopened correspondence. (It never ceased to amaze me how he knew instinctively which letters to deal with and which to leave, for whenever we posted a cheque to him it would go through our account right smartly.) There would be at least one pile of drawings which he would show us lovingly, one by one, spending a long time over each. There was often his cheque book, and a few five-pound notes – just about anything he had happened to deposit there. The table was never used for dining – picnics only.

Directly behind the table was his mother's upright piano, closed now and never used except as a prop for some small canvas. A pile of records occupied an upright chair with the odd *Playboy* magazine hidden among them; there was an old gramophone and everywhere lay objects which had gravitated there over the years.

Opposite the door was an extraordinary fireplace which would have looked more at home in some Lakeland pub in the thirties. Drawn near to it was his huge shabby armchair, with a similar one across the room. A mirror hung over the chimney breast, and upon the mantel shelf stood a clock and bits and pieces of modern bric-a-brac, given him, so he said, by various young friends over the years. 'And bloody awful, aren't they, Mrs Marshall? But I can't hurt their little feelings by getting rid of them,' he would chuckle. There was a roll-top desk and, to the left of the fireplace in an alcove, a dark oak chest with a narrower glass-fronted cabinet resting on it, full of his mother's now dusty collection of china. The narrow net-covered window was to the right of the room upon entering, and a long chest was to the left against the wall; this he used as a sort of sideboard. And everywhere stood clocks – Victorian dining-room-type clocks, a strange china thing and some carriage clocks. There were a few pieces of Staffordshire pottery, an odd paperweight, a piece of carved wood, an Epstein head on the chest in front of the china cupboard. The walls looked damp and in dire need of decoration. 'It's a bonny room, isn't it?' he would groan.

Even in the height of summer I always felt chilled and Lowry would switch on a small electric fire, usually stumbling over the flex. In winter his housekeeper, Mrs Swindles, would have lighted a couple of coals in the grate but it never amounted to much warmth. It was small wonder he constantly reiterated that he had to get out of that house. The marvel, sometimes, was how he ever got into it.

Pictures hung everywhere. His own portraits of his father and mother and his self-portrait hung above the sideboard. Beneath them hung various Rossettis, including a study for *The Loving Cup*. Lowry had picked it up in an antique shop in Chelsea years before and insisted it was genuine; on the verso it certainly stated that it was a study for *The Loving Cup* by D.G.Rossetti, but to me it smacked in every way of Treffrey Dunn and I was of the opinion that this was the copy Dunn made which secured him his job as Rossetti's assistant. In any event it disappeared on Lowry's death.

On a wall to the left of the fireplace hung the large Rossetti chalk head of Alexa Wilding which Lowry left to his solicitor. There also hung in this room a small Rossetti drawing which we gave him, a design for *Benedick and Beatrice* dating from 1850. Lowry delighted in the figure drawing of the girls. 'Just look at that line,' he would breathe, moving his forefinger over the outlines, drawing in his breath and expelling it. 'Just look. . . .'

Among this assortment of pictures hanging in his sitting room, Lowry was never without two, and maybe three, of his portraits of Ann.

Further along the passage directly behind this front room was a smaller one he used as his studio. In his paintings, Lowry worked with a great deal of white – it might have been supposed that a flock of pigeons had recently roosted here. It was about as ungrand as it could be – paint spattered and in splendid disarray, squalid, with bare floorboards; but it served his purpose. In this workroom hung one or two more Rossetti pastels and, of course, various of his own works in assorted stages of completion. A little french window at the back of it opened into a ramshackle something which I suppose might once have been called a conservatory. Very tiny, it appeared appallingly insecure and later he had to have it boarded up.

Further still down the passage was his awful kitchen where he could make himself a cup of tea, boil an egg and even achieve, on occasions, so he said, a piece of toast, hopeful that Mrs Swindles had not forgotten to buy some butter. There was seldom anything else.

The staircase went pretty steeply up from the left of the hall. At the top, straight ahead, was his loo and separate bathroom with bare floorboards. Turning along the landing to the right, above his sitting room, was his bedroom. This was always tidier than the other rooms and it was here that he proudly showed us *Proserpine*. Since his death it has been said that this great oil painting hung in all sorts of peculiar places, but in fact it hung on the left-hand wall of his bedroom, just beyond his wardrobe, and could barely be seen until one was well inside the room. Lowry's single bed was behind the door, in the centre of the room, from where he could just see and enjoy his great Rossetti. He never tired of it and would maintain that it was a comfort to see the painting last thing at night and upon wakening.

Opposite the bed, above the small fireplace, was yet another Rossetti, which he claimed he regretted having bought. This was a watercolour, *The Return of Tibullus to Delia*, and the only 'soobject' work of his favourite artist he owned. It was not one of the beautiful early watercolours of Rossetti but a later replica, for which our friend had no fondness, and he was delighted when it was stolen. He rather hoped that he had seen the back of it but, like a bad penny, it was recovered. After this he moved the painting from his bedroom. When his collection was posthumously exhibited at Manchester's City Art Gallery as 'A Pre-Raphaelite Passion', the catalogue to the works stated that the model for the central figure of Delia was Fanny Cornforth. This is erroneous, for the model was a domestic servant called Ellen Smith.*

On the small chimneypiece in Lowry's bedroom stood always a small framed photograph of Carol. She had been 'snapped' standing prettily in one of the Manchester parks, and the painter much preferred this to the Rossetti watercolour which for years hung above it.

His dressing table was by the window with a tall oak chest of drawers beyond, and another fine Rossetti pencil drawing above it, *The Laurel*. And at the foot of Lowry's bed stood a small carved oak chest, filled to overflowing with his press cuttings. Years later I was to see the companion to this chest in the bedroom of his cousin May.

Above his bed there hung for many years one of his own works which had been a favourite of his mother, so he told us. This was *Yachts at Lytham*, and there came the day when he asked me if I would mind climbing on to his bed to take it down as it was due to go for exhibition in his 1966 Retrospective at the Tate Gallery. Doing as he requested, I replaced it with a Rossetti study for *Aspecta Medusa*, a newly acquired pastel from the Stone Gallery.

Next to the painter's bedroom was a small room in which he kept mostly finished works of his own. I was never inside this holy of holies but on occasion he would take Micky in.

In the Manchester catalogue already referred to, it was said that a certain Rossetti coloured chalk, *Reverie*, once hung in Lowry's 'lounge' but it never did. After Lowry bought it from the Stone Gallery my husband hung it for him just inside his bedroom door, to the left, with the wardrobe and *Proserpine* beyond it, and *Reverie* was never moved from that position until it was carried from The Elms after our friend was dead. The same catalogue claimed that the pastel *Pandora* by Rossetti hung in Lowry's bedroom, but this picture was never inside his house. He acquired it as a present for Carol and it went straight from our gallery to her mother's flat in Rochdale until it was loaned to the Manchester exhibition.

* See *The Diaries of G. P. Boyce*.

There is an interesting anecdote connected with Lowry's purchase of a small watercolour entitled *The Parting of Herwig and Gudrun*. One day an elderly lady brought this charming and colourful watercolour to our gallery. She told us that her uncle had owned a large collection of Pre-Raphaelite works and this was his bequest to her. She cared nothing for the Pre-Raphaelite painters and wished to sell the work. On the verso was written 'Ford Madox Brown – William Morris'. She had taken it to a well-known London gallery to have it valued.

The London gallery had valued it at eighty pounds, but was unable to say whether it was a work of Brown or Morris. Looking at it I said, 'Well, it's not Morris!' while my husband doubted if it was by Madox Brown. Anyway, it was a delightful work and I immediately offered her a hundred pounds for it, which she was glad to accept.

It was unframed and I put it face to the wall on the office floor, where it remained for several days until Lowry arrived. Whenever he returned from his home for another visit he was always at his most fed up. He sat back groaning and moaning as usual in his chair and, searching for something to interest him, I spied the watercolour still face to the wall. Picking it up I said, 'Come along now, Mr Lowry, and tell us who painted this.'

He grabbed the picture from me, did not look at the back but sprang to his feet, saying, 'Oh, Mrs Marshall, I'm ashamed of you! You don't know? Not after all my teaching? Why it's Madox Brown – who else? Oh, Mrs Marshall, had you only studied those murals in Manchester Town Hall, you'd never have been asking me. How much d'you want for it?' I told him the story of the woman bringing it in, and that the gallery had paid a hundred pounds for it. 'Well, I must have it!' he exclaimed excitedly. 'What'll you take for it?' I suggested that by the time it was framed he could have it for a hundred and twenty pounds.

After it was framed it hung in the office awaiting his arrival. One day another client who was an avid Pre-Raphaelite collector saw *The Parting of Herwig and Gudrun* and said, 'How much d'you want for that Madox Brown? It's one of the loveliest things I've ever seen.' We had to explain that Lowry had already bought it and when he arrived, a short time later, the client offered him six hundred pounds for it. But Lowry would not part with it. He took it home and hung it in his living room (next to a Rossetti drawing of Annie Miller –

a study for *Helen of Troy*) and never ceased to castigate me for not having been as certain as he that the work in question was by Madox Brown.

Some little time after Lowry acquired the painting I found a reference to it in a Rossetti letter to William Bell Scott, where he tells the latter that Brown is busy with a lovely small watercolour illustrating one of Morris's Icelandic sagas. This was just before Brown and Morris fell out.

After Lowry's death, *The Parting of Herwig and Gudrun* was valued by Christie's at two and a half thousand pounds and rated a work of national importance.

After November 1965, when the Stone Gallery began gradually to specialize in Pre-Raphaelites, our exhibitions brought to the gallery a new clientéle, and we made many friends amongst new collectors and various academics from all over the world. One of the collectors was a young lecturer in law at Newcastle University, who was to meet Lowry more often than any other of our friends. He was a bachelor, with an invalid mother for whom he had to care, and Lowry and he had this experience in common. Many times the painter would console Ian when he was unduly depressed over his mother's condition, and the artist would describe again how he nursed his mother through the days and nights – passionately telling of the burden he had found it to be, with no other help at hand.

Much has been made of Lowry's attachment to his mother, and it has been claimed that in some measure this affected his entire life. But in all the years we knew him, when he spoke of her there never appeared any great fondness on his part, but rather a resentment at the burden she had been. It was apparent that his mother's illness and helplessness was a situation with which he had found himself encumbered and a problem which he recalled with rancour rather than love.

Certainly Lowry would not have been human had he been without regret that neither parent lived to see his fame. On the other hand, it would not have been in character had he not considered that it was an economic saving for him with them gone.

Before she died, Ian's mother built up a remarkably important collection of Pre-Raphaelite works over a short period of time, and it was their common interest in the Pre-Raphaelites which became a second bond between Lowry and Ian – one of the few people whom Lowry addressed by Christian name only. Despite a long and close friendship with the painter, Ian was never tempted to buy his work, and Lowry showed no sign of resenting this fact. Rather, it made for a happier situation in as much as he could not list Ian as being among the throng who always wanted something from him. Nevertheless, occasionally we wondered about his inner reaction to Ian's attitude. I once completed some sentence with, '. . . knowing Ian as we do.' And Lowry smiled across the room at me, 'So you think we know the gentleman, do you, Mrs Marshall? I have a feeling we don't, you know. And, what's more, we never will. Bully him as you like, and indeed as you do – but he'll never buy a work of mine!' And he never did.

Another who continued to meet Lowry constantly, although they did not become close was Dr Chalmers Burns. Good conversationalists never went down too well with Lowry, and Chalmers could keep us in gales of laughter, when the painter would doze rudely in his chair, occasionally opening one wicked eye to wink at one or other of us.

Chalmers was another who refused to buy a Lowry work of any description. Lowry once tried to tempt him by saying that he would even sign one 'MacLowry' so that it might not disgrace the musical gentleman's collection of Scottish painting. But Dr Burns would have none of it. Later, however, when some of Dr Burns's students from Newcastle University approached Lowry to ask whether he would make a special drawing for them as a retirement present to Dr Burns, it was the artist's turn to remain adamant. And he delighted in getting his own back.

After the painter's death Chalmers regretted his lost opportunity with, 'Dear me, just think – I could have had the only MacLowry in existence.' I recall a day when Dr Burns had been talking incessantly of his great-great-uncle until, to bring Lowry into the conversation, I turned to him with, 'You like Dyce's work, don't you?'

'Dyce? Who's Dyce? I've never heard of him,' replied Lowry without hesitation.

'Never heard of William Dyce?' I asked astounded, for there was no painter, seemingly, of whom Lowry had not heard and with whose work he was unfamiliar. 'I was sure I'd heard you say you admired Dyce.'

'No, you're quite mistaken – who was he?'

'The great nineteenth-century painter,' I started in all innocence to explain, but was interrupted with, 'Can't have been – never heard of him.' At which point Chalmers launched forth once more, and Lowry apparently fell sound asleep.

Eventually our friend left. He had hardly got out of the room when Lowry turned to me with a broad smile, 'God, the man does go on, doesn't he? We want our lunch.'

'Yes,' I agreed, 'It's high time we had it. Gosh – I'm really surprised, though, that you've never heard of William Dyce.'

'*Never heard of William Dyce*? Of course I've heard of Dyce. I'd heard of him before his great-nephew had heard of him! I just didn't think it was good for the gentleman to know I had – that's all.'

'You monster!' I exploded with laughter. 'Why, you even had me fooled. Ye gods, you should have been an actor, not a painter!'

'D'you really think so, Mrs Marshall? I fancy I'd have rather enjoyed it. Although you and Ann both agree that it's rather a sordid existence – still, I'm very fond of sordid things. After all, most of m'pictures are sordid!'

There was another evening we were sitting with the painter over drinks in the office. Ian was with us as expected, and Chalmers had dropped in. It was getting rather late and Lowry kept looking pointedly at his watch as his dinner was overdue. Eventually, feeling I could do no other, I asked Dr Burns whether he would care to join us at Tilley's, and he promptly accepted.

Walking round to the restaurant Lowry took my arm, saying, 'Did you have to ask that gentleman?'

'Yes, I did. And you needn't complain – you're not paying. Anyway, I don't know what you have against him.'

'He does go on so.'

'Yes, but he's bloody funny, which is more than some people are,' I said.

'Well, don't sit me next to him, Mrs Marshall – that's all.'

'Oh no, you can sit and whisper to Ian.'

Chalmers was ever a guest who paid his way, to my mind, by being entertaining. Dinner was much more amusing than it would have been, but Lowry refused to contribute to the conversation, and after my little dig he refrained from whispering to Ian as they sat together on the banquette. Only when Dr Burns was leaving to board his sleeper for London did Lowry manage to raise a little charm and was more amused by the, to him, welcome departure of

Chalmers than by Chalmers's pronouncement that he must not forget to warn the guard on no account to waken him if there was illness or death during the journey. 'Always have to warn them I'm not that kind of doctor!'

'Now I can enjoy him,' said Lowry when he had gone.

The lack of rapport between the painter and Chalmers Burns was reciprocal. One day when Chalmers came in to see us, on learning that Lowry was upstairs, he exploded with, 'My God! Is he still with you? It's like having Beethoven on your hands – trouble is, this man isn't dead.'

Years later when Lowry was dead and Dr Burns talked of old times, he reminded me of a day when a young dealer, David Hughes, (aware of Lowry's constant presence with us) sent from London an oil painting which he was certain was a Lowry. It was unsigned and undated; he wondered whether we would be good enough to check with the artist whether or not it was his work. Lowry gave a cursory glance and immediately proclaimed that it was not his. A little surprised, for we had thought otherwise, we put it away on an easel in a store room. Later, when Chalmers looked in, in an effort to include Lowry in the conversation we mentioned the work and all decided to go and have another look at it. Seeing it again, Lowry crossed slowly towards it; gently he began to move his hand over it here and there; back and forth, up and down that beautiful hand of his moved over the painting, until suddenly he started back to announce, 'Oh yes, it *is* mine. Someone's done something to it here and there, but you could say it's mine. As Mrs Marshall will say – bloody stupid of me. Yes, very stupid of me, but I had no memory of it at all. *The Doctor's Visit*: pretty early it is. I'll sign it.' As Dr Burns was to recall, Lowry read that painting as a blind man might have read a piece of music.

Since his death it has been said that the mischievous side to Lowry's character allowed him upon occasion to say that a work was not his when he was fully aware that it was – intending to displease or annoy a friend. This I find impossible to reconcile with the man we knew. Mischievous he certainly was, but never, so far as I'm aware, did this element enter into his approach to his art. If he said a work was not his, then it was his honest opinion at the time.

Lowry's art was his life. He looked upon painting as a job like any other, certainly. He had no use for artists who felt they had to wait for inspiration. 'Get on with it,' he would exclaim irritably. 'Get on with the job – pull it through. If you've made a mess of it, you can still work at it and pull it through. Work at it, work at it, it's only a question of work – it's not God-given inspiration – there's no such thing. Genius? What's genius? Don't talk to me of genius – it's just bloody hard work, begging your pardon – thank goodness I don't ever have to beg Mrs Marshall's!' He would dissolve into sudden laughter as he realized he had given a glimpse of the inner man.

Lowry could be mischievous, oh yes; but he cared far too much about his art to lie deliberately about it.

One day we received a telephone call from a child psychiatrist who said that she was about to be given a Lowry oil painting. Before accepting such a valuable present, she felt she ought to have it valued. We asked her to bring it in the following afternoon about 3.30, 'For then Mr Lowry will be here, and I'm sure he would be fascinated to see it.' The lady arrived in the gallery at three o'clock. After unwrapping the fairly large oil painting, I exclaimed, 'Oh, that's not a Lowry, I'm afraid.' Simon emerged from the office and did likewise.

Micky merely looked at the back of it, and said, 'Oh, I'm sorry, but that's not a Lowry!'

The lady looked appalled. 'But you haven't even seen it yet.'

'No, I don't need to, for he doesn't work on that sort of canvas.' The woman remained unconvinced, so we tried to show her that the texture was wrong, and that it had a subtle green undertone, rather than a luminosity.

'Well,' she said, 'it's like all the Lowrys I've ever seen!'

'Oh,' said Micky, 'it's a very clever fake, and the best bit of all is the signature and date – they're perfect. But I fancy it's a composite picture; you know, bits taken from this painting of Lowry's or that one and put together to make an "original" whole. Look, come into the office, and I'll try to show you what we're talking about.' He led her through to the room where hung a fair display of Lowry oils. He pointed out texture, underpainting of white, lack of varnish, and a few of the rather more obvious points in question, but the woman remained totally unconvinced.

Ian came downstairs and I said, 'Ian, come and have a look at this Lowry, and tell us what you think of it.'

Ian stood looking at the painting, then announced in his splendid legal drawl, 'Ooh, I'm afraid I do not care for it. Indeed, I should be surprised if it were indeed by our friend, despite that very fine signature, madam.'

I said to Simon that we had better gather up the painting from the reception area, as Lowry was not going to be very thrilled if that was the first thing he set eyes on. I went to remove the offending object, but before I could do so the gallery door was flung wide and in walked Lowry.

His eyes went straight to the picture and, taking a step back, he tore off his trilby. Turning to me with a face of thunder he demanded, 'My God! You haven't bought *that*, have you?'

'Heavens, no, Mr Lowry.' I tried to pour oil on the troubled waters, and lowering my voice said, 'There's a woman in the office who has brought it in for valuation; we've told her it's not one of yours, but I'm afraid she won't accept our opinion.'

'My God!' he repeated, picking his hat off the floor where it leaned against a stool. 'I've seen that before.' I looked at him very sharply, for this was a phrase he would often use when looking at a work of his which he hadn't seen for a long time, or even at a photograph of some work which was genuinely his own. 'You've seen it before?' I asked.

'Yes, I saw it six months ago – but you're quite right, of course, it's not mine. It's a fake.'

Micky was ushering the lady out of the office and introduced her to the painter who announced firmly that the painting was indeed none of his. He was not smiling, nor were his eyes twinkling. Still apparently reluctant to accept even the painter's opinion of what was and what was not his work, she said that at least it would make a nice decoration for her loo. She took her departure and we didn't see her again.

As our secretary took Lowry's hat and raincoat, we trooped into the office, and Lowry said, 'As we're dealing with a fake, Mr Marshall, just put that machine of yours on – it would be nice to have a record of this conversation.' We were joined in a few moments by Philip Robertson, who had driven Lowry from Mottram and had by that time parked his car. What follows is a recording of the ensuing discussion.

'Well, well! Just fancy seeing that again,' laughed the painter.

'Gosh, when you said you'd seen it before you had me puzzled . . . you went positively purple!' I announced.

' "What *again*," I said . . . Well, sir, and how are you?' asked Lowry of Micky.

'Fine, thanks, and what about you?'

'Oh God, I'm nearing the end you know – it won't be long now. I'm *dying*. I'm *fed up*. But I feel more cheerful, when I come to think of it, at seeing that old friend.'

'Well, you didn't act cheerful,' I laughed.

'Oh well, you've got to allow for my surprise at seeing it in here . . . well, no question about that!'

'No, no bloody question at all,' agreed Micky, 'I had the female on the phone twice yesterday, and suggested she bring it in today as I thought you'd be interested – not that I knew in advance that it was going to be a fake. But it had me puzzled. She gave me the size and the subject and said that a friend wanted to make her a present of it. I told her that if it was genuine it was worth about eight thousand. Well, she rang back after a few moments saying she had accepted it and could she bring it in for insurance valuation. She'd got the picture so quickly it meant the friend must live locally; and who had a painting of that description of which we were unaware? But when she brought it in today I saw the back first and thought you certainly never use that canvas.'

'Oh, that was clever of you – that's right enough, people invariably fail to pay attention to detail. Now start at the beginning and tell me the story again.'

[This was always the way with Lowry; once didn't suffice, one had to go over and over things.]

'Did I see a photograph of this a few weeks ago?' asked Mr Robertson.

'No,' murmured Lowry.

'Not in Huddersfield?'

'*Yes* – you did,' recalled the artist.

'That's the one, is it?'

'Yes – that's the one. That's the one. Six months ago it was brought to my house by a gentleman who's a collector and has a lot of my things, and he said, "Look here, this *is* yours isn't it?" And I said no and he said, "Well, I've bought it." So he went back to the people – you know them well enough – and he said; "Look here, I'm cancelling my cheque and here's your picture back." '

'And what had he paid for it?' I queried.

'A lot of money.'

'A lot? Can you tell me how much, Mr Lowry?' asked Micky.

'In the event it turned out he'd paid twelve hundred pounds.'

'Well of course, that was ludicrous if it was right,' I announced.

'It is ludicrous, ludicrous,' said Lowry.

'Mad,' I continued. 'Because if it was genuine it's a fraction of what it would be worth, and as a fake it's robbery at any price.'

'Well, I must say Mr Marshall was clever to know without seeing it – still, he's a clever lad, I always say. People invariably fail to pay attention to detail. They do 'em on the wrong side of the canvas, they do them on canvas I never use.'

Not to be outdone I said, 'I told the woman this was wrong and that was wrong and, look, it's as dull as ditchwater, and it's been painted yesterday . . . this should be fourteen years old by the date . . . '

'What was the date on it?' asked Lowry.

'Fifty-six.'

'Oh no! Oh, ho-ho.' He mocked again.

'I pointed out that it wasn't painted over white – there was no luminosity. I showed her the too regular windows, the stupid curtains, the figures with no weight to them, toppling over here and there – no balance – you never get that in a Lowry. But she couldn't understand.'

'Oh no, nothing would convince her,' added Ian.

'Yes, well then,' murmured Lowry, 'If she's buying it and not been given it she may be sensible and take it back and say it isn't mine.'

'Well,' I said, 'if I'd got one like that I'd take it back to whomever I'd got it from and say it ought to be destroyed.'

'It'll not be destroyed,' laughed Lowry yet again, 'that's quite certain – it'll turn up again somewhere. Oh yes, it'll turn up all right – it's like an old friend – there's no question about that.'

'Where did you see it last time?' asked Simon.

'Oh, about six months ago in Mottram,' repeated Lowry. 'Mr L— had bought it, and I said to him, "I'm surprised at you. I can't believe you've done it. It's not mine,". I said, and he said, "You're certain?" I said, "Yes, look at the damned thing – sorry, look at the thing." And that's the last I saw of it; he took it back and stopped his cheque and he told them it wasn't genuine.'

'Blooming funny – you walking in like that and seeing it again. I'll never forget your face!'

'Ah, Mrs Marshall, well, it seemed like an old friend. I wanted to shake hands with it.' Lowry was chuckling merrily. 'If that lady didn't believe you, d'you think she believed me?'

'Well, she'd no alternative, had she?' I ruminated.

'Can't we find an independent opinion?' scoffed Micky, remembering one of the painter's famous stories, when a man refused to take his word that he was not the originator of a certain picture, and suggested they find an independent opinion. Philip and Ian were familiar with the tale and we all joined in the general fun.

'Well,' Lowry was still at it, 'I was a bit startled to be greeted by that. "What, again?" I said – first in Manchester, now here. Oh yes, it'll turn up again. It's been travelling around. To think I had it brought to me by a fellow who ought to have known better, but he bought it, and I said that's not my picture, so he got very busy then, and he stopped his cheque and took them back their picture and he told them to do what the devil they liked. So it's an old friend is that picture. A very odd thing, isn't it? Like meeting an old friend as you might say, in a far off country . . . ha, ha, ha.'

'I think you're very tolerant,' I said, 'I'd be livid, wouldn't you?'

'I think so – yes,' agreed Mr Robertson.

'I'd be furious,' announced Micky.

'I don't care,' said Lowry, 'it doesn't worry me.'

'I'd put my foot through it,' said Micky.

'I presume,' contributed Mr Robertson, 'that you get to the stage where you accept these things as inevitable.'

Simon continued the theme with, 'I suppose in a way it's a compliment.'

'Yes, well it's a compliment I'd put my foot through,' said his father.

'I don't think you would,' said Lowry thoughtfully.

'Oh, I'm sure I would. Well, I mean, dammit – it's not just your picture, it's your signature which has been forged as well.'

'Yes, but that's the easiest thing of all to forge, Mr Marshall!'

'You're not getting my point. Anyone can paint a picture and anyone can debate who's painted it. But the moment someone other than you puts your signature on it, it is an offence – it makes it unlawful. It's an appalling liberty to sign someone else's name.'

I turned to Ian as the legal expert. 'Would you be angry, Ian?'

'Well,' was the tactfully drawled rejoinder, 'at least I could take it as a compliment that I was worth faking.'

'Ah, yes. I must take comfort from that, sir. But, I say, could she have been daft enough to have bought it?'

'I suppose we must accept her story that she's been given it.'

'Well,' said Lowry, 'could anyone be daft enough to spend good money on a painting without taking every possible precaution first?'

'Oh yes, Mr Lowry,' said Micky, 'I think from my experience people do, because the public is naturally so greedy, everyone is looking for bargains and finds.'

'Well, she found one there, didn't she?' hooted the elderly man. 'Well, well, well, what an interesting afternoon. Always something going on here to keep me going.'

Suddenly he felt in his inner pocket and pulled out the usual bulging notecase. 'D'you know, I've just remembered, I believe I have – yes, I have, I've got a photograph here of that painting the lady brought in.'

'You've what?' I asked.

'Look, here you are, here's a photograph of that picture.' And he produced a snapshot of the fake.

'How do you come to have that?'

'Well, I had this photograph taken as a record, but I'd quite forgotten I had it in m'pocket book all the time.'

'Oh, you stupid old fool,' I snorted. 'D'you realize that, if you get run over, or kick the bucket suddenly, as you're always telling us you're about to, and that's found among your things, it's going to take a hell of a lot to convince people that it's not one of your own paintings. Here, come on, take this pen and put a line through it, and write "fake" over it – for God's sake. . . . '

'Not for God's sake, Mrs Marshall – for mine. Aye, it's a good idea. D'you know that thought never struck me? I wouldn't mind wagering that it comes out pretty quickly after I'm gone! My word yes, I'll do as you say.' And he did.

This little episode was typical of time spent with Lowry. As his art was repetitive, so was the man.

Some little time later I saw a certain painter's work for the first time. I looked carefully at it and, turning to our friend, announced, 'Ah – there's the perpetrator of that fake the woman brought into the gallery.'

Lowry looked at me closely. 'What makes you think so?'

'The subtle green undertone. Look at it – it's exactly the same.' Lowry looked.

'Well, I believe you're right. But *he'd* never fake my work?'

'Why not?'

'Well, he's got plenty of money.'

'Yes, but one painter doesn't fake another for money – not as a rule. Envy is the motivation. You're famous and he's not, but he fancies he can paint just as well as you so he paints in your style to prove it and signs the work with your name. Ninety-nine people out of a hundred are fooled by it and he'll continue to suppose that he's just as good as Lowry.'

'Eh, folk will do some strange things,' and then he remembered an amusing experience he delighted to relate. One morning he had been looking around in an art dealer's shop when a man entered. He eventually admired a watercolour said to be by Birket Foster but it was not signed. Had it only been signed, the man told the dealer, he would certainly have bought it.

'Oh, not to worry,' the dealer was quick to reassure him, 'Mr Foster comes in most lunchtimes, and I expect him today as usual. I'll get him to sign it, it's just an oversight.' The prospective customer was delighted at this information and said he would return about three o'clock in the afternoon.

Finding this situation irresistible, Lowry himself returned to the shop shortly before the appointed hour. Sure enough as he filled in time prowling around, the gentleman of the morning returned. 'Oh, splendid,' the shopkeeper greeted him, 'Mr Foster looked in as I expected, and he's signed the watercolour with his monogram in his usual manner; he was delighted to know that you admired it.'

The customer bought it, went happily upon his way and Lowry went happily upon his. He had never cared much for Birket Foster's work but from henceforth he admitted the artist to be something of a genius. It showed remarkable ability to return to the world most days at lunchtime, having been dead since 1899.

As our knowledge of the Pre-Raphaelite painters grew, so did the demand. As we were selling works to collectors from all over the world, it became necessary for us to extend our search area. This required a lot of travelling; it could be disappointing at the end of a long journey only to find a fake, a copy, or a wrong attribution on offer. Stockholm may be a beautiful city but it is cold in winter, and the effort of trying to cut through the bureaucratic web of the civic-controlled Swedish saleroom, only to find what is called a painting by Dante Gabriel Rossetti to be nothing of the kind, was, in that temperature, a very low point in our constant searching.

We had successes, of course. A couple of drawings in Berlin; and, with assistance from Virgina Surtees, the Rossetti authority, we were directed to Florence to visit the granddaughter of one of the Pre-Raphaelite associates. She lived in a flat in the centre of surely the most beautiful city in the world. The walls were hung with works whose whereabouts had been a mystery for years but of which there were documentary records. At last here they were in the possession of a small Italian lady who had a passion for bridge – and who wanted to sell. Alas, owing to export restrictions, the Italian government would not permit her to part with certain paintings – but it was wonderful to see them.

It was always a delight to visit Rossetti's great-niece, who lived in an old house at Woodstock. She did not wish to part with very much of her remaining small collection, but the few items she was prepared to let us acquire we were pleased to have, particularly a large drawing for Rossetti's famous painting *Found* – the only existing drawing of the same size as the oil. Imogen Dennis bore a remarkable likeness to her great-uncle, just as her granddaughter resembled Christina Rossetti.

Lowry was totally delighted when we were able to tell him that Rossetti's great-niece preferred his work to that of her famous ancestor.

But major Rossetti works have always been hard to come by, and there came the time when certain of our clients had perforce to take turn and turn about when making an acquisition. Very occasionally one person alone cared for a certain painting or drawing, which simplified the matter, but for the most part it was a question of would-be buyers taking their turn in the queue. Out of this sometimes amusing situation the Rossetti Society came into being. It was purely a fun activity attached to the Stone Gallery. There was no entrance fee, and only one rule of membership – ownership of a Rossetti work bought from the gallery. Lowry was unanimously voted President of the Rossetti Society, and from that time on a number of our friends seldom referred to him as anything but 'the President'. 'Well, and how is the President today?' Ian would ask upon meeting him, and Captain Michael Clark, another member, would invariably inquire, 'Well, what has the President to say about the matter?' And the President lapped it up.

There were many people in and out of the gallery who met this man addressed as 'the President', and left without having the slightest idea that they had been talking with Britain's most popular painter. It speaks volumes for Lowry's modesty regarding his own work. A young Canadian, Dr Allan Life, who for a number of years was research assistant to the Pre-Raphaelite scholar Professor W. E. Fredeman, spent an afternoon and evening with us all, and told us years later that he had no idea at the time that the man with us and constantly referred to as the President, was the distinguished painter, L. S. Lowry.

Ian became the society's Secretary and, taking a leaf out of the President's book, he seldom replied to letters. My husband was voted Chaplain – I cannot imagine why one was required and no one could ever recall how he came to hold the position, but it was suspected that he proposed and voted himself into it. I was referred to as the Librarian, for the simple reason that I was the only one to open anything other than a picture book on Rossetti. Michael Clark, who was interested in owning and breeding race horses, was unanimously voted Master of the Horse – after all, Rossetti had been extraordinarily fond of animals and for some years had a positive zoo in his garden at Cheyne Walk.

The reader may think that there is much reference to food and maybe also to drink throughout this narrative, but in an elderly person's existence food becomes of major importance and Lowry was no exception. The long days and evenings were relieved of some of their monotony by the periods given up to 'sust', as Ian would call whatever meal we were about to consume. It was therefore taken for granted that any activity such as the Rossetti Society must revolve around a dinner party. And, of course, the venue for the most part, had to be Tilley's. Lowry by this time was totally attached to Tilley's, claiming that there was no restaurant in the land to equal it. In some respects he was right. We all mourned it deeply when it closed.

How we laughed, and laughed again, during those Rossetti Society dinners; it is impossible to relay the sheer stupidity and fun we all enjoyed. I have seen Lowry sitting in his favourite spot on the banquette, scarlet in the face, with tears of mirth pouring down his cheeks, pleading with my husband or some other member to stop his nonsense until he could get his breath. Ian kept the minutes, and though possibly they cannot be appreciated at this distance of time by any who were not a part of the merriment of the moment, I will quote one or two:

The inaugural meeting of the Rossetti Society was held on 25th June, 1967.
The members impugned the authenticity of each other's pictures.
The members impugned each other's learning.
The members impugned each other's judgment.
The President spoke at much length of his impending demise.
The President spoke at even greater length of his onerous tax burdens.
The gravy was abominable and the Chaplain's bill enormous.
An enjoyable time was had by all and it was resolved that the Society should assemble frequently.

July 8th 1967. The absence of the Master of the Horse was noted with much regret, some fear being entertained for his personal safety. The project of hiring at enormous expense detectives Poirot, Maigret, Sherlock Holmes, Sexton Blake and others was discussed, but it was resolved that this be deferred pending further local inquiry. Fortunately it was discovered next day that the Master of the Horse had merely miscalculated the date of the meeting – a beauty contest had also been on the telly!

The meeting was a little subdued as the President did not care for the new location of the Gosforth Park Hotel. He tried three tables and still could not find one which met with his approval. He did not care for the beautiful view from the window, but expressed approval at the splendid hot pudding.

September 13th 1967. The Chaplain (as befitted his office) raised the issue of Rossetti's use of coarse language upon occasion. Recoiling in horror he moved that the Society be disbanded, and the members' works sold forthwith, to the end that the chastity of the members remain unsullied.

The Librarian asserted without hesitation that the use of these words in their context demonstrated the extreme purity of Rossetti.

The Secretary explained, with a variety of literary allusions, that the use of oaths was common around that period.

The President pointed out that it was common at any period; and then with his customary incisiveness pointed out that, owing to the credit squeeze, the market was not at present propitious for a realisation of the pictures which might in time be expected to command a higher figure.

This point proved decisive. The Secretary called for a vote and the motion was lost with no support, the Chaplain bowing, as other wearers of the clerical garb have been known to do throughout the ages, to a discreet appreciation of the need to temper the worship of God with a discerning eye to the merits of Mammon.

The project of acquiring further Rossettis by marrying their owners was urged with enthusiasm by those members who would not have to do the marrying. The President pointed out the need for circumspection; the quantum of the estates of these females had not been ascertained, nor the artistic merits of the works they were reputed to own. Some might well be the possessors of 'subject' pictures, and he wanted none of those.

The Secretary stated sadly that *Rosa Triplex* which had been mentioned as a star acquisition was not one of his favourites. The President concurred, and spoke of the poignant anguish which any defection to the matrimonial stakes on his part might be expected to cause in another female bosom. It was agreed that, pending further and fuller particulars, consideration of this project be deferred.

The President spoke of his tax position with unwonted brevity, having not yet regained his spirits after a meeting with his accountant.

The meeting terminated at 11.45 p.m.

September 18th 1967. The character and actions of some new members of the Society gave rise to much discussion among members present.

The President was invited to address the gathering once again on the subject of his taxation, but was too sunk in sorrow consequent upon his accountant having intimated his inability to secure any reduction in the demand notes which fall like leaves in autumn around the revered head of the President.

The Secretary was asked to render his version of 'Come into the Garden Maud', in the tones and accent of the Bard. The restaurant appeared to empty more speedily and earlier than usual, except for the Society table, which received some odd glances from departing diners. It had always been recognised that the Secretary had the ability to empty any restaurant with his particularly fine rendering, and the Society was not disappointed upon this occasion.

The President was seen to be wiping what appeared to be tears of mirth from his eyes, but it was thought that this could hardly be the case.

The meeting was revived with more coffee, and the President with more cream which he drank only because 'it was good for babies and young children'.

March 12th 1968. Simon Marshall was welcomed in the Society after acquiring a very small watercolour of which he was extremely proud, but which did not meet with either the President's admiration or the Secretary's. It was agreed that it let the Society down somewhat, in as much as it was Rossetti pre-chloral work and not a post-chloral.

There was much discussion of the type of people who liked early Rossetti works, and the type who liked his later. It was agreed that there was something wrong with those who liked the early work, but something infinitely more wrong with those who liked later Rossettis of which the President and the Secretary were perfect examples.

Discussion became rather acrimonious and centred round the activities of Mary the housemaid and the reason for Rossetti's dismissing her. The President had a nasty gleam in his eye as he gave his usual opinion on this touchy subject. The Librarian insisted that it was Madox Brown who dismissed her as he considered Rossetti's staff too large for his means at the time. The President would have none of it.

The President wished to know why Hall Caine was instructed to have his meals in the wash-house when Mrs Morris visited Cheyne Walk. Again this was a touchy matter between the Librarian and the President, as the latter was well aware. The Librarian pointed out as usual that Hall Caine was merely asked to have his dinner in his own room, and she expressed her displeasure with the President who, as she said, should know better.

The President put it to the meeting that he considered it unfair that he could be assessed for tax as a trader if he sold a painting not of his own manufacture.

The President described himself as 'a cold fish', forgetful that he could not hope to get away with this claim with any who really knew him.

The Librarian described the President as a 'sly old fox', which at any rate was less terse than her description of the Secretary as 'a poor bloody silly nit'.

Projects were discussed for expeditions to Oxford to sit on a certain commode, (an obscure reference to Rossetti's now bedridden niece aged ninety), and to the abodes of members of the Society in order to inspect and criticise their collections.

The meeting ended at 11.30 p.m.

6th April 1968. Miss Carol Lowry was welcomed into the Society. She gave a description of a visit with the President to see the Rossetti collection owned by the Secretary. It was noted with disapproval that Miss Lowry had been more impressed with the silver goblet out of which she had consumed a large amount of sherry than with the works of art.

This serious matter was discussed at length. The young lady vehemently denied the charge, stating that the Secretary's collection of Pre-Raphaelites was more important than the President's. Uproar. The President expressed displeasure, the Secretary his great approval of the young lady's judgment.

During the course of the meeting Miss Lowry expressed the view that the Master of the Horse reminded her of Rex Harrison – adding, Rex Harrison when young. The President looked displeased and called the meeting to order by congratulating the Secretary on his newly acquired Madox Brown mural cartoons for the paintings in Manchester's Town Hall.

The Librarian brought the meeting to order, reminding the members of the Society that this was a Rossetti Society, not a Madox Brown one. She asked what had been thought of the Secretary's *Venus Verticordia*, an enviable acquisition in her opinion. The President said the 'tit' upset him not a little. He would have liked it otherwise, 'but oh, that tit!' He was afraid it was a 'pot boiler', to use Rossetti's description of some of his works. The Secretary affirmed that it was a boiling pot of which he was very fond. The President feared he was a dark horse, and the Master pricked up his ears, wondering what the spring sales would produce.

The Chaplain informed the Society that an American newly arrived to this country had boasted that any future Rossettis coming up for sale at auction would be knocked down to him. A cloud descended on the company. It was agreed that all had done remarkably well pricewise to date, but this was bad news.

The Chaplain cheered the company by saying that the American had just paid a high price for a work he had been sold in London as a Rossetti but it was a Walter Knewstub. The Librarian confirmed this fact as the work in question was reproduced in Knewstub's grandson's autobiography.* The Society's spirits were much raised, and the Librarian congratulated upon her research.

More coffee was called for and a jug of cream for the President as it was important to keep babies and young children nourished.

Simon Marshall once more extolled the virtues of his watercolour as was his wont. He was quickly silenced with cries from the President of 'pre-chloral, sir!'

The President then gave a short talk on pre-chloral and post-chloral Rossetti works. The Society was very familiar with it. The President then summed up his discourse by stating that the Secretary might be forgiven his *Venus* – tit or no tit, it was at least post-chloral, but said again that he would have preferred either two tits or none. The Secretary said he would have preferred two.

The President's tax problems were aired with grievance. The Master of the Horse said in his opinion it was worth paying high taxation for the benefits of living in England. The President told him it was time he went home and thought the matter over again.

The meeting ended at 11.45 p.m. It was noted that the President muttered something about 'one tit' as he collected his hat from the cloakroom attendant, who was seen to eye him with some concern.

Over the years as we travelled the country with Lowry to visit various public galleries, we noted that he was quite correct when he constantly bemoaned the fact that the works he most wanted to view were so often stored in some cellar. For this reason he continued to maintain that he was glad of his decision to leave nothing of his own nor any of his collection of other painters' work to a public gallery.

On one of our visits to Manchester's City Art Gallery Lowry wished to show us his two favourite Madox Browns. He wrote to Micky on the 14 October 1967, 'The Art Gallery in Manchester say that if you give them say a day's notice they would be pleased to show you those two pictures, the *Cromwell* picture and *The Body of Harold* which are in store – 2 of Ford M. Brown's greatest pictures – the latter – *The Body of Harold* is going to America at the beginning of next year – (They are in the cellar here now.)'

Micky made arrangements in advance, and with Lowry we were taken to a cellar where we could view the works only in a dim light.

* Sir John Rothenstein's autobiography, *Summer's Lease*, 1901–38. Sir John's grandfather, Walter Knewstub, was Rossetti's assistant for some years.

The pictures in question were *The Body of Harold brought before William the Conqueror*, and *Cromwell, Protector of the Vaudois*. Later, Lowry was extremely caustic in his comments at having to see them under such conditions. 'Laughable, simply laughable. Fiendish, Mr Marshall! And now you understand why they'll get nothing of mine.'

We called in at Bradford's public gallery unexpectedly one day; Lowry wanted to show us a large oil painting of his own. The director arrived and had it brought out of store for us to see. Walking to the car, Lowry exploded, 'Fiendish, isn't it fiendish? But just as I thought – in the cellar as usual.'

One bright October day in 1967 my husband and I pulled up in the car outside The Elms. We were to take our friend on a three-day jaunt to Birmingham. The main objects were to visit the City Art Gallery, where there is a splendid collection of Pre-Raphaelite works – with over two hundred and fifty Rossettis, inclusive of drawings – and Wightwick Manor, just outside Wolverhampton. Micky is as punctual as Lowry was in his habits, and so we arrived exactly at the moment expected for we knew the painter would want to show us all sorts of things, and above all, I would have to be shown *Proserpine* again. There would be little stories he would want to relate – once a splendid equipage had drawn up to his door and, answering the knock, he had found a gentleman standing on the doorstep who announced, 'I want to purchase one of your good paintings.'

'Oh, I'm sorry, sir, but I only paint bad ones,' replied Lowry, closing the door in the ducal face.

As Lowry gathered himself up for his departure, he never failed to tell us with glee how in his absence Mrs Swindles would be answering the door and telling callers no, no, she'd not the faintest idea where he had gone; he would be away for quite some time; it might be weeks before he returned and, of course, he never told her where he was going. Then she would close the door, go into the sitting room and redirect his post. This always amused him.

It was about an hour before we were off and speeding down the new M6. Lowry was not fond of motorways, as he was unfamiliar with them, and he always had a preference for the familiar. He had also found from experience that it was impossible to stop the moment he decided it would be convenient to pop behind a hedge – and he appeared to desire a pop behind a hedge more frequently as a consequence. We always drove to the refrain, 'What speed are we doing now?' and 'What would happen if a wheel came off?' Lowry was not exactly comforted when I related how one had once come off a car my father was driving – and how surprising it was to see it bouncing down the hill ahead of us.

On this particular October afternoon we stopped at one of the service stations for a cup of tea. Coming down the last six stairs from the café Lowry took a most terrible fall. I can feel again the overwhelming sense of pity and affection for him as I recall him lying crumpled on the floor. We rushed to his aid, but were beaten to it by the manager of the place, who happened to be standing near. 'I do hope you're none the worse?' he inquired anxiously, as we all helped the elderly man to his feet.

'Well, if I am, I'll sue you!' barked Lowry. But he recovered immediately; he was no stranger to heavy falls, but was always stoical about them. I have seen him take some shocking ones. Once coming up the gallery steps he fell heavily with his right hand and arm beneath him. It appeared a miracle that he had not broken anything. Another time he fell down four stairs from the exhibition gallery, banging his head on a window ledge; a consultant in the gallery at the time thought he might well have killed himself, but again he showed his remarkable courage and physical resistance and would permit no fussing.

It was dark and raining by the time we reached Birmingham. We had arranged to stay at the Midland Hotel there and after unpacking I went down for dinner to find Lowry and my husband ensconced just inside the entrance to the lounge and as near to the front door of the hotel as possible – a most uncomfortable spot to have chosen, but throughout the visit it proved to be the painter's favourite.

His object in this choice was to observe every coming and going, and he would discuss every good-looking girl in sight. 'That totty has splendid legs, Mr Marshall.' Or, 'D'you think she's in love with him? What d'you fancy her name is? – I've an idea it's Maureen!' This was not my idea of enjoyment at all. Micky could always play Lowry's little games with him so well, but I never attempted to. I could stand a certain amount of this nonsense but the prospect of three days of it, without respite, was daunting.

I suggested that we go and eat – with any kind of luck I would be able to keep him in the dining room for most of the evening ahead. He was going through a cold beef and chips phase, and for a great change would alternate it with cold beef and boiled potatoes.

We were shown to a delightful table in an alcove from which he had a good view of the room but the public, alas, had no view of him and this would not do at all. After trying two other tables, we returned thankfully to the first. Lowry realized that he was unrecognized so he might as well sit in the comfortable alcove after all.

Our first morning in Birmingham we were in the City Art Gallery shortly after it opened and the first picture to meet our eyes, near the entrance, was one of Lowry's paintings – *An Industrial Town*. We stood beside it and awaited the arrival of the assistant with whom we had corresponded when making arrangements to see the large collection of Rossetti drawings. These were not normally on view to the public unless a request was made in advance. After a while we left word for her at the reception desk that she would find us in the Pre-Raphaelite room. 'Ah,' breathed Lowry, looking across to *The Last of England*, 'there's good old Ford Madox Brown – the greatest of them all, y'know, but of course I *like* Rossetti better – not that I think much of that one!' He was pointing to Birmingham's *Proserpine*, a truly dreadful work, a replica completed just before Rossetti's death. 'Oh no,' I agreed, 'it's positively bloody, isn't it? And that *Beata Beatrix* over there is almost as bad – perhaps it's worse.'

'Aye, it's strange, Mrs Marshall, that this gallery should happen to own the two worst replica Rossettis I've ever seen.' I asked him how he liked Millais's *Blind Girl*, and he replied, 'Need you ask? You know what I think of Millais – but please don't tell Miss Bennett.'

The assistant we were waiting for had still not arrived, so we went back to the entrance hall. She came hurriedly to greet us and as we gathered beneath Lowry's painting I thought how very tactless it was of her to make no mention of it, or comment that it was pleasant to meet him.

We were taken through various corridors to an old gallery, a door was unlocked, and we found ourselves surrounded by framed Rossetti drawings.

'I'll lock you in,' the assistant told us, 'and when you've seen all you want, just use this phone on the wall here, and I'll come and let you out.'

This area of the old gallery was now used only as a store. Lowry promptly thumped himself down on an upright wooden kitchen-type chair moaning, 'Let me out. Let me out. Mrs Marshall, ring that phone and tell them to come and let me out!'

'Oh, bloody hell! What on earth's the matter with you now?' I turned on him angrily.

'Oh, Mrs Marshall, all these Rossetti drawings – and *not one for sale!!*'

'Well, just sit yourself there while I enjoy myself for once,' I laughed – relieved. It was only a moment before he was on his knees, tilting one framed drawing forward after another as they were stacked two and three deep along the walls, with the larger works hanging above them.

Lowry picked out one here and another from there, praised this one and rejected that. He coveted the studies of Rossetti women, and discarded the medieval subject works. He expressed his excited admiration in his usual way: a sucking-in of breath reminiscent of the old steam trains going into the tunnel under Saddleworth Moors and then an explosive comment as the train emerged just before Huddersfield.

'Oh, dear me – and they say he couldn't draw – bloody fools. Look at those eyes, the curve of that jaw. Look, there's a study for the little black girl in *The Beloved*. I wonder why he changed the girl for a boy in the finished picture. I prefer the girl. Oooh – just look at that, my word he could do it!' He made his expressive train noises again.

Behind him on the wall hung a large pastel of Fanny Cornforth. 'I don't ever care for Fanny,' Lowry muttered. 'There's not the same mystery there.'

As we waited to be let out after a long morning, Lowry took my arm gently. 'You want to know something?' he whispered, as though all the world were listening. 'They say Rossetti couldn't draw; they even say he didn't draw or make studies. Well, I'll let you into a secret – they're talking through their hats. Take Holman Hunt f'r instance, I've never seen many good drawings or studies of his – too academic by half; I reckon the fellow was jealous of Rossetti. Then Burne-Jones, well, you know I've a great regard for him. I'm very fond of a lot of his work, I'll show you those paintings in the Southampton gallery I want you to see, even if you don't want to see them – but Burne-Jones's drawings weren't a patch on Rossetti's. Oh no, not by a long chalk. But there's no convincing folk. But you and I know, Mrs Marshall, don't we? I fancy it was all that Ruskin's fault – took up with Burne-Jones because he was a tactful yes-man, and Rossetti wouldn't be bossed by Ruskin. That's why there's such a regard for Rossetti's early work – just because Ruskin liked it.'

The gallery assistant arrived to take us to freedom and we went with her to the large Burne-Jones room, where his colossal *Star of Bethlehem* was hanging. Lowry announced to me that he considered it laboured, uninspired and rather dead. 'No magic,' I heard him sigh. In the same room were more case-files of Rossetti's unframed drawings, but after some little while I noticed that our friend was tiring and guided him to a seat. He was never fond of spending hour upon hour in a public gallery – there were few more tiring places. He pulled me gently down on to the seat beside him (every touch of Lowry's was always strangely gentle) and whispered, 'Oh, couldn't they offer us a cup of coffee?' I had seen a small cafeteria on our way to the Burne-Jones room and we went back to find it. Alas, we had not realized how very late it was and there were numbers of young people queueing for lunch.

We returned to the settee. Lowry was whispering again, 'Oh my God – you'd have thought they'd have offered us a cup of coffee, now wouldn't you?'

'No, I wouldn't,' I laughed, 'not at the rate payers' expense, you understand. You're not in the Stone Gallery now, you know!'

'I'll tell you something, Mrs Marshall, if they'd have given me a cup of coffee I'd have given them a picture.'

'Of course you wouldn't.'

'I don't know, I've given a lot to Salford in m'time.'

'Yes, I know you have.'

'Well, all I can say is I wish I was back in your gallery in Newcastle.'

'Well, you wouldn't be having coffee now – you'd be having some of Ella's chicken.'

'Oh, don't, Mrs Marshall, I can't bear it. Why wouldn't they give us a cup of coffee here?'

'Because they've been good enough to let you see a whole lot of drawings which few of the public ever see – and that's your lot.'

'Well, they've got something to learn, that's all I can say.'

'No, you keep forgetting the rate payers.'

'The rate payers don't run this gallery.'

'Indirectly they do . . . anyway it's always the excuse when a public gallery requires one.'

'So giving a poor old fellow like me a cup of coffee would be a waste of public money?' Suddenly he was impatient. 'Oh, I've had enough – let's go.'

I moved over to Micky, who was still talking to the gallery assistant. 'Darling, Mr Lowry's rather tired, he's had a long morning, I think we should be going. . . .'

We returned to our hotel and Lowry was soon revived by his late luncheon, but over coffee he continued his moan, for that was his way once he got something on his mind. 'A bonny hospitable lot in that gallery this morning, Mr Marshall – oh yes, I'd have given them a picture if they'd have liked one, if only they'd given me a little cup of coffee.'

Our visit to Wightwick proved a much more hospitable time. Lady Mander had asked us to take Lowry to this house, which is a perfect example of William Morris decor. The house had been left to the National Trust by her late husband and Rosalie Mander remains as custodian. It was not open to the public on the October afternoon of our invitation. As our car drew up, the front door was opened and Rosalie Mander stood on the step, flinging her arms wide in welcome of the painter. He had a pleasurable delight in her charming greeting which set the seal on his afternoon's enjoyment.

Rosalie Mander had met Lowry previously when she visited his own little house with Virginia Surtees during the course of the latter's work on her great *Catalogue Raisonné* of the works of Dante Gabriel Rossetti. In Lady Mander's study the books piled high everywhere reminded me that she had written, amongst other things, the fascinating *Portrait of Rossetti*, which was published in 1964 under her maiden name of Rosalie Glynn Grylls. In company with Virginia Surtees and Mary Lutyens (the Millais expert), Lady Mander and her friends were known in certain academic circles as the 'Pre-Raphaelite Sisterhood'.

Looking around this splendid house with its untouched Morris decorations, I had tended to lag behind at one point. I was gazing at a tablecloth made from the green stuff curtains of Rossetti's bedroom at Tudor House, Cheyne Walk, when our old friend sidled up to me to whisper mischievously, 'Just as well you haven't a little pair of scissors with you or I fancy you might be snipping off a bit of that cloth as a souvenir of your hero!'

'Now stop teasing, but just imagine, that hung in Rossetti's bedroom. . . .'

'Come along now, Mrs Marshall, and I tell you what, when I'm gone I give you full permission to have a bit of those lovely curtains in my bedroom.'

'Perish the thought!' I retorted, regretting it instantly as I saw Lowry's slightly hurt expression. 'Oh, I didn't mean it like that – I just mean your curtains are a bit grim.' I was making matters worse.

'Well, I can't say *that* speaks much for Rossetti's,' he replied, pointing to a rather unattractive cloth.

'You're such a blooming modest person about your work, you know, that when we're all joking on together we tend to forget you're a painter. It's your own fault, of course, because you dislike talking art, as you put it – at least when it comes to your own things.'

'Now stop making excuses, and continue your hero worship – what a pity the poor fellow can't meet you.' Lowry was laughing again.

There were many interesting Pre-Raphaelite works in the house, and we came upon a remarkably beautiful drawing by Burne-Jones of a head of a lovely woman. I recognized the model immediately as Maria Zambaco, a Greek lady. She and Burne-Jones had been passionately attached to one another, even contemplating a suicide pact. They had meant to drown themselves simultaneously but, on stepping into the water, Burne-Jones found it too chilly and chickened out, so both lived on. Lowry always revelled in this story.

'I don't know how you came to recognize her – you don't care for the gentleman's work.'

'Yes, but that doesn't mean I don't know anything about it. You can't help knowing about Jones if you're researching Rossetti.'

'Aah, that's right, Mrs Marshall, I'm glad you call him by his proper name.' Lowry disapproved of the 'fellow' for having accepted a title and for using the hyphenated name. If Brown could be Brown, Jones should have been good enough for Jones, he would say.

Tea was taken in the dining room, sitting up to table just as Lowry preferred to have it and, what is more, Rosalie Mander sat him in Rossetti's famous painting chair. Inwardly I prayed that he would not see fit to indulge in one of his fidgeting acts and break it, but he was on his best behaviour until the moment when he got up and his hostess said, 'There, now, Mr Lowry, you've sat in Rossetti's chair,' whereupon he pushed it back more than a little irritably.

Sensing his thoughts, I promptly sat myself in it for a moment saying, 'Ah ha, but now I'm sitting in a chair in which both Rossetti and Lowry have sat!' He beamed. Looking back from this distance of time, there must have been numerous occasions over the years when he might well have felt more than a little put out by our absorbed interest in Rossetti, to the complete exclusion of himself as a painter. On the other hand it is equally possible that herein lay a part of the attraction our friendship had for him. So many of Lowry's friends and acquaintances were interested only in his own work – that is, how much of it they could acquire for themselves, at how small a cost.

On our return journey to Mottram we stopped for lunch at the Royal George, Knutsford. It was an ancient inn, one that Lowry knew well, quiet and comfortable. As the luncheon progressed, however, Lowry became increasingly silent and morose; this tended to occur sometimes when a jaunt was nearing its end. He was always in the highest of spirits when we set out on our travels but a depression would descend on him as we neared his home, which he never failed to describe as 'that awful house'. As we came from the dining room to the reception lounge, Micky collected and handed to him his battered trilby. Lowry grabbed it, threw it into the air and as it fell he gave it an almighty kick across the room. He ran after it, took another kick at it and yet another. Backwards and forwards, up and down he pursued that poor headgear, while I looked around fearfully, thankful to see that we were alone as the unpleasant thought passed through my mind that he'd gone off his head at last.

'Oi, m'lad, what's the matter?' queried Micky, for this was no pleasant sight to observe; there was ill-temper and vehemence behind every kick.

'Surely you don't object to me kicking m'own hat around if I want to? It's not yours.' Picking it up at last, he turned with a beaming smile and said, 'It's quite some little time since I was here. This hotel's gone off. It used to be better. I've got a young friend lives near here – shall we call and see her?'

'You've got a young friend lives near here?' asked Micky.

'Yes, that glamorous one, what's her name? Pat Cooke. Let's call on her, shall we?'

'She won't mind?'

'Mind? Why should she mind? Come along, let's go; I think I know the way.'

'It won't be you if you don't,' I laughed.

We found our way very easily and pulled up at a pretty little modern house. Pat welcomed Lowry with shrieks of enthusiasm, sitting him down in a chair with herself on the floor beside him, gushing with joy at seeing her 'dearest, dearest Mr Lowry'. This was quite a different girl from the one I remembered. Gone was all the elegance, here was the 'arty' girl working hard for a coming exhibition in Manchester. She wore a home-spun crafty sort of skirt, schoolgirl-black stockings, sweater, long hair brushed back with a band round it, and no make-up other than heavy mascara, which made her eyes look dark and enormous in her colourless face. Her gestures were wide and sweeping, and her personality in complete contrast to the one I remembered, but none the less entrancing. Lowry sat back, lapping up her adoration, listening to Pat's news, chortling, laughing, and delighted. Eventually Lowry looked at some of her completed work at the other end of the room. We all admired it; it was very slight, but very charming. For an hour or so all was excitement and gaiety, waving hands, more worship, laughter – dearest, dearest Mr Lowry!

What a man of parts our friend was: with Carol one man, with us another, with 'Lofty' Robertson another, with Ian another, with the painter Harold Riley yet another ('we'll just talk football to him Mr Marshall – watch me'), with Pat here was yet another man; while with the press he was always the same po-faced old bore.

At last it was time to leave. As we neared Mottram our friend began to fidget and demanded, 'Can't you go a bit faster, Mr Marshall?'

'Well, I can't go against the lights – not even for you. Hold on, we won't be long now.' At The Elms Lowry was out of the car almost before it had stopped. He was away and up the stairs in a flash, calling, 'Go into the sitting room, I won't be a minute!' True enough, in a moment or two he was back, 'Ah, that's better – thought I wasn't going to last out. Now come into the back room.'

He led us through to the little painting room. We looked at this and that, and Micky picked up a tiny oil sketch from the mantel-shelf. 'What a little gem of a seascape!'

'Well, take it then,' was the immediate reply.

'No, you know we don't play at that game. I can admire without greeding it from you.'

'Well, you're the only one who can then! But you're not as you say "greeding" it from me, Mr Marshall. I don't want it.'

'All the same, we'll leave it there if you don't mind,' said Micky firmly and replaced it.

Propped against a wall were two remarkable paintings of a very young girl with long straight hair. Both paintings of the child, one back view and one front view, were in shades of black against stark white backgrounds. I thought them breathtaking in their dramatic effect. I had never seen anything in the least like them and I said so.

'Now that's very strange, Mrs Marshall, you should say that. You like them? You really do?' I assured Lowry that for me they were pure drama. He appeared unduly pleased, pulling them from their position the better for me to see.

'Well, I *am* interested in your reaction. . . . I must have got something that I set out to get. You see, it's the young girl from Pirandello's *Six Characters in Search of an Author*. I went to see the Zeffirelli production one night and I was enraptured with it, and I went the next six nights running – seven in all. Ralph Richardson, Vivian Leigh and the others – oh, they were all right, but it was the young girl who never speaks who enthralled me. Oh, she was wonderful, wonderful – and this is her. But you know one night I saw her understudy – and the whole play fell to pieces – never forgotten it. So you like them – and you picked out the drama in them. Oh, dear me, that's interesting.'

Picking my way across the little painting room I reached the opposite side and saw two small canvases face to the wall. I picked them up, but with a couple of strides Lowry had crossed the room and snatching them from me he replaced them face to the wall. Inwardly I had frozen, but I turned a blank face to him as though I had not seen them. I was not intending to deceive, it was simply better so. I learned a lesson never forgotten – I have never, since that evening in his grubby little grey house, ever looked without permission at a painter's work which is facing a wall.

'Come along now, Mrs Marshall, *Proserpine*.' While I was looking yet again at his proud possession, Lowry and Micky went into the small room next his bedroom. I heard Lowry suggesting that he would like to show his last oils the following year – so long as Micky was prepared to have a non-selling exhibition. These last friends he said he wanted to keep by him.

It was dark as we waved farewell to the elderly painter, who stood on the doorstep of The Elms calling to us that he would be over to see us again shortly. I sank back into the front seat of the car with something like relief. It had been a hectic three days – always on guard against Lowry's small irritabilities which could spring up with no warning; trying to keep him sunny and happy; never quite certain how, and at what, he would react. And I certainly never wanted to eat cold beef and boiled potatoes again. Once Lowry had decided that cold beef was the thing to eat he would glower and sulk if we looked at the menu, disapproving if we decided to have anything other than his choice. This appears rather ludicrous in retrospect but it was certainly the case at the time – and it was easier to suffer the cold beef than a Lowry temperament.

6

In the mid-1960s the north-east and its politicians were still seeking popular favour by fostering their policy of regionalism. Almost overnight Newcastle, in the minds of its councillors and public relations officers, ceased to be a provincial city and became the capital of a region. But to hand central government funds over to a political clique of career-seeking adventurers was like handing over the tote to a committee of warned-off trainers, welching bookies and disbarred jockeys. Lowry can be accused of many things, but gullible he was not. He would stand at one of the gallery windows, hitching his baggy trousers higher around his loins as he peered at the local politicians passing on their way to the civic centre. 'My word, but he looks an honest gentleman, Mr Marshall – and just look at that one; I'll get him to look after m'wallet. And this one coming along – I'd give him the key to The Elms any day, everything would be safe in his hands.'

The national media joined in the regional game. Journalists, TV producers, chairmen of committees, PR men, up-and-coming failures and metropolitan rejects all saw salvation writ large. No necessity to go to Damascus – just refer to 'Geordies', 'bairns' and 'ha'way the lads' and your fortune was made. And so, as the media got to work, North *v.* South became a vibrant issue. At least it did in the north – the south may have remained unaware of it.

At this time Lowry was invited to luncheon at the civic centre by a very well-meaning Labour alderman. He was accompanied by Micky and Carol. Our friend did not care for it at all. Despite the fact that he was a well-known teetotaller, he felt played down to by being offered only fizzy lemonade, and he was never to forget that on the menu was *place and ships*!

Of course neither Lowry nor my husband could get emotionally involved in this partisan approach to what was essentially a national problem of revitalization. Lowry accepted that there was little difference between the rogues of Manchester, London or Newcastle. Because he did not choose to move to London or become a part of its 'art scene', it must not be thought that he found all well in either his native city or in Newcastle, where in his later years he spent so much time.

My husband was with Lowry more than the rest of us. Day in and day out, the elderly man sat with him in his office, never thinking for a moment that he might be *de trop*. One day in 1966, having egged one another on, they decided that they were going to engage in the North *v.* South controversy by putting on an exhibition called *Painters of the North*, with the sub-title *The Ambience of the North*.

Lowry proposed various painters and offered to act as guide to introduce my husband to a few with whom Micky was unacquainted. I never knew our friend to be other than remarkably generous towards his fellow painters with the one exception of Norman Cornish. Lowry would buy works at exhibitions which he did not really care for because, possibly as a result of his own early experience in life, he recognized the importance of encouragement. In view of some of the things which have been written about him since his death, his generosity to those who despised and laughed at him during his youthful struggles was completely unselfish. He frequently urged us to show works by Manchester's academic painters, or his fellow Royal Academicians; he would accept it without rancour when we argued that they were not up to the standard we wished to show – with the exception of Sheila Fell.

In the spring we took Lowry home to Manchester. We stayed as usual at the Midland, where he would join us for his meals. One evening he took us out to meet Harold Riley and, after much talk between the two painters on the subject of football, when it might have been supposed that there was no subject dearer to Lowry's heart, we selected five slightly disappointing works for the forthcoming exhibition. We were given no choice, if we wanted to include his work, for Riley had no other paintings available.

Next we were introduced to an interesting contemporary of Lowry's, John Bold, a charming and delightfully gentle man who had a studio in central Manchester. We liked his work but, to our surprise, it did not have any success with or meet approval from our clients. It was austere, with an uncontrived and honest vision and without concession to possible buyers. Lowry was later disappointed that none of his old friend's work had sold, so he bought one himself and gave it to Carol.

For some reason which I cannot recall – perhaps because Lowry did not totally approve of Theodore Major's political views – he decided to let us call on this painter without accompanying us. Certainly Theodore Major's assessment of Lowry's work was generous in the extreme, rather to Lowry's surprise when we told him. (We were later to put on an exhibition of the work of Major's invalid wife – which was enormously successful.)

My husband and Lowry went together to visit Norman Adams, who lived in Yorkshire, and chose five of his works. As they neared their destination Micky said, 'I can't see where we shall get a cup of tea Mr Lowry, I haven't seen anywhere as we came here.'

'Leave it to me, Mr Marshall – I know a good place.' Micky gave it no more thought until later in the afternoon when, the works chosen, he heard Lowry saying to Mrs Adams, 'D'you know of any place we could get a cup of tea?'

'Why, I'll make you a cup right away,' she smiled. Micky was more than a little shocked at Lowry's practised artfulness.

The '*Painters of the North*' exhibition was generally well received. M. G. McNay wrote in the *Guardian*:

An exhibition of English painting called *Painters of the South* is inconceivable: Southerners are not that self-conscious. Why then should we have *Painters of the North*? . . . This exhibition is a success. Lowry, for instance, has a painting of *The Shot Tower* at Newcastle whose intervals are as carefully enunciated as an early Italian masterpiece – just how carefully you can see by comparing it with the drawing of the same scene which lacks the final harmonising touch of the figures in the foreground. But the exhibition really works because the less-known artists look thoroughly professional in this exacting company.

Donald Gow, *The Times* correspondent, wrote:

The exhibition, including, as it does, such northern painters as Sheila Fell, Norman Cornish, Theodore Major, and Jack Simcock, all of whom favour a figurative approach to their work, could hardly fail to portray the physical features of the landscape and its people. Indeed in this it succeeds admirably. . . . The essence of the North is there for all who wish to savour it: the sharp moorland air, the sea's pervasive presence, valleys and fields shrouded in mist: all contrasted sharply with an industrial ugliness compounded of pits, slag heaps, and semi-derelict buildings. But a visual record is insufficient in itself. . . .

The outstanding artist in the exhibition, the archetypal northern painter, the man whose work and problems presaged all that were to follow, is Mr L. S. Lowry. For years he failed to gain recognition for his unique vision, but with stubborn persistence went quietly on with his work until he made others see the world as he saw it. Two canvases in the show, painted last year in Newcastle, are examples of his ability to come to terms with the industrial scene and, without in any way seeking to obscure its grotesque ugliness, produce something of sheer beauty. His *Shot Tower* is an exquisite rendering of possibly one of the most uncompromising constructions he could have found. [That particular shot tower no longer exists.]

When we had to be in London on business Lowry would remain in Newcastle with Simon and upon our return the old man would avidly question my husband on what he had bought, whom he had met, and generally what was going on in the capital. Once we returned with a very large watercolour, *Satanic Mills*, by William Gawin Herdman. 'What did you want to buy that for?' Lowry demanded.

'One, because it's bloody good – and secondly to show that someone did the industrial landscape before you did!' laughed my husband. Herdman, born in 1805, the son of a Liverpool corn merchant, was a clever and proficient draughtsman, and this colourful industrial scene, painted in 1862, was a strong argument for the case that there is perhaps little new in figurative art. After seeing this particular picture, Lowry was always careful to stress that his own intention had been to 'put the industrial landscape on the map'. Certainly no one could quarrel with that.

A painter Lowry much preferred, and with good cause, was John Atkinson Grimshaw, an artist whom my husband actively promoted. For, although it may be supposed that very little took place in the gallery other than the entertainment of our friend, despite all hindrance Micky still managed to put on eleven exhibitions a year in those days. One of these featured the work of Grimshaw.

Lowry particularly enjoyed sitting around the office while this exhibition was prepared, and he revelled in Atkinson Grimshaw's life story. The artist was born in Leeds in 1836, and died at the age of fifty-seven. As a young man Grimshaw worked as a railway clerk by day and painted by gaslight in the evenings. Eventually he achieved something of a national reputation and was able to concentrate upon his art. He rented Knostrop Hall, a seventeenth-century mansion near Leeds, where his wife entertained a good deal, one of their friends being George du Maurier. About 1876 Grimshaw was able to build a most lavish house on the promontory at Scarborough. Unfortunately he then lent a considerable sum of money to a friend who let him down, and this house had to be sold. As a result of bad sanitation at Knostrop Hall, eight of Grimshaw's fifteen children died as infants. It was always at this point in the painter's story that Lowry would bellow with laughter. He also made much of the fact that, while Grimshaw was hard up after his friend's defection, when he took his surviving children out in the carriage he made certain that their feet were well hidden, so that it could not be seen that they were without shoes.

Our old friend would chant the last catalogue note with eternal glee, 'Grimshaw painted up until the week before he died, when he crawled upstairs on hands and knees to bed. His last words to his wife were, "No sun, no moon, no stars." He is buried in grave No. 12005 in Leeds Cemetery.' Having learned those figures by heart, Lowry once mistook them for a friend's telephone number and could not understand why he received no reply. But he considered Grimshaw to be no end of a fool to paint right up until a week before his death, although it would remind him that the gentleman had not suffered, as he did, from the avid attentions of Chancellors of the Exchequer.

Atkinson Grimshaw was the only nineteenth-century painter of whom Lowry appeared never to have heard, and with whose work he was entirely unfamiliar. This was strange because, in his time, Grimshaw enjoyed considerable success. When Lowry eventually saw the Atkinson Grimshaw exhibition hung, he ceased to be quite so amused by the artist.

The reviews were widespread and extremely favourable, and the finest painting in the exhibition was sold for one thousand pounds. An inferior work recently sold at auction for twenty-six thousand pounds.

During 1968 Lowry was seldom parted from us, and as month after month passed we thought up all manner of jaunts and trips which might keep him out of the gallery so that work might be less interrupted.

He had always wanted to visit Portpatrick, where his great-grandfather, Jacob Lowry, had landed from Ulster and Simon offered to take him there for a few days' visit. The painter then declared that it would be nice if Carol went with them. The trip was arranged to take place during her half-term holiday from teaching.

On 17 June, having eaten his favourite chicken and strawberries with pints of cream, Lowry was in splendid form as he sat over coffee in the gallery office after luncheon. Carol was shortly to arrive by train, ready for the journey to Scotland the following day. The telephone on Micky's desk rang and after a moment or two Micky said with consternation, 'Yes, yes that's right; it belongs to L. S. Lowry of The Elms, Mottram; Staleybridge Road. Well, as a matter of fact he's sitting right here beside me – I'll put him on to you.' Turning to the painter he said gently, 'Now don't worry yourself, I don't think it's anything too serious, but it's the Mottram police – they're trying to trace the owner of some pictures. I think you've had a burglary at The Elms.'

Showing no concern whatsoever, Lowry took the telephone, and started with his usual, 'Are you there? L. S. Lowry speaking.' And after a moment, 'Yes, that's right, that's mine. Yes, and that's mine too.' He listened again for a few moments, and said, 'Oh yes, those are all mine. Oh well – that's very good. *No*! No, I can't come back, I've got an important engagement to keep – it's business you know. Well, you'll be keeping the stuff there just now, won't you? If I were to come over, there's nothing I could do, and m'housekeeper, Mrs Swindles, will identify them. She'll give you every possible assistance.' He gave them her address, asked them to get her to ring him at the gallery, and continued, 'Well, I don't know when I'll be back. But I'll get in touch, or Mrs Swindles will let you know.

'Thank you very much – *very* good of you to have rung. And don't hesitate to ring here again if you want to know anything further. M'friend Mr Marshall will help you if I'm not here. Goodbye.' And as cool as a cucumber he replaced the receiver, sat back and rocked with laughter. . . . 'Well, well, they've stolen old uncle's calendar!'

'What on earth's happened?' I asked with concern.

'Well,' said Micky, 'the police at Mottram rang here because this morning a van was reported stolen, and a couple of policemen saw it, and gave chase. Two men in it, suddenly aware they were being followed, jumped out, and made off over the moors. They weren't caught, apparently, but the police took charge of the abandoned van and found a lot of pictures inside. Oddly enough, only one had a label on the back – you remember that nice little Hans Janisch Mr Lowry bought? Well, that was among them and, as it was our label, they rang to see if we could tell them who owned it.'

I turned to Lowry and said, 'But my goodness, hadn't you better go back?'

'*Good God no!* What could I do?'

'Well, if you've had a burglary. . . . '

'If I've had a burglary, then I've had one. No use going now. It's no use closing the stable door. . . . It can wait. Carol's due any moment. Besides, they haven't taken anything of much importance. A couple of nice Sheila Fells, some of those daft canvases from the hall, Rossetti's *Return of Tibulus*, and, oh dear me, you'd never believe it,' and he began to laugh all over again, 'they've taken an old calendar of me uncle's. It's been framed and hanging up as long as I can remember – a woodland scene m'mother was fond of . . . the fools, just fancy taking old uncle's calendar.'

'What of yours have they taken? Your own work?'

'Good God – Mrs Marshall, nothing of mine! They wouldn't care for them at all; wouldn't think they were worth taking. Probably think a child had done them.' He rocked back in his chair with further bellows of mirth. We teased him unmercifully about it for a long time. Often the public was sufficiently misguided and rude to say in his presence that they did not care much for his works, but they would usually add that they might well be a good investment. We would laugh them to scorn with, 'Don't you believe it – even his burglars wouldn't touch his work!' And Lowry took all this in very good part.

That afternoon nothing so mundane as a little break-in was going to worry him or send him scurrying back home. He put the matter out of his mind after Mrs Swindles rang to say that apart from the pictures nothing was missing from his house: the thieves had apparently entered through the back door, which she had forgotten to lock.

We took him to the station to meet Carol and later, when Ian had joined us, we took them, for a change, to the Gosforth Park Hotel for dinner. But the dimly lit, comfortable bar in which we had drinks as we decided to order infuriated Lowry, even with Carol present, when as a rule he would behave rather better. 'Carol – I can't read this, what the devil do they want to write these things in French for? If there's one thing I can't stand, it's a menu written in French. We're English – this is an English hotel – why can't they write everything in our own language!'

Micky tried to calm him down by asking why all musical instruction wasn't written in English; there should be an end to *fortissimo* and *pianissimo* – only directions to play loudly or softly; and what could replace *scherzo*?

'Playfully, of course,' barked Lowry.

'Doesn't sound so good though, does it?' quipped Micky.

'It sounds better.'

'Never mind,' I consoled him, 'I'm sure I know what you're going to have, Mr Lowry. . . .'

'What?'

'Well, melon to start with, then cutlets – you've had chicken already today, and doubtless it'll be strawberries to finish with.'

'Aah,' and he pointed a Kitchener finger at me. 'But that's just where our clever Mrs Marshall is wrong, see? I'm going to have a little mushroom soup, then egg and chips, and then that pudding I had last time we were here. It was very good . . . the only thing I liked about the place.' I looked across at my husband; egg and chips were the last thing we would be expected to order – very trying. Of course he got his egg and chips but was disappointed over the 'pud', as the chef whose speciality it had been was no longer there. So the old boy settled for *crêpes suzette* and, looking darkly at me as he demolished the last mouthful, announced that the pancakes were very poor.

Simon's next few days were not enviable. It was a swelteringly hot day as they drove to Scotland. Lowry never allowed a window to be lowered when travelling in a motor car, although his fellow passengers might stifle. Simon, used to his open car in fine weather, had to fight off a continuous drowsiness.

Their first port of call for morning coffee was the George Hotel at Chollerford – this place was always something of a favourite with Lowry. I have the little bill for it in front of me as I write – seven shillings and sixpence.

I have seen it argued since his death that Lowry was not mean. He was. Indeed, he was the meanest man I have ever known. He and his protégée, invited by the artist, were to be Simon's guests on this trip to Portpatrick, and Lowry began as he was to continue – he permitted our twenty-four-year-old son to pay every expense.

The road over to Carlisle was one which Simon had travelled often enough – frequently, of course, with Lowry. It is an undulating road across the Pennines with occasional glimpses of the Roman Wall crossing bleak stretches of moorland. Few artists have been able to paint the moors and capture the awesome atmosphere of solitude, but Lowry was one who could and did. He had no sense of the picturesque, and his few paintings of the moors are quite different from the usual romanticized interpretations. His breast-shaped hills stand out against a grey sky and convey a feeling of natural majesty, basically repelling to any comfort-seeking observer. Like Lowry's seascapes, they are uncompromising, uncomfortable but utterly authoritative – almost abstract painting, and the greatest example of Lowry's primordial sense of loneliness. The more popular and better known mill scenes did not portray the same innermost Lowry.

The road from Carlisle to Dumfries (where they lunched) was straight and narrow. There was invariably a lorry in front and another coming in the opposite direction. This could be tedious and infuriating to a fast driver, and not conducive to idle chatter. But with Lowry, trivia must be talked all the way. It never occurred to him that a driver occasionally needed to concentrate. 'What will happen if the wheel comes off? Where are we now? You're not doing more than thirty, are you? Are you all right in the back, Carol?' As our son remarked later, it didn't matter a damn if she were not, Lowry wouldn't get into the back, and Carol at that time did not drive. Then there were the place names, and the expected comments: 'Lets go to Kirk-coo-bright', or 'Gatehouse of Fleet? Where's the gatehouse?' And again; 'Are you all right in the back, Carol?'

At this period Lowry's continuous pandering to Carol was at its height. He began to say that Carol too was descended from Jacob Lowry. He was fully aware that there was no truth in this, but he seemed to feel that it made a common denominator between himself and the girl in this relationship he had set up to the exclusion of all others. The manner in which he achieved this was strange and difficult to analyse, but left one with the feeling that he and Carol, and they alone, were God's chosen. Other people were there on sufferance, because they were of interest to Carol, and she found 'Uncle' easier to cope with if others were there to assist. But Lowry gave the impression that one must not presume for an instant that one entered into this relationship in any way. There was a sense of exclusion, as though one were looking through a window into a warm room on a snowy night, fully aware that one could never enter. One might freeze to death outside and, when it suited him, Lowry would kick the corpse out of his way. It had not always been so and it did not remain so, but in 1968 Lowry's obsession with his 'niece' was abnormal.

At the umpteenth time of Lowry's asking what would happen if the wheel came off, Simon replied, 'You'll probably die, mate!' The old boy shut up for a while and Simon was much relieved when they came into Portpatrick and his elderly passenger showed his first signs of real enthusiasm.

The Portpatrick Hotel was a jolly one, much frequented by holidaying families all apparently enjoying life, but at dinner Lowry achieved a couple of moves around the dining room before he was settled. He went on to complain throughout the meal that his friend, the Reverend Geoffrey Bennett, had once promised to take him to Portpatrick, but eventually had not even seen fit to drive him to Dumfries. This rankled with the painter, while Simon mentally congratulated the reverend gentleman. Daylight was already fading when they left the dining room and Simon was taken aback when Lowry suggested that they should drive to the headland, some twenty-five miles away. Simon in no way relished the thought of another fifty-odd miles driving to the tune of 'What happens if the wheel comes off?' But there was no getting out of it and he took up his role of chauffeur again. He drove the car as far as possible along a single-track road and ahead of them they saw a lighthouse, beyond which was the end of the promontory. Imperiously Lowry ordered the driver to turn about and go straight back to the hotel. However, Simon needed some fresh air and suggested that they walk to the lighthouse and on to the headland. Lowry would have none of it and he and Carol remained in the car while Simon walked on alone.

The hotel was full of life when they returned and Simon, who by this time should have known better, had hopes that Lowry would, as he termed it, 'bugger off' to bed. But Lowry was never one to retire early, especially if there was a little life to observe.

Next morning the painter decided that they would visit Stranraer.

While they were having coffee there Lowry proposed they should take the ferry across to Ireland. It was another beautiful day and he thought the sea breeze would do Carol a power of good. Simon was dispatched to find out what time the next boat left. Lowry then said they would, of course, take the car with them and Simon could drive them around, showing something of Northern Ireland to Carol. Simon discovered that it would cost an extra twenty-seven pounds to take the Volvo, and he had not bargained for this added expense for four hours in Ulster. He stated firmly that he would not take the car.

Lowry was outraged. Simon argued back. In a fury, Lowry raised his stick and gave his side door of the new vehicle a tremendous crack with it. That Volvo carried the mark of Lowry's disgust and anger as long as we ran it. Inwardly fuming, our son obeyed the painter's command to go and park the offending object and get their tickets. They lunched on board, but later the old man regretted this. He remembered having been told by friends that there was a good hotel in Larne and he would have liked to have sampled it; he certainly had a passion for hotels. This deprivation rankled for years.

Upon landing, Simon immediately found a taxi and Lowry ordered the driver to take the coast road to Carrickfergus. It was drizzling and blowing a gale. Lowry had no scenic sense for anything other than the sordid, and looked fixedly ahead of him as they travelled. This trip was totally wasted as far as the painter was concerned; it was apparently being undertaken entirely for Carol's benefit. At Carrickfergus Simon was directed to show Carol the castle while the painter, the only one equipped for the weather in his raincoat and flat cap, remained in the car. In the course of time, the taxi driver eventually returned his passengers to the ferry.

The weather cleared but rather than enjoying the sea breeze on the ferry most of the time was spent having dinner. When they landed at Stranraer Simon went to collect the car. He returned promptly to where he had left Lowry and Carol but there was no sign of them. He waited and began to worry. Suddenly they emerged from a little café in very good spirits, having fortified themselves with a cup of tea. There was no apology for going missing, nor any thought that Simon might have enjoyed a cup.

On their return journey to Newcastle the following day they called for lunch at the Douglass Arms in Castle Douglass. Lowry insisted on moving from table to table until Simon longed to hide beneath one of them. The painter complained of everything possible and created an unpleasant scene when it was found that there was no red-currant jelly with his lamb, only mint sauce. He thundered at the young waiter who stood helplessy stammering that no, he was very sorry but there was no red-currant jelly in the hotel. Well, could they send out for some? No, he did not think they could. Simon intervened quickly with an assurance that it didn't matter. His guest shouted imperiously that indeed it *did* matter and they should worry. Our son dug his toes in, saying mint sauce was quite correct with lamb in summertime. Looking at the lunch before him, Lowry angrily inquired of Simon which fork he should use to eat it with. 'Well, that's what you'll be telling me next, isn't it? That I don't know what is what!' For long years afterwards Lowry would occasionally demand of the gathered company at a meal, 'Now what do I use to eat this with?' I have even seen Carol become embarrassed and annoyed with him when he indulged this humour.

After the lamb minus its red-currant jelly had been heartily eaten, there was more trouble to follow when it was discovered that no hot pudding was on offer that June day. This was fumed over until the coffee arrived, which Lowry voted extremely disappointing. Simon vows to this day that the luncheon was delicious, the surroundings attractive, and the staff helpful. The boy looking after them was about eighteen and obviously scared out of his wits by the demon customer. Simon found it extremely difficult to come to terms with Lowry's treatment of waiters. Alas, there was no assistance forthcoming from Carol who, up to a point, had the same contemptuous attitude, obviously influenced by her mentor. This was very strange considering that she herself had worked in a hotel for a year.

When Lowry chose to be ungracious or arrogant his behaviour had to be seen to be believed. Although we found him constantly nerve-racking, my husband and I usually contrived to prevent a situation getting out of hand. Lowry certainly took advantage of our son, however. His unreasonable attitude was at its worst in places he did not expect to be visiting again. We were always amazed that Lowry chose to stay so frequently at the Seaburn Hotel, for he was ever full of complaints about it. Either his egg at breakfast had been hard boiled, his toast burned, or his haddock unsatisfactory. Carol on one occasion cared little for their idea of a chopped salad and sent it back with directions how to make it in future. But it was the same wherever he stayed.

When they reached Chollerford for tea, Simon rang us up. We had had a busy day, so we suggested that he drive slowly for the remainder of the journey to give us time to leave the gallery before their return. Simon could then take his companions round to Tilley's for dinner before taking them back to the Seaburn.

We almost made it. Just as we were locking up the gallery they descended on us. Greetings and dyings over, I took Simon aside and demanded why on earth he had not managed to delay their return for a few moments longer. Now relaxed, he roared with laughter at me. 'Not a blooming hope! Driving as slowly as I dared, the old boy decided something was up and kept saying, "Drive faster – drive faster, can't you? My God! You never drive as slowly as this!" So I'm sorry – he even rushed his tea to get back before you left. He didn't mean you and Pa to go home.'

Simon went off to collect his own car which we'd been using, and we put Lowry and Carol into ours, with its nice new dent in one side, and went to Tilley's. My two menfolk were still parking the cars as Lowry lowered himself on to his favourite banquette, drawing Carol down beside him. In my chair opposite, I leaned my elbows on the table and smiled across at them. 'Well, I'm so pleased you had a nice time.' I can see Lowry's venomous expression now, and feel again my sense of shock as he spat out, 'Your son makes me sick – your son makes me *sick*!'

Carol had the grace to jump in quickly with, 'But Uncle Laurie, he drives wonderfully, you must agree he really does. He's a wonderful driver.'

'Uncle Laurie' didn't agree at all, but merely repeated, 'He makes me *sick*!'

I never react as I would wish when taken by surprise, and stupidly I sat there smiling. 'Really? Why?'

But I only received yet again, 'Your son makes me sick.'

After Lowry's funeral, Carol's mother turned to me and said, 'Oh dear, why did you prevent my Carol from marrying Simon?' I all but fell through the floor. 'Good heavens, I never did any such thing,' I exclaimed. 'There was never any question of it. They never got along in that sort of way. Why, I remember Carol telling me that you were insistent that she marry someone with tons of money! That alone would put Simon out of the running. In any case, Simon married the only girl he ever wanted to marry – and she's standing just behind you.'

But Mrs Martha Lowry was not put off, for she continued, 'I've been telling Carol all this week, since I met him last Sunday, that she should have told me what a lovely boy he is. And she said, "Oh, but mother, he never was – all he thought about was fast cars!" So I told her, "Better than fast women, Carol." When they went to Portpatrick, I said to Mr Lowry beforehand, "Oh, maybe there'll be an engagement – maybe when they come back there'll be an engagement." I *was* so disappointed.'

'Well,' I retorted, 'Mr Lowry certainly wasn't!'

During the summer of 1967 we took Lowry to luncheon with the Rossetti Society's Master of the Horse and his wife – Michael and Bridget Clark. They lived in a beautiful house, Fallowfield, which stood peacefully secluded on the hills above Hexham in Northumberland. Lowry was in remarkably good spirits, and knew his host and hostess well. They not only collected Pre-Raphaelites and Symbolists, but also Lowry's paintings. He loved to look at what he termed 'old friends' again; enjoyed seeing them hanging in someone's home; he was always on his best behaviour with a client.

There were mighty few people living in Northumberland who cared for Lowry's paintings. Occasionally the Clarks came in for criticism from their friends when they acquired yet another. This can be off-putting to a collector, who very naturally enjoys showing a new acquisition to visitors. Once Michael Clark was persuaded by a friend whose opinions he valued to sell back to us a small Lowry oil. We gave him twice as much as he had paid for it, and later we resold it for another 300 per cent on that price. On this occasion we shared the profit with Lowry, although we didn't have to do so, as we had originally, of course, bought the painting from him. Here again was a cause of our feeling no small sense of injustice at the artist's continuous public statements that the art world was full of rogues.

As we sat sipping our pre-luncheon drinks in the orangery that lovely June morning, Michael told us that he and his wife had been trying to dissuade his father-in-law from buying a new morning suit for Ascot that month. He had bought one in 1914 which had done splendid service until 1939 when he had bought his next; for obvious reasons, it was imperative that he never bought a third. His appearance might well not be all that was desired at Ascot the following week, where he had a horse running, but it must suffice.

Lowry's eyes gently closed in slumber, but this never mattered with the Clarks. Michael well understood the painter's little idiosyncrasy and murmured, 'Ah, The President is just recharging his batteries. When he wakens we'll have luncheon.' At the magic word, Lowry promptly opened his eyes. Luncheon had been carefully planned with Lowry's 'private-house chicken'.

Lowry was usually extremely disparaging about homes with modern furnishings, but he had a remarkable eye for antiques (always being on the lookout for items he might purchase for Carol). Lowry really enjoyed good things and it was strange that he put up with the conditions in his own home, which were primitive in the extreme. He delighted in this visit and commented later on the lovely silver and china. The great silver mustard pots particularly took his fancy, and as he ate I noticed his eyes flicker from one lovely painting to another hanging on the walls.

On the way back to the gallery in the afternoon I heard Lowry murmur, 'They're fond of racing, I think, aren't they?'

'Yes,' I answered, hardly giving it a thought, 'I suppose they are.'

Despite the fact that Lowry would so often close his eyes and assume slumber, as a rule he was giving the company his close concentration. The old boy was always observant, and very little escaped his attention. On other occasions he would appear alert, asking questions, digesting the answers, nodding now and again, and later he would admit that he had been curious to note a person's reaction to the question put. When Michael next appeared in the gallery I felt somewhat stricken that Lowry had observed this interest while we had never given it consideration, so purely out of politeness I asked how their horse had done at Royal Ascot. 'Oh, we won the Gold Cup,' was Michael's nonchalant reply.

As the years passed art was no longer the all-absorbing topic of conversation when the Clarks came to the gallery. When their horse won the Cambridgeshire there was much rejoicing. Racing is in my blood; my paternal grandfather was a horse dealer. Micky's paternal grandfather did much better – he won the Irish Sweep. One of my uncles ended in the workhouse as a consequence of backing horses, while another became a wealthy man as a result of pursuing the same occupation. Lowry always put my own success down to luck, and he refused to have it otherwise. I put it down to researching form, but never risked much money. Lowry always prophesied dire consequences. . . . 'It's only beginner's luck – just you wait and see, the day of reckoning will come.' He was a little annoyed that it never did.

Unfortunately for Lowry, racing on television occasionally took over in the gallery office. We often wondered what the painter said of our telly when we were not there to hear – for he certainly said all he dared to our faces. In this respect he was made to suffer. Watching the horses going down to post, Lowry would inquire impatiently, 'Hasn't that Pigglet won yet?' To him, every jockey was Pigglet. When told to shut up, they hadn't even gone into the stalls yet, he would complain bitterly, 'Oh, isn't it ridiculous, simply ridiculous?'

'You won't say that when I take you out tonight,' I'd laugh, and at the thought of the evening ahead he would cheer up.

The only fillies which interested our friend were the two-legged variety playing tennis. Occasionally when Wimbledon was on the box Lowry would give the screen his full and undivided attention, as he watched the girls serve, in their minute skirts – showing lots of frilly pants. The men, however, had no right to play.

One afternoon in 1973 we were all sitting in the office with our coffee, and racing was due on television at any moment. Veral, by then our daughter-in-law, opened the *Sporting Life* and suddenly exclaimed, 'Oh, Mr Lowry, here's just the horse for you! Portpatrick – you really must put fifty pence on it.' The old man glowered in Veral's direction and suggested she get back to work, muttering he was not going to start backing horses at his age – he would not be lucky like Mrs Marshall. For the hundredth time I argued that luck had *nothing* to do with it and, just to show him, Veral and I would put fifty pence each on Portpatrick. I didn't believe in association bets and assured him it wouldn't win.

It did, though – at 14 to 1. Lowry awakened to new life and rocked with laughter. 'Oh, you silly old sod – you should have backed it – it's obviously you who's the lucky one. Portpatrick's nothing to do with me.'

He treated us to further gales of mirth, interrupted by a small yelp from Veral, 'Oh, Mr Lowry, I'll never forgive you if you don't back this one – My Drifter. You'll never believe it, he's out of Christina Rossetti. Come on now – fifty pence.'

Our friend was obdurate. So to show him it wasn't a question of luck I said, 'OK Veral, here's fifty pence, you put on the same, and we'll go halves.' There was much worse to come this time. The horse had never been out before and Veral had a habit of placing her little bets at tote odds, which on this occasion paid 318 to 1. This was becoming too much even for Lowry. At the sight of the money he sat up, his blue eyes glinting behind the gold-rimmed greasy lenses. He wouldn't risk fifty pence even for fun nor, on principle, contemplate a bet of any description. Nevertheless he intended to have that money.

'My word, you mustn't waste that.'

'Oh don't worry, we shan't,' said Veral.

'Oh yes, but you might – you'd better have one of my drawings with it.'

'What good's one drawing between us? What are we supposed to do with it? Cut it in half?' Veral is a match for most painters and we eventually got one each.

The following afternoon, Veral once again opened the untouched *Sporting Life*. 'Now Mr Lowry, you saw what happened yesterday – here's another chance for you – the very horse – Uncle. Come on, be a sport.' But this was a game the artist had no intention of playing. Again Veral and I went shares: again the horse won at long odds. This time, however, we noticed that Lowry was sitting up and cheering it ever so gently upon its way.

A couple of months after the artist's death we were gathered again in the office with our coffee after lunch and were recalling Lowry's disgust, albeit amused disgust, at our interest in racing and the television to which he had been subjected. Once again no one had studied form and, when I picked up the sporting press, I laughingly suggested to the family that we see whether Lowry was still with us in spirit. 'Right,' said Veral, 'I'd better vacate his chair and give him a chance.'

'Let's see if we can find a horse with any association with him – we'll back it for fun – *oh*!' I shrieked, 'I'm sure we can't do better than this one . . . Elm. It's never been out before, it hasn't a hope.' It had though. The four of us this time contributed fifty pence each and amid raucous mirth we watched it win at 25 to 1.

Lowry was determined I should write about him and suggested that we have the occasional record of how his days were spent in the gallery. To this end he thought it an excellent notion to tape record conversations, unless they were private. He fancied posterity might be interested in his views; hence many Lowry commentaries on art, politics, and his acquaintances are in our possession. What follows is a transcript.

One August afternoon in 1968, Micky was away on business, and Carol arrived with her mentor after a visit they had paid to the British Ropes factory – Lowry having accepted the invitation of one of the directors who hoped a conducted tour would interest the painter.

After greetings were over, Lowry asked Simon, 'Where's mother? How is she?'

'Mother? Oh, she's not too bad you know.'

'And how are you?'

'Same as ever – happy, fit and healthy.'

'Happy?' queried Lowry gloomily.

'I'm sure you'll be ready for a cup of tea – one of the girls is making it. Ella's gone off early.'

'Ah,' sighed the artist, 'that'd be nice. I'm a bit late getting here – I was on the telephone – the *Daily Mail*; they want a question answered by well-known people – I blushed at that you know, sir. . .'

'Did you really?'

'Did I think the trouble in Czechoslovakia . . . blast it, now what was it . . . ah yes, should we break off cultural relations with Russia?' At that moment Jean, a girl working in the gallery during her university vacation, brought in the tea, greeting Lowry by asking how he was.

'Oh, I'm very tired you know – it won't be long now. I'll be demising very soon.'

'Jean, have you announced to my mother Mr Lowry's arrival?'

'Aye, that would be a great comfort, sir.'

'Is she downstairs?' asked Jean.

'Yes,' answered Simon. 'It's the accountant's day – she's in her office.'

'Yes, it would really be a great comfort, sir – please tell her I'm here,' rumbled Lowry, as Simon took up the matter of the telephone call where they had been interrupted. 'So what did you say?'

'I said I didn't know!'

'The latest I heard was that the Czech leaders are escaping and fleeing. . . .'

'Well, the *Mail* asked whether I thought it advisable for us to break off relations with Russia,' Lowry repeated.

'Would it do much good?' asked Simon.

'I didn't go into it. I said I didn't know. "I'm not a politician," I said. I can't say. "Well, what do you really think?" So I told them I didn't think about it at all.'

'Isn't it ridiculous?' laughed Carol.

'Well, personally I think we should send a gunboat – that's the answer,' announced Simon, while the two girls roared with laughter, asking what age he supposed he was living in.

'A gunboat, now I didn't think of that,' said Lowry. 'I just said, "I can't say, I don't know," and the fellow said that he'd give me a few minutes to think it over. "Oh, that's no use," I told him, "I've got to go out now – I'm busy." So then he said he'd ring me up again tonight, and I told him I wouldn't be in tonight. "I'm really very busy indeed, and I haven't time to think about it, but in any case, I don't know." And he laughed heartily and I laughed heartily – so that subject's closed now until I see what they say tomorrow morning. Ridiculous isn't it to ask me such a question – they must ask Mr Wilson . . . he's paid for it. *I'm* not paid to answer questions like that. And where *is* mother, Simon? And what are you doing tonight?'

'I'm taking a bird out,' announced Simon firmly. 'Rather a nice one actually, one of the better examples of the female sex – not the common or garden ones you see around here!'

'Hello everybody – how are you?' I asked, rushing into the room.

'Now Mrs Marshall, has Mr Bennett suggested I take that picture home with me?' demanded Lowry.

'Well, if you're counting on a lovely present from Mr Bennett you've got another count coming to you,' I laughed. 'I don't think it's in the gentleman's mind to be making you any present of a nice Pickersgill – so Baba's going to be disappointed if Baba was expecting a present!'

'Oh yes, Mrs Marshall – but I was. I was sure he'd give it to Little Laurie.'

'Mr Lowry's been rung up by the *Daily Mail*.'

'Seriously?'

'Yes, seriously,' said Carol.

'Well, whatever it was about, I bet you stepped out of it nicely,' I laughed.

'They were asking well-known people, and I blushed at that you know – what their views were on the situation in Czechoslovakia in view of the Russian invasion.'

'And what did you say?'

' "*I don't know*", I said. "I'm not a politician – I don't know." ' By this time Lowry had worked himself up into a right old paddy.

'As if it mattered anyway,' said Carol.

'No, it's not our matter really,' muttered Lowry.

'No, it wouldn't have been our matter if Hitler had invaded really, would it?' exploded Simon in fury.

'Except, my friend, Russia is not Germany!' shouted Lowry.

'Germany invaded Czechoslovakia – and we had to do something about that in the end.'

'You weren't born at the time Simon, and the Germans are a different race from the Russians,' snorted the artist.

'Never mind, Mr Lowry, you haven't disappointed me – masterly inactivity as ever.' I smiled a little unhappily.

'According to the news this morning, the Chinese have been expressing their displeasure,' pursued Simon.

'Well, that's going to be a serious thing for Russia, that y'know – one day. Lord Roberts said once upon a time, then Lloyd George, and to a degree, I think, Churchill said the terrible thing of the future would be the Chinese,' said Lowry and, continuing his gloomy train of thought, he announced, 'But I know one thing, it doesn't matter the nationality – all human beings are the lowest form of animal life – we *are* y'know. You've heard that, haven't you Carol?'

'Oh yes,' agreed Carol, and certainly she and we had been treated to Lowry's favourite cliché often enough.

He was pressing home his point as he continued, 'The lowest form of animal life; and yet we're one of the most advanced, the cleverest – and we put it to the least use. Look what's going on in Czechoslovakia – and what's that for? Lust, isn't it? Look at what Hitler did to the Jews. No animal would do that. No, I'm sorry to bring this sad note in on a Saturday afternoon, but. . . .'

'It's Friday,' corrected Carol.

'Oh yes, I think you're right there, I'd forgotten. But just you analyse it; through the ages it just won't bear thinking of – what we do to each other. Who was that man who said, "The more I see of human nature, the more I love my dog."? A great man that – but

I forget who it was.'

'And do you like dogs best of all animals then?' asked Jean.

'Well, I do look on them as superior to humans. I'm sorry but I do. And they're so dependent on human beings – that's another sad thing. And you agree with me Carol, don't you?'

'Yes.'

'And then humans talk about religion,' continued Lowry, now in full flow. 'Yes, they talk about religion, and in the name of religion there've been more atrocities committed than for anything else in the world – in the name of religion!'

'Oh yes, that's absolutely true,' agreed Carol.

'There's been a hell of a lot of good done in the name of religion also – if you don't mind,' I said.

'Oh lord, are you lot still talking drivel?' queried Simon, returning to the office. 'It's time the accountant had some tea. He's worn out – just built himself a six-foot garden wall – saved himself two hundred pounds. You'd be much better building a garden wall, Mr Lowry!'

'My word, sir, that's an idea. I believe I would,' laughed the painter, beaming at the young girls draped about the office, for we had been joined by another student who was helping out.

'Your accountant must be potty,' said Carol. 'D'you like my new shoes, Simon?'

'Yes, they're very nice. Better than the ones you bought yesterday. You haven't told us how you enjoyed your visit to British Ropes.'

'I thought you were rather upset at first, Carol,' said Mr Lowry.

'I was. It floored me. I couldn't believe it. Oh, the dust . . . the air was full of it. Five minutes there and I felt I wanted to choke. I wanted a cup of tea.'

'Aye, they've seven hundred girls in that place – the largest of its kind in Europe,' said Lowry. 'It was an education for you to see that Carol, wasn't it? I thought it might be. I've been in quite a few of these places – and it would do a lot of people good to go through one of them – make them realize how the world lives,' he added fiercely.

'Yes,' agreed Carol. 'It would make them realize how lucky they are. I felt enormously lucky. When I come out of school at a quarter past four, I think, "Oh dear, I've had a hard day" – thirty kids all day, you know – and then I realized, when I went there. . . .'

'Yes, you learned a lot there, didn't you? Thought you would,' announced Lowry with conviction, adding, 'I once went round a chocolate factory to do a picture; and they were very, very nice, but when they took me round, and I saw them doing the same job day after day – I found I couldn't do that picture. So I rang up Mr Corcoran of the Lefevre Gallery, and said, "I can't do it. I shouldn't have gone to that factory. You shouldn't have sent me. I can't do it. I don't want to do it." And he said, "You don't want to do it?" "*No*!" and I wouldn't do it – I wouldn't have it. So you saw it today, didn't you Carol? And the conditions today were very good compared to what I've seen in the cotton mills. *You* haven't been in any of these places, Mrs Marshall – you haven't lived!' Lowry scowled disagreeably.

As Simon again returned to the room Lowry shouted at him, 'It would do *you* good to see what Carol's seen. You want to do what she's done – you want to see the conditions, and then you'd know how lucky you were.'

'Yes, it's the conditions that are important,' agreed Carol. 'And they're doing a lot of plastics there now – but we couldn't go into that building. Look they've given us each one of these. . . .'

'A free sample?' asked Simon hopefully.

'Yes, look – a cure for wasp stings. A doctor gave them the formula, but it didn't pay, so they sold it.'

'Oh, how marvellous – can one buy those?' I asked with interest.

'Yes, but under another name now, I think.'

'Oh, I must try and get one for Micky – it's death for him if he gets stung by a wasp – he swells up like a mountain,' I explained.

'I shall take mine with me to Switzerland next week,' said Carol.

'That's right, and you can have mine as well if you like,' said Lowry.

'Oh no, I don't need two – give yours to Tilly.'

'No, I'll keep it then,' and our friend put his away in his pocket. 'You don't know how the other half lives, Mrs Marshall.' Sanctimoniously he closed his eyes, suddenly to open them again to inquire of me, 'Have you ever read Henry Mayhew, the mid-Victorian?'

'No.'

'Well, it would do you a lot of good – a lot of good. You'd learn a lot,' he spoke rather viciously.

Our accountant came smiling into the room. 'They've been having a tour of British Ropes today,' I said.

'Oh, indeed? And what have you been doing there?' asked Mr Groves.

'Seeing how the other half lives,' replied Lowry sourly.

'Well, I've been watching it here,' retorted Mr Groves.

'What d'you mean?' asked the artist. '*Where?*'

'You sitting up here with all this charming company, whilst I have a cup of tea on my tod downstairs.' Suddenly Lowry's ill-humour left him; he dissolved into bellows of mirth.

7

In 1968 Micky suggested to Tyne Tees Television that they should make a film on L. S. Lowry. No colour film of him or his work existed. Lowry was most happy at the idea, provided that Micky was the interviewer and that he and I were the art advisers.

Tyne Tees did the job very thoroughly, sparing no expense. It was made in Eastman colour, and the company retained their award-winning producer, Robert Tyrrell, to direct, despite the fact that his contract with them had recently expired.

We arranged for Bob to meet Lowry for the first time over dinner at Tilley's. Lowry gave him a brief account of his life – the same old commentary he had churned out for the press over the years. Again we wished he could find something a little more interesting to say about himself, but it was the usual 'nothing's ever happened to me, there's nothing in my life except what I've said. I've never robbed a bank, or shot someone, or married. . . . I often think I should have been a stockbroker.' Eventually Bob Tyrell put his head in his hands at the dinner table, saying in despair, 'I really don't think I can make it!'

Lowry had shown no enthusiasm until then for the project but, sensing this new piece of publicity to be sailing away, he put his ever gentle hand on Bob's arm and said, 'Now don't worry – we'll see you through.'

And I comforted with, 'You'll find when it comes to filming, Bob, that Mr Lowry's a natural. He may be sitting here unrelaxed because he's meeting you for the first time, but I've seen him in front of TV cameras – he becomes a different man.' Bob gazed at me in disbelief, then, accepting another glass of wine, resigned himself to his fate.

Dinner over, Simon took Lowry back to his hotel. Tyrrell still had misgivings. 'But if only the old bugger *had* ever *done* anything but paint! How can I make his life interesting? How the hell? Just paint, paint, bloody paint. I wish to God he had robbed a bank, shot someone – why, he hasn't even got a woman in his life!' Bob despaired again.

'We'll have Carol in the film,' I announced.

'Who's Carol?'

'His heiress – she must be in it for the record.' After further discussion Bob inquired whether this could be managed. I told him to leave it to me.

Originally Lowry wished the film to deal only with his last ten years, as he particularly wanted his later work presented to an ever wider public. Tyrrell overruled this idea, and got Micky to talk Lowry into consenting that it should cover his whole life.

The film was to refer to his childhood, his cultural background, his first impulses towards art, his art school, his teachers, his curriculum; the First World War; his paintings of industrial scenes; his continued years of obscurity; his development in style; his method of drawing figures as human notations rather than representationally; his habit of working in electric light to the music of Bellini. It would go on to describe his recognition at the age of fifty-eight; his eventual change of style and what impelled him to paint the down-and-out solitaries; his dislike of artiness and art talk; his love of the Pre-Raphaelites; his dislike of Rembrandt and the Impressionists; his love of Vanbrugh and Congreve; and finally his philosophy – 'Man is the lowest form of animal life', 'Trust no one'; and what he would wish his epitaph to be: 'He worked for others and there was no rest.'

Once we had overcome Tyrrell's first fears, he decided that he wished to use Lowry as his own commentator – for the most part. At that time I felt this might be an error because Lowry's rather ill-fitting teeth occasionally made his speech slurred. In retrospect, however, despite a slight incoherence in the painter's commentary from time to time, the producer's decision was undoubtedly a good one. Since the artist is no longer with us it is a most valuable record. This tape was made as Lowry sat in his usual chair in the gallery office, with all equipment and technicians out of sight.

Everything was going nicely to plan. Contracts were ready for signing; casting sheets received. There were to be filmed sequences in the auction rooms of Sotheby's and Christie's; Mr A. J. McNeil Reid was to describe his discovery of Lowry and Sir John Rothenstein to give his opinion. The film unit was to go to Aspatria to film Sheila Fell at work; to Salford, Oldham, Bolton (with Carol and Lowry), Mottram-in-Longdendale, Manchester, Seaburn and South Shields. Lowry was to be filmed in the Stone Gallery before the opening of his last exhibition. All was planned for the weeks and months ahead and the painter was most happy with the arrangements when Philip Robertson arrived for a part of his annual holiday at the Seaburn Hotel.

Carol was staying with Lowry and her visit overlapped for a day or so with Philip Robertson's. Until then, these two had not met. On the Saturday after Carol's departure, Lowry and Robertson arrived at the gallery with Lowry in a storming rage. He had been discussing the film with his friend, and his friend agreed with him – we were going to kill him off. Lowry's opinion of Tyne Tees was low. They did not know what they were about and, turning to Mr Robertson for support, Lowry got it in no small measure. Mr Robertson was apparently well informed on amateur film-making and he was in entire agreement with the painter: he would never stand up to the rigours of making an hour-long film.

We tried to explain that this was no amateur effort. The producer had won two international awards. We were aware of Lowry's stamina, and during the past six years we had not been the end of him. I was used to safeguarding his comfort down to the last detail and I should continue to do so. It had already been arranged that I would supply the necessary sustenance, keeping him well fed at frequent intervals, and in a good humour, which I was reasonably adept at achieving.

No – nothing availed. Argument was useless. Mr Robertson warned that he was going to be killed off, and, if Lowry had decided against it, that was that. The television company was paying Lowry seven hundred pounds for his pains plus expenses but, if he wanted neither that nor the free publicity, he could stuff it.

My husband rang Tyrrell at his home. Tyrrell would need to have all due warning: it affected him personally as he had been retained for this one purpose. An extremely professional young man, so good a union member that nothing but a crisis would have induced him to work that afternoon, Robert was in the gallery in half an hour. He handled Lowry with tact, understanding and extreme kindness, giving him every assurance that he would be safeguarded from any over-exertion. After some time, all was sunshine and smiles again

– the film was on. Lowry had managed one more dramatic little scene to amuse himself. Taking Tyrrell aside, I comforted him considerably by saying that this was nothing to what we might expect before the film was completed. By that time, six years of close association with our friend had left me with no illusions with regard to his temperament. There would be endless fireworks before the job was done.

Later, over dinner in Tilley's, Lowry started up his refrain once more. On Monday morning the film was off once again. To Tyrrell it seemed necessary that, if the film were to be made, Lowry and Philip Robertson must spend every second of their time with us when they were not sleeping. And as far as possible this was achieved; if we were not in the gallery they visited us at home. Once the contracts were signed, Lowry, to our relief, ceased his threats.

The London filming took place from 16 to 19 July. David Bathurst at Christie's proved more helpful than Sotheby's auctioneer, who complained of the bright lights and the distraction of the TV crew. Lowry did not forget this.

On 29 July, when filming began in Lowry's home, he insisted on a long break at lunchtime, and he, with Micky and Tyrrell, joined me at the Midland. As we ate our hefty midday meal, I asked Tyrrell what he thought of Mr Lowry's great Rossetti. Lowry informed me at once that he had recently sent it into store and, therefore, the producer could not see it. I was more than surprised, having supposed that it, with others of his collection, would be included in the film. 'Where have you sent *Proserpine* then?' I asked.

'Deep under ground, Mrs Marshall,' was Lowry's answer, 'in a nice vault.'

Long after midnight Micky and I drew up to the door of The Elms to deposit our friend. I was tired and longing for bed. 'Come along, Mrs Marshall,' I heard Lowry commanding, 'come along now and see *Proserpine*.'

'*Proserpine*? I thought you'd put her into store?'

'Good heavens, no! I just didn't want that fellow to see it, that's all. Security . . . don't want her in the film.' I got to bed at three o'clock.

The painter decided that things were going a little too smoothly and, when one particular sequence was due for shooting which necessitated the hiring of a bus and various bit-players, the old boy decided that he was not available. The producer rose manfully to the occasion and switched his schedules. As a result it transpired that the bus sequence, which entailed Lowry taking a number nine bus from outside his hotel at Seaburn to travel to the gallery took place on 19 August, possibly the hottest day of that year, instead of in July as had been originally arranged. Accompanying Lowry on this bus trip, but well out of sight at the back, were Carol, Simon and my husband. The painter and Micky had planned one of their small surrealist episodes. At one of the bus stops they wanted a woman to be pushing a pram and, when Lowry looked down into it, there was to be a small pig inside instead of a baby. But Tyrrell felt this was either too much of a good thing, or too difficult to achieve. Instead, he arranged a wedding party at the gates of a church. It was a rather splendid affair, with the bride looking exactly like Lowry's portraits of Ann.

Although Lowry's perversity had its amusing side, it could be dreadfully trying, as it was during the making of this film. It was Lowry who insisted on our including a sequence with a lavatory attendant. He had discovered this man, Sam West, painting pictures in a gents' at South Shields and had promptly bought two for ten shillings each. He brought them to the gallery, maintaining they were excellent when they were no such thing. We all ragged on and what had started as something of a joke ended in a shouting match between Lowry and Simon. The old painter, besides being perverse, could be extraordinarily persuasive and Lowry talked the producer into including the amateur-painter sequence in the film, despite the fact that Micky and I were credited and contracted as the art advisers. As a result Sam West got a nice leg-up, an article or two in the national press, and began to move his paintings like hot cakes. Later Lowry was to admit that he had made rather an ass of himself, but he only admitted this to us. I suppose that this particular film sequence stands as an example of Lowry's encouragement of the amateur. The smaller Sam West painting he eventually took home; the larger one he presented to Simon, who threatened to crown him with it.

That extremely hot August day the filming went without a hitch; the painter stood up to the rigours remarkably well – he always preferred heat to cold. During the late afternoon he had a well-earned rest; the gallery was full of people, and Lowry wandered out to have a word with this or that person who took his fancy. On these occasions he behaved angelically.

We seldom closed promptly; the secretary had left long since; part-time helpers had departed; Simon took Carol off in his car for a jaunt before dinner. Micky put the bolts in the door and went to change his suit. I was left alone with our friend.

His demeanour altered in an instant. The man who had done everything asked of him by the film producer all morning, who had laughed and enjoyed his day and never put a foot wrong, who but a moment ago had been smiling pleasantly and talking in a civilized manner to the public, gave way to a demon incarnate. Hurling himself into a chair he yelled, 'I'm sick of it – *sick* of it, d'you hear? Bloody sick to hell of it. I'm not going to do any more. They can take their film and stuff it anywhere they want. I'll do no more. I'm sick to *death*! They don't know how to do it – don't know how to do it. I'm sick and fed up with the lot of them.'

All summer long I had seen to it that he did not over-exert himself, and watched over his creature comforts. True, he had had a strenuous morning, but I had made sure that he had had a good rest during the afternoon; I'd pampered and spoiled him all I knew how. He was not the only one to be sick to death of it. My nerve broke and I yelled at him, '*You're* sick of it? Well, I'm sick of *you*. Sick and tired to death of you. Get out this instant, and never you dare return within these walls. Your pictures will be sent on to you. Now *leave* – get out, and don't you ever dare come back.' All my pent-up irritation with him over the years welled up and I burst into tears.

Suddenly he was out of his chair and sitting beside me on the window seat. In an instant he had changed again. 'Oh now, Mrs Marshall, don't take on like that – dear, dear me, you mustn't upset yourself.'

With the tears running down my face I looked at him, 'Not upset myself? *I* haven't upset myself, it's *you've* upset me. I tell you get out and take your bloody pictures with you.'

'Now, now,' he laid his hand on mine, 'you've been overdoing it. Yes, you've been looking after us all, and it's been too much for you – now don't take on like that.'

'I'll take on any bloody way I want!' Living over the scene again, I remember my subconscious astonishment. Here was Lowry, who had so often had my nerves frayed almost to breaking point, a moment ago an old fiend, now a near-angel offering comfort. I could not believe my ears. Wickedly and purposefully I continued to cry.

My initial shock was past but I decided that the tears were going down so well it was a pity to stop them.

I bellowed with rage. Micky appeared from below to ask what the dickens was going on. 'Oh,' Lowry soothed him, while I cried ever more loudly, 'poor Mrs Marshall has been overdoing it.' I told my husband that the moment Simon returned he must take me home. He could give Lowry and Carol dinner as arranged, and then the old man could take himself out of the gallery once and for all, pictures and all.

'No, no, that won't do at all,' I heard the artist saying, 'now you're not going home until you've had some dinner first, Mrs Marshall. You'll come along with us.'

'I'm blowed if I will – don't want any dinner,' I sobbed.

'Oh, but I know what's best for you – you're not going home without at least a bowl of soup first,' he consoled. My husband looked from one to the other of us, still wondering what it was all about.

'I'll tell you what it's about,' I continued to sob, now thoroughly enjoying myself. 'Mr Lowry's been marvellous all day – I'm the first to give credit where credit's due. He behaves like an angel when Bob Tyrrell or any of the public's around, and then, the moment they're gone, he starts playing me up. Says he's sick to death of everything – well, it's nothing to what I feel about him!' The old blighter started to roar with laughter. 'And you can stop your laughing – you can always laugh when it suits your purpose!' But he continued to laugh and then Micky joined in, and in the end I began to smile as well. Eventually I departed to tidy up my face and to my amazement I heard the teetotaller suggest to my husband that he should have a nice drink ready for my reappearance.

For three days Robert Tyrrell and my husband were in the west country doing research for the film, while Lowry remained with Simon and me in Newcastle. One afternoon Ella provided a birthday cake as a surprise for me. Lowry promptly asked what nice presents I had received. Well, I laughingly admitted, it was the first occasion my husband had forgotten the day – 'too busy, you see, over your affairs!'

To my surprise, he rose from his chair, took down two small paintings of his own from the office wall, handed them to me with, 'There, for you. Happy birthday!' These were the small version of *The Sixth Character in Search of an Author* – back and front view.

He had just recently given the larger version, so admired by me, to Carol. The smaller he had brought to the gallery, saying he did not wish to part with them, so they remained his and were not for sale but were hanging in the office.

'Good God! I couldn't take those,' I announced at once, 'Micky would kill me.'

'It's got nothing to do with him – they're mine, and I want you to have them. Take them home. And don't tell anyone. If anyone asks where they've gone tell them to an exhibition at Runcorn.' We laughed together but I still refused to take them. We argued back and forth until he finished the matter with, 'You're discarding m'work then?' When I realized that he might misunderstand my refusal, I accepted them with great pleasure. 'And you'll take me out for dinner, won't you?' he added, hunching his shoulders up and giggling like a small boy.

So, for the three evenings Micky was absent with Tyrrell, Simon and I took Lowry round to Tilley's as usual. At the end of the first dinner, I asked Mr Redman to call a taxi for our friend. When it arrived Lowry turned and said to me, 'You must come with me. Simon can follow in his car, and pick you up from the hotel.' It seemed a damned silly idea but, as ever, we fell in with his wishes. For three consecutive nights this was the routine. These were the only occasions I recall Lowry travelling in the back of a car. I felt something of an imbecile as I turned my head to glance out of the back of the taxi to see poor Simon following at a snail's pace, while I sat bolt upright with the elderly painter's beautiful hand lightly resting on my own rather rigid one. Lowry smiled his approval as I paid his taxi fare each evening.

The summer moved on its way and eventually the film was finished. One evening it was time to take Lowry to the television studios to see the completed *Mr Lowry*. In the viewing studio the painter sat himself next to me, with Micky and Carol on his other side. In the course of his researches Tyrrell had unearthed an ex-landlord of Lowry's, a Mr Dufty. This man had evicted the painter from the house in which he had lived for so long with his mother – 117 Station Road, Pendlebury. It has been said that Lowry moved from there because of the sad memories it held for him but, according to Mr Dufty, the painter had let the house become so filthy and run-down that the landlord had no alternative but to have him evicted – nine years after his mother's death. I was aware that neither Micky nor Tyrrell considered that this fact should emerge in the film and Mr Dufty is recorded in it as saying only nice things about the artist. But as Mr Dufty's face appeared on the screen Lowry didn't know that his secret was safe. He jerked upright in his seat, and I felt him go rigid. Out of the corner of my eye I saw him about to explode with rage. He opened his mouth as if to scream, but his moment of panic passed as Mr Dufty faded out. Lowry sank back, relaxing with relief; it had been touch and go.

The film stands as the finest record there is of the painter's life. But as he left the studios that evening he was muttering constantly, 'This lot didn't know how to do it.' When Carol told him how good she thought it was, for once he disagreed with her. During the following months Lowry continued to air his dissatisfaction with the production until, one evening over dinner at the Station Hotel, he beamed on the Rossetti Society and announced, 'Very good about the film, wasn't it?'

'What was?' we asked.

'I've had a press-cutting – it won the silver medal at the Venice Film Festival,' he informed us. 'I always said it was magnificent.'

In the spring of 1970 we purchased at Christie's auction rooms Rossetti's watercolour, *Sweet Tooth*. At the time the price was a record for this artist's work. It was by no means the top price for a work at auction that day and so we were surprised the following morning to see the national press highlight the acquisition. For some reason we were constantly rung up by various newspapers and asked further questions about it. It is possible that they thought we had bought it for Lowry and there might be a story behind it, but we had merely bought it for stock.

We had barely arrived in Newcastle the following Saturday when Lowry descended on us. Apparently the news of the purchase had reached him in Mottram and he could not wait to see it. It was a small painting, circa 1864, and interesting in as much as it tended to be a link between Rossetti's earlier and later work. It portrayed a single figure of a girl sitting eating a bunch of grapes with the background in the artist's earlier style. Rossetti's single figures of women are usually either large oils or pastels: there are few small watercolours, and these tend to be highly valued. It was in good condition and could be hung forthwith, which is not always the case with works purchased at auction.

Lowry expressed his immediate pleasure with it and kept returning to the outer gallery every now and again to view it once more. He would stand before it constantly expressing his approval and then return to the office to exclaim over and extol its merits. We were expecting one of our most important clients in at any moment to see the Rossetti. This man was not a member of the Rossetti Society but had often met Lowry in the gallery, and was fully aware of his interest in the Pre-Raphaelites. We were therefore delighted that the artist so heartily approved our purchase.

The client arrived punctually. He viewed the Rossetti at length and asked what we wanted for it. We kept the profit to a minimum and he appeared impressed. We took him into the office and gave Lowry his cue to be as enthusiastic as he had already been. Micky and I were speechless when, without hesitation and giving me a dirty look, he announced that he did not care for the painting at all. I do not find myself speechless very often, and I didn't remain so for long.

'But you said you considered it was splendid . . . you've been saying you thought it very fine indeed!'

'Well, Mrs Marshall . . . I didn't want to depress you. Oh no, I don't really care for it at all,' heaving a sigh of satisfaction.

Other people arrived and drinks were handed round the office, while Lowry handed round his opinion that the new acquisition was a very poor thing indeed. Our client departed, saying in the pleasantest way possible that he would, in view of Mr Lowry's opinion, wait for a better Rossetti. He is still waiting.

During this time, Ella had been working overtime in the kitchen preparing the favourite chicken for our unexpected guest, and we were joined by Ian and Bill Taylor, our young company secretary. Throughout the meal the artist talked ceaselessly to Ian of the Rossetti watercolour, his teasing and outrageous comments becoming ever more mischievous. Ian, seldom averse to leading the old boy on, joined in. They finally agreed that five pounds would have been too high a price for *Sweet Tooth*. The denigration continued as Lowry and Ian drank their coffee. Micky sat behind his desk with an expressionless and unconcerned face until he eventually got to his feet saying he needed some fresh air and some cigarettes.

At last Lowry commented that Micky had been a long time gone. I told him that my husband was not the sort of person to enjoy the sight of small boys pulling the wings off flies. What was I talking about? His and Ian's behaviour over the new acquisition, of course, and that he had deliberately prevented the sale of the Rossetti that day for the sheer devilment of it. 'I suppose you thought we should have bought one of your own works instead?' (We quite often had – when we saw his works going too cheaply in the sale rooms we had done our bit to keep up his prices.)

'Oh well, perhaps I'd better stay out of the gallery in future!' he retorted.

'Perhaps you had.'

We took him out to dinner as usual, and a day or two later he returned to Mottram. But before very long he was back, bringing with him Philip Robertson. We welcomed them as merrily as ever, and with tea over they went to the main exhibition rooms to view the works. As they came down the stairs Lowry promptly demanded his hat and, to our surprise, they hurriedly took their departure. This had not happened previously: normally we would have taken them out to dinner. Simon took his current girlfriend to Tilley's before going on to the theatre that evening, and who should be eating at the usual table but Lowry, Philip and Ian.

Attack always being the best form of defence, when Ian came to see us next morning, he told us that Lowry had been sad at the poor welcome he had received the previous afternoon. He had spent his time during dinner bemoaning the lack of new acquisitions on exhibition.

'Oh, what a crying shame,' I said. 'He wanted to see lots more Rossettis, did he? Poor old pet – how disappointing for him!'

Lowry had a sadistic streak within his character. He admitted that his pictures of cripples, bearded ladies, the paintings and drawings showing the suffering and disabilities of others, were made without compassion. His love of creating difficult situations for the purpose of observing the results was a continuous enjoyment and amusement to him. He undoubtedly got some sort of kick out of these experiences. My son informs me that I was a splendid objective for his sport. 'Oh Ma – you were a sitting target for him. You've always been such a worrier. Lowry saw this and played you up as a consequence. He knew exactly how to make you suffer.'

Looking through some correspondence, I see that Carol makes reference to a certain fascination I held for 'Uncle'. This appears very odd. I don't have a beard, and I'm not yet a cripple, so I can only assume that Simon is correct when he stresses the fact, 'You're such a fool at times – you were grist to Lowry's mill.'

Nevertheless, Lowry if he chose could behave like an angel. There was something within his personality which made him the veritable charmer, if charm was his intention. There was a power within the man which could twist and turn one's guts.

In the long run none of us resented Lowry's prevention of the sale of *Sweet Tooth*. It was sold, if I remember rightly, for about seven thousand pounds. As I write, it has just come on the London market again – the asking price is thirty-six thousand.

Increasingly the Stone Gallery's character changed. Now it had become more of a dealer's, than an exhibition gallery. From 1971 we had to have a London base, because collectors could not be persuaded to come to Newcastle to see one important work.

In London we met our friend Philip James, then librarian at the Royal Academy. He told my husband that the Academy had just been let down at the last moment with regard to a Chagall exhibition planned. Micky said, why not put on a comprehensive show of D. G. Rossetti's work? Virginia Surtees's great *Catalogue Raisonné* had recently been published – if she could be persuaded to assist, the work was already done.

Lowry made infrequent visits to London, when he would stay at Brown's Hotel because it was reasonably close to our flat. For the Rossetti exhibition in the winter of 1973 he arranged to meet us at the Academy, bringing with him Carol. The old man refused to spend very long in the first rooms where hung most of Rossetti's earlier work; he moved pretty quickly to the last room where an attempt had been made to recreate the claustrophobic effect of Rossetti's house and studio. Lowry in no way approved of this idea and laughingly wondered what his own works might look like if hung one day in an effort to reproduce their effect in his own little house. He felt, on the contrary, that it mattered not a damn under what conditions the paintings had been produced – all that concerned the spectator was that every painting should be given the space and setting due to it. This he considered had not been afforded to the later, larger paintings and studies.

Lowry had been asked to loan his great *Proserpine* to the R.A. exhibition, in preference to the almost identical version which is in the possession of the Tate Gallery. At first he had hesitated to lend his pride and joy but he agreed when I pointed out to him that, some time in the future, when it became Carol's, it might well be worth more to her if it had been included in this particularly important exhibition. And now here he was, on this winter's afternoon, gazing at the painting in its unfamiliar surroundings. Then his eyes moved to *Astarte Syriaca*, always in Lowry's mind the greatest Rossetti of all – on to *The Bower Meadow* from Manchester's City Art Gallery – very well known to him, and again much beloved. He wished endlessly and, of course, hopelessly, to own it. There was the *Pandora* oil, once ours, and the great pastel *La Girlandata* which had passed through the Stone Gallery when, alas, it had not been his turn to buy. But it appears in his Tyne Tees film, where he is seen to admire it and gives his reasons. *The Blessed Damozel* (not one of his 'top ten') was here, and *Dante's Dream*, from Liverpool's Walker Art Gallery, but he never cared for that one either, just as he did not admire Rossetti's *Beata Beatrix*.

As he gazed enraptured at many favourites and familiars, he was spotted by Mr Hutchison, the Royal Academy's secretary – not a favourite of Lowry's, who much preferred his predecessor, Mr Humphrey Brooke. The elderly academician had been observed by many and he was delighted when Yvonne Mitchell asked me for an introduction and the actress's young daughter dropped him an old-fashioned curtsey. There were many that afternoon who asked us if they might meet him which did not occur very often in the north-east. Mr Hutchison returned to say that the president, Sir Tom Monnington PRA, would like Lowry to go upstairs to the Diploma Gallery; that day an exhibition of watercolours from the Mellon collection was opening and it would be appreciated if Lowry would go and meet Mr Paul Mellon. But Lowry had come for one thing only and that was to see the Rossetti exhibition. Wild horses were not going to drag him upstairs. Sir Tom, whom I already knew, came down in a few moments and we looked at the exhibition together. He rather preferred the earlier work so I moved back to see some of it with him, while Lowry remained with his favourites.

Carol was a room or two further back still, but eventually we all repaired to the public tearoom in the basement, led by the president. When he had departed to his duties in the Diploma Gallery, Lowry sat back and stretched out his long legs, still rather enjoying being something of an attraction, as others looked across at him. He had pleasure in renewing the acquaintance of Mrs Roderic O'Conor, (great-niece of Dante Gabriel, granddaughter of William Michael Rossetti, and great-granddaughter of Ford Madox Brown), a charming person with whom Lowry had once stayed.

At dinner that evening, as Lowry dived into his favourite 'starter', he announced, 'Ah, this is the way I like my melons – eating them, not meeting them!'

Previous to this occasion, when Micky and I were dining one evening with Willy MacTaggart at the Arts Club, the then President of the Royal Academy came across to have his coffee with us. Remembering that we were friends of Lowry, he told us his side of a visit to the Academy by its elderly academician. We were aware that our friend had called in as he wanted to show Burlington House to Carol. They had then joined us in the flat for tea. We knew that Lowry had introduced Carol to the president, which was something of a surprise, but it transpired that he had not wished to buy a catalogue for the current exhibition and, rather than do so, had to make known who he was. In a moment or two, he and Carol had been taken to meet Sir Tom Monnington. In the president's room Lowry introduced Carol as his niece, which by this time had become second nature to him, and Sir Tom, fully aware that his fellow academician had no brothers or sisters nor, so far as he knew, any living relative, quizzed him. 'Oh – well, what sort of a Lowry is this, then?' To which he received no reply. Sir Tom, still in the dark as to the relationship, if any, asked whether we could throw any light on it. I told him the girl was no blood relation, but her name was Lowry.

'Do you happen to know how Lowry is leaving his estate?' we were asked. I fancied that a shadow of disappointment crossed the president's face when he learned it was to go to Carol, so, to comfort him, I told him that once or twice Lowry had muttered that, should Carol pre-decease him, or anything untoward occur, he would then leave everything to the RA Benevolent Fund.

Some time later Lowry received a letter from Sir Tom Monnington on behalf of his committee, saying that they would be happy to give Lowry a Retrospective Exhibition at Burlington House in due course. Lowry would be the first living RA to be so honoured. Once more Lowry asked Micky to draft a letter of acceptance. Sir Tom visited The Elms to discuss matters further, and went to see Lowry works at Salford.

It was sad that neither man was to live to see the exhibition. Had they done so, at least three paintings would not have been shown.

We wondered what kind of a scene Lowry would have created had he heard the GUS (Kettering) Brass Band playing, quite superbly, in the courtyard of Burlington House during the private view. Those of us who knew Lowry can only congratulate Sir Hugh Casson PRA that the artist was absent. There was only one thing Lowry disliked more than the current Chancellor of the Exchequer – and that was what he would refer to as 'background music'. It was his constant, continual, eternal, raging anathema, and if he had been there to hear that splendid brass band the president of the Royal Academy would not have known what had hit him.

Lowry was certain that he and he alone knew what was best for his career as a painter, and on the surface it would appear that he was proved right, for he died a famous and wealthy man. In his last years the directors of his London gallery and we were averse to his signing the mass of coloured reproductions, marketed as original prints, which were not 'original prints' by any manner of means as the term is understood in the art world. Usually, the artist makes the original print himself or is, at least, concerned in its process from start to finish, maybe working with a lithographer and examining each print as it comes off the stone, which is then usually destroyed when a small edition is complete. But Lowry's so-called 'limited editions' usually ran to many hundreds so there are in existence thousands of perfectly ordinary reproductions signed by Lowry. At one time it was possible to buy an original Lowry drawing for little more than the cost of one of these signed reproductions of his oil paintings, and we constantly begged him not to be party to this activity which to our minds did not comply with the Trade Descriptions Act.

After the visit to the Rossetti exhibition, back at the flat Carol beckoned me to follow her into the bedroom and turning to me with great anxiety asked, 'Oh Tilly, will you and Micky try and persuade Uncle to stop signing these endless reproductions? They're going to land him in trouble one day, I'm sure, and they're so bad for his reputation.' I told her that Micky and I had advised him strongly against the course he was pursuing for long enough but to no avail. Nevertheless, perhaps if the three of us tackled him that evening he might listen; since she felt as strongly about it as we did, there was certainly no harm in having yet another try.

Lowry's favourite eating spots were seldom ours. He had not cared for Prunier's, which was a pity for it was so handy; he considered the Connaught overrated and inferior to Tilley's; he had sat in a draught at the Vendôme, and we had had to move tables three times; he did not care for Wilton's as there he could neither see nor be seen; he preferred the St James's Overtons, but got impatient when he had to have a drink while we ordered, as he'd already had his orange squash in the flat. He would, of course, have had a fit if one had taken him to the more off-beat places like Peter Langan's Odin's, so on the evening in question, we decided to take him to the newly opened Lafayette in King Street which was just around the corner from us. It is a long time since I have been there, indeed not since that occasion; in those days it was quiet. I realized immediately that it was not the happiest choice when we were shown to an alcove which was not sufficiently in the public eye for the painter's liking. However, coming into the restaurant we met a one-time managing director of Tyne Tees Television, who recognized him and the evening was saved for the moment.

Carol regaled us a little tactlessly with an account of a holiday she had recently shared with a friend in Greece, and she talked a good deal of her companion, John, whom she was later to marry. This did not augur too well for the idea we had of tackling Lowry on his print signing, but after a time Micky managed to change the subject and the matter of the reproductions was introduced. Carol pleaded with the painter, I pleaded, and Micky, who would never plead – not, I fancy, if his life depended upon it – put to our friend the dangers of overpopularizing and overexposing his art; even, eventually, the dangers of the Trade Descriptions Act. All argument was useless; in no way could Lowry be dissuaded. We asked him why. Because, he said, he got two pounds a signature (it may well have been more), and he had never earned money so easily in his life.

And anyway, he argued, if some poor people couldn't afford an original painting, why shouldn't they have these hanging on their walls at a lesser price? Yes, we said, but he was merely adding a pencilled signature (over and above the printed one on the reproduced oil painting) so these 'poor' folk were paying from a hundred and fifty to two hundred and fifty pounds for a reproduction worth perhaps twelve pounds. If he felt so fervently for the poor who were going to hang these (in the belief that they had bought an excellent investment for the future), then in our opinion it was time he thought again.

Suddenly Lowry had had enough and, despite the presence of acquaintances nearby, he banged his fist angrily upon the table time and time again, thundering, 'Let's leave it shall we? Let's leave it.'

'Oh yes,' retorted Micky. 'We'll certainly leave it – but don't come whimpering to me in the future saying I didn't warn you. For I'm warning you now and for the last time – I shall hope not to see you in a court of law before you die.' And I think had Lowry lived longer there was some danger of that. But nothing prevailed against the cheques that rolled in for doing no work – although we were not to learn until much later just how large some of those cheques were, including, as they did, copyright payment.

A good deal was told in his day about Lowry's enormous love of music – but try as we would we could never persuade him to come to a concert, an opera, or a play – not with us. He had gone to these things with Sheila Fell and Pat Cooke, but it must have been only to please them. His seven attendances at the Pirandello production were the outcome of his rapture at the performance of the young actress, and he always maintained Ann had taken him in the first instance. By the time we knew him these wider interests were a thing of the past, if they had ever been a genuine part of his make-up, which I doubt.

Looking back objectively, perhaps Carol was not after all the only one to whom he would show his possessiveness. He became possessive of us too, I think, for he would get frightfully disgruntled if we were away. As year after year passed, he was not the only one growing older. Sitting with him night after night in Tilley's, Mickey and I would long to be at home restoring our energies. We always had to rise at 5.45, hence he could not stay overnight with us – and I never invited him to. We continued to harken to his interminable stories and memories, gently prompting him when he forgot his lines, until he took up his role of raconteur with renewed vigour – pouring the endless cream into his cup, to the endless refrain.

Regardless of work – and it must not be forgotten that Lowry was only one painter for whom we dealt – we also had certain social obligations. Dinner parties would be hastily cancelled at the last moment on some pretext other than the real one – caring for Lowry.

Good clients became tired of meeting Lowry so constantly in the gallery.

Of a morning I would warn my husband that I really must get home at a reasonable hour – we couldn't look after Lowry that evening. Come evening, Micky would turn to him and say Tilly was tired – we must get home. I would look into the old man's disappointed blue eyes and relent – he would hunch up his shoulders in his particular fashion, giggle, heave a huge sigh of satisfaction. 'Ah . . . that's a good Mrs Marshall – Little Laurie's happy now.'

Nor did we ever take a holiday from work.

I was discussing it recently with the family, asking how the dickens we managed – and above all *why*?

My daughter-in-law smiled again at her memory of Lowry. 'Well, we couldn't not look after him, could we? Like you and Micky, Simon and I would have done anything, almost, rather than disappoint him. He had a quality which could bring out all one's sympathy. He was also an incredibly powerful personality.'

My husband will explain that, difficult though it so often was for him to work with Lowry constantly alongside his desk, nevertheless, when the old boy arrived, and the first 'dying' had been disposed of, his mind was alert. He knew the art world. He knew what everything was all about. There was no painter, sculptor, or art movement they could not and did not discuss. Sharing an interest in early Italian painting and certain of the Surrealists, they spent hours studying books and catalogues. It was perhaps not difficult, if one had that type of mind, to vacillate between the early Italians and the Belgian, Paul Delvaux, whose work is classical in method but Surrealist in spirit, and René Magritte, who was as interested as was Lowry in the world about him, but who represented it in surprising ways.

Magritte painted many canvases exploring the relationship between the tree and the leaf, the landscape and the picture, and even the shoes and the feet. Lowry, in his single figures, explored the relationship of unfortunate individuals, firstly, with the industrial background, and finally against a blank background. In some ways, Lowry shared the opinions of Magritte. For instance, when the latter was asked about the relationship between his life and art, he replied, 'I really couldn't think of any, except that life obliges me to do something, so I paint.' Both Lowry and Magritte adopted the same form of dress – dark grey suit, white shirt and collar, with black tie. There is no great significance in this similarity of dress but it existed nevertheless, and in both artists it indicated a workmanlike approach to their 'job'.

Lowry made much of this non-arty attitude; he would quote Bach (usually it amused him to pronounce it *Batch*) dashing away from a party of friends and an evening's enjoyment to knock off a cantata for the following day; or Brahms reluctantly leaving a convivial gathering to finish off a symphony. Lowry had little patience with artists who wanted to discuss aesthetic problems. 'Never mind all that – just get on with the job!' he would say and this was a logical element in Lowry's character. Aesthetic pertains to the beautiful and he had no sense of beauty as the world accepts the term.

When Micky and I had returned to Newcastle in 1969 after seeing the Magritte exhibition at the Tate, Lowry quizzed us about our reactions, and pored over the catalogue for days. One morning he came into the gallery in some excitement, for once not immediately proclaiming his early demise, but as a painter bursting with ideas.

'You know that Magritte picture we like so much, Mr Marshall – the one with the girl with those fine legs but the body and head of a cod fish, washed up and lying on the beach with the sea behind? Well, this morning I looked out of my bedroom window at the Seaburn – the beach was quite deserted, except for something that caught my eye. I went out to have a look, and there, just above the water line, what d'you think I saw? A fine well-upholstered settee – facing the sea – oh! what a picture it would make. Give me a bit of paper. Oh, for goodness sake find me a pencil – you never have a pencil – you're an awful man! Wait, I've got one myself today. . . .' He scrabbled through his pockets, found what he wanted, Micky gave him some paper, and he produced the little sketch.

Lowry was a man who had excelled on his own. During the earlier years of the century when Duncan Grant, Augustus John, the Nashes and the Spencers, Nevinson, and so many others were already well known, Lowry had been working away in Manchester unheard of. But in the end, as a painter, he was to outdo all for fame. He was a man who had excelled on his own for the reason that he could never tolerate direction from others. This was an innate characteristic. Perhaps in Micky he found a man of a similar temperament. He had been present throughout the days when Micky had turned down direction or interference from city councillors and representatives of local government. Lowry saw the period ahead when, under cover of Regional Arts Associations, this sort of unknowledgeable body might wield too great an influence over the artistic life of the country. In conjunction with the Arts Council, there was now the full machinery set up in Britain for censorship of the arts. And Lowry smelled danger. So occasional irreverence for authority became an added bond between the two men.

One evening Micky was to speak on television against the activities of town planners. The following morning he received a telephone call from a well-known London-based architect, warning him of 'the dangers of speaking against the angels'. Lowry was in the office when the call came through. Going into the room a moment later, I found both men helpless with mirth.

There was a sophisticated side to the painter's character which neither presented normal behaviour nor expected to receive it from us. Sometimes when I interrupted a serious discussion between Lowry and Micky their reaction was to cease all interest in their subject, and they would take off into *folie à deux* art improvisation. Once they decided that Lowry would do a series of drawings, signing them all Percy Smith. 'He's related of course to Percy Park!' (This was an allusion to a place in Tynemouth.) ' "Holiday Drawings of the North-East". The BBC's bound to like that – it'll lap it up.' So an entire exhibition was planned around Percy Smith's drawings. None would be dearer than ten pounds – 'And not one will sell!' vowed Lowry. The rest of us were in agreement. But when the cost of framing was pointed out the idea sank like a stone, while he and Micky were away extemporizing anew.

Once, at the Wilson Arms in Grassington, Micky and Lowry amused themselves with one of their typically nonsensical jokes. After an excellent lunch they were given coffee in the lounge, an extremely narrow room with tables close together, resembling a rather splendid railway carriage. Taking their time, for Lowry's coffee had to grow cold before he could bring himself to drink it, the artist spotted an appalling 1920ish amateur watercolour drawing of the hotel.

'D'you think they know what they've got?' Lowry asked Micky, who eyed the thing with some inner horror but nevertheless knew what was expected of him.

He replied, 'No, I shouldn't think so.'

'No, I shouldn't.'

'Early period, isn't it, Mr Lowry?'

'Oh *yes*, Mr Marshall, of course – goes without saying. Early, yes, and very rare now, of course. What d'you think it's worth?'

'My God, I daren't think, but all of five figures.'

'Oh, my God yes, Mr Marshall, all of that. I wonder if they could be persuaded to part with it? We might try!' Out of the corner of his eye, behind those glinting glasses, Lowry watched a man near them get rapidly to his feet. 'Well, I fancy I'd better drink up, and we'll be off, Mr Marshall. Don't want to be late for our appointment, do we?' They left rather hastily. Neither man dared glance in the direction of the manager's office, where they had glimpsed the fellow who had just left the lounge gently closing the door behind him. 'Ha, ha, that'll teach the fool to bargain hunt!' laughed Lowry.

During another such journey the two mischief mongers called in at the George Hotel in Huddersfield, a favourite port of call of Lowry's. On this occasion they were late arriving; it was almost two o'clock when they went into the empty dining room. Settling himself at their usual table Lowry announced, 'Very popular place this – lucky to get a table.'

'Yes, just as well we came early. Shall we have claret, or would you prefer burgundy? You can sleep in the car after lunch – you usually do.'

'Oh, I'd rather have a Château Kia-Ora,' answered the painter.

'Any particular year? D'you mind having London bottled – I'm a bit short of the ready today!'

'Not at all, sir. I'd see to it m'self, but my remittance hasn't arrived yet. As usual I'm a bit impoverished.'

'If they pay you to stay away – why don't you threaten to go back? They might raise your remittance with luck. She lives in a respectable neighbourhood – Wilmslow isn't it?'

'No, no, she's moved.'

'Where? Southport? Well, that's posher still. She won't want you turning up there! Oh yes, you'll get that remittance raised without a doubt if you play your cards right.'

'It's not I who play cards, Mr Marshall – it's she who does.'

'Oh, yes, how stupid of me. So long as she doesn't see fit to pass you off as the gardener, of course. . . .'

'Oh, she couldn't – no garden.'

'Well, we shall have to give all this careful thought. We must put our minds to it.'

'We could, if only we had minds, Mr Marshall – ah, here's the waiter.'

'An orange squash and a lager, please.'

'You're very busy today. If you have time I'll have melon and then cutlets and chips – just a few chips.'

'And a few peas, perhaps, with them, sir?'

'*No* – just cutlets and chips, or do I mean french fried? Mr Marshall, do I mean chips or french fried?'

'Have sauté for a change. But never mind about you, I'll have paté and then steak. Oh look, how nice, we're not going to lunch alone after all.' At that moment a group of people entered the dining room and made their way to a specially prepared table in one corner. As fortune would have it, there were splendid mirrors on the walls which enabled both men to observe the whole party. Lowry gave the newcomers his undivided attention. 'They're very quiet, Mr Marshall, what d'you make of it?'

'A funeral party, perhaps?'

'Oh no, Mr Marshall, I don't think so; you're not very observant in these matters. Looks more like a wedding to me, they're obviously suffering. Po'r things – look at 'em, not a smile on their faces.'

'The one to be most upset would be his mother – which d'you think's his mother?'

'Now, Mr Marshall, you haven't got the way of it at all. You're not experienced in these matters, I can see. It's *her* mother you've got to think about. The po'r little wretch – well, I hesitate to say.'

'Oh, dear! That had not occurred to me.'

'You're a novice in these things, Mr Marshall. Where's that waiter?'

'Where d'you think they're going for the honeymoon then?'

'Oh, need you ask – Majorca, where else?'

Before luncheon was over, they had the bridegroom in this innocuous wedding party in love with his mother-in-law, the bride in love with the best man, the bridesmaids in love with each other, the best man in love with the bridegroom, and the mother-in-law in love with the head waiter, while father was in love with a lesbian bridesmaid. And, as the party proceeded to eat in a gloomy and self-conscious silence, it was decided that Majorca was after all completely out of the question – the whole lot were heading straight for the divorce courts.

On these occasions, when the two men returned to the fold, as it were, all the events of the day were relived and the entire conversations were gone through time and again – what Lowry had said to Micky, and what Micky had said to Lowry. If one left a bit out the other would prompt him. The old painter would chuckle and chortle and splutter with bronchial coughs, dabbing his eyes with a fortnight-used handkerchief. He would ask permission to lie on the floor and, when given, he failed to have the courage to carry it out. Instead he would look slyly out of mirthfully watering eyes to announce yet again his impending demise. Whereupon we would all cheer, telling him to get on with it, comforting each other volubly with the prospect of a little peace once our tiresome friend had 'kicked the bucket'. Hearing our hilarity, Ella would wander in from the kitchen on some pretext, fearful lest she was missing the fun. She would urge Lowry to hurry up if he were going: after all he'd been talking about dying for far too long. She had the sheets handy for the laying out and she would like to get off home in good time. Lowry counteracted by demanding whether his lunch or tea were not ready yet. Just a little something before he went.

Year after year, nonsense of this kind continued. But one afternoon he appeared genuinely depressed. The end wouldn't be long now. He had a premonition that this would be his last visit – we wouldn't be seeing him again. 'No such luck,' I assured him. 'You'll be turning up again like a bad penny.'

His instant guffaw rocketed through the gallery. Up on his feet, out he pranced to the kitchen to tell Ella, 'Mrs Marshall doesn't think I'm for the next world yet. She thinks I'll be turning up again like a bad penny.'

'Why yes, so you will,' agreed Ella, 'I'd like to see the day you don't turn up.'

He was laughing helplessly as he returned to the office. 'My God! She's worse than you are – whatsername's worse than you are,' (Ella was usually 'whatsername' to Lowry). 'Oh, this is a rum place – my word, I do enjoy myself here.' His depression had vanished. Ella followed him into the room with a special cup of tea for his added comfort.

Lowry was not kept happy or equable by accepted methods. If the character of the man is to be understood this fact must be accepted. He loathed people to be obsequious, as they often were. I have quoted occasions when people were derogatory to his face about his work, and his modesty. Perhaps the same modesty prevented him from caring for overpraise.

'What are they after?' he would ask.

Once when Alice Bennett left the gallery, I exclaimed, 'Oh, I do enjoy seeing her!'

'Do you really?' he queried. 'I've never cared for her manner much m'self. I fancy she's too fulsome – aye too fulsome for my liking.' I remember looking at him with some surprise – I'd thought her charming. I was very sorry when she died.

Recently I asked Donald Gow who, for a number of years, was northern art correspondent for *The Times*, what his outstanding memory was of Lowry as a man.

'Oh,' he replied without hesitation, smiling widely, 'the first occasion I met him – in the Stone Gallery. He was sitting in a chair in the corner of the office. His suit was very food-spotted, almost as though he'd been painting. Then when I was introduced to him he sat back and promptly went to sleep. Well, it was a bit unusual to say the least. I was there to review his exhibition. I should have liked to talk to him but there he was, eyes closed and gently snoring. I never saw a man go to sleep so quickly! It was a bit of a shock, for I was a great admirer of his work. I've never forgotten it. I admired him the more!'

I recalled the occasion well. We had wanted Lowry to show to good advantage but alas, there he was being gloriously rude for he wasn't asleep at all. His brain would be ticking away ten to the dozen behind those closed eyes. But he loathed to be taken unawares by the press.

It may be thought that there were times when we dealt hardly with Lowry – but I think none knew better than he that for the most part we tried to see things went his way.

One night, Micky and I were returning him as usual to Seaburn. It was a dark wet night and my husband concentrated on the road ahead through the rain-swept windscreen. Lowry hitched himself around on his seat next to the driver, possibly trying to arrange his raincoat more comfortably. He shoved and pushed and pushed and shoved himself about. He was a big man of very considerable weight and he broke the back off his seat. It descended with a flop into my lap with Lowry after it.

Quickly I pushed the back of the seat and him forward, and over the miles to Sunderland I continued to hold both in position. For the life of me I cannot imagine why, rather than disturb him by suggesting that he get into the back of the car, I preferred to continue under this strain until we arrived at our destination. My arms and hands were numb, and I almost in tears. Perhaps it would take a psychologist to explain why I would not hesitate on more than one occasion to tell him to leave the gallery, never to return, and yet would go to a length such as this that he might not be put out. Equally it might require a psychologist to explain why, after that evening, Lowry never got into the car when I was present, without trying to break the back of his seat.

When Tilley's closed its doors for the last time, we had to look for another restaurant, close at hand if possible, to take its place. We were never to find another restaurant where the manager would have a cake specially made for Lowry's birthday. (Dinner finished, this was brought as a surprise to the table while restaurant and kitchen staff came to gather round and sing 'Happy birthday, Mr Lowry – happy birthday to you.')

There was a newish one nearby and in the hope that it might fill the gap we tried it. Never again. The tables were placed in cubicles and Lowry could neither see nor be seen. In place of his favoured white tablecloth, there were unaccustomed table mats. Lowry eyed these with an evil glint, and his mat eventually ended up under his feet. Despite instructions, the old man was served with sprouts. Quickly he pushed them off with his fork all over the table while I tried to scoop them up. Then he announced that it was ludicrous, simply fiendish (always a favourite word of disapproval), the table was far too close to him, and he did his utmost to push it over. To my relief it happened to be bolted to the floor, but his disappointment was immense.

Micky and I collected Lowry from Mottram one day and the three of us called at the King's Head in Darlington, where we were met by Simon, who after dinner drove Lowry on to Seaburn. It was quite a pleasant meal but for some reason the painter took an instant dislike to the head waiter, although he was giving us excellent attention. I mentally congratulated him upon bringing, unasked, a jug of water to the table.

'I hope you've diluted that water?' Lowry inquired of him fiercely, adding, almost before he was out of earshot, 'the fellow looks none too clean to me.' This was entirely untrue and, glancing at our guest, I thought he did not look too clean to me. But that is not entirely true either. Lowry's hands and face were always spotless – it was his suit that was the problem. His hair was always perfectly cut and cared for, and it was thick and silky to the end. As Simon began to lose his, he was envious of Lowry's hair.

Dinner continued; Lowry became more disgruntled and moody, his mind preoccupied – he was not himself. All was explained when, towards the end of the meal, the head waiter turned to ask, 'It is Mr Lowry, isn't it?' Grudgingly the painter agreed that it was (and he was not usually grudging in the admission). 'Do you remember, I wonder, I used to look after you at Berwick? And what a very nice young lady that was with you, in those days.' Lowry looked unhappy, his cheeks slightly flushed. I remembered there had been talk of a landlady's daughter at Berwick.

One winter night in February, I left my mother with a night nurse while I returned to the city to give Lowry dinner. I never saw my mother conscious again, and she died twenty-four hours later.

We hardly supposed that with the shock of my mother's death father would outlive her long but he lived for another six years, dying just short of his hundredth birthday. On his housekeeper's day off, he looked forward to lunching with us in the gallery during four of these years. He continued to take an interest in the visual arts and enjoyed seeing whatever exhibition we were showing. Aware that age bored Lowry, we asked the painter not to arrive until the afternoon on the days father came to lunch. Nevertheless, one day both had to be in together, and during luncheon father chatted away, smiled and talked of things he supposed might interest Lowry. As far as the painter was concerned the older man might not have been present. We tried to carry off the situation as best we could in an effort to prevent father feeling *de trop*.

It was a busy day and first Simon had to abandon his lunch, then Micky was called away, and finally I had to rush upstairs to help, leaving the two elderly men to demolish their pudding together. I returned some time later to find them chuckling and laughing, as Lowry turned in good humour to inquire, 'Any more of that very good pudding? Oh dear me – your father's been making me laugh, Mrs Marshall. He says you're very bossy, and what's more, you always were!'

'Thanks very much.'

'He's been telling me that when you were about three you were sent on some errand, and were too small to be seen over the top of the counter, so you banged on it with your money, shouting "Tum and serve me, please." '

'Oh, that's one of his old favourites.'

'And the lady who told him about it complained you were too young to cross the road alone.'

'I was very good at crossing roads. My brothers and I played lasty across and I always won. Once my knickers fell down and I was all but run over by a lorry. I can remember the driver yelling at me now and threatening blue murder, while my brothers pretended they weren't with me.' I thought Lowry would never stop laughing. After that he got along very well with father.

I was by no means the only one to find Lowry nerve-racking. There were occasions when the painter was a heavy burden for Carol to cope with, and there could be little doubt that the time spent with us eased the burden for her. Seeing the tension she was under one winter when they were staying at the County Hotel in Newcastle, and Lowry's habit of sitting up in her bedroom until all hours had got her down, I told her either Micky or Simon would run her home there and then. All she craved was her freedom: she cared neither for what she was to inherit, nor for Lowry's well-intentioned organizing of her life. I admired her greatly for the manner in which she saw the visit out. Shortly afterwards Micky, Ian and I pleaded with the artist to be less demanding. We were aware that Carol was his heiress but we had no means of knowing how he was placed financially. We begged him that, if he could afford to do so, he should make Carol financially independent. This he did in some measure when she went to the Isle of Man to work and, until she married, Lowry enjoyed occasional visits to the island. He had known it as a younger man, and found that it had remained very much as he remembered it.

When Lowry said we might expect him at a certain time he was invariably prompt to the minute. One bank-holiday Saturday he failed to put in his expected appearance during the morning and we became anxious. Micky rang his hotel to learn that he had gone out as usual – apparently in the best of health. We put off lunch as long as possible, but still he failed to appear. We had visions of the poor soul either in hospital or some cold morgue.

In mid-afternoon he landed in as large as life and full of apology. He had taken the train to Newcastle that morning instead of his number nine bus. At the city's crowded central station, with its mass of holiday makers, he had become so engrossed observing the comings and goings of the public that he had sat himself on a seat and forgotten the passing of time.

He'd been fascinated by one couple who could not have been more than twenty-one or two. She carried a baby, he had a tot in his arms, while another not much older clung to his jacket. The girl turned to look at her husband with an expression of hatred so all-consuming that Lowry was expecting to read of a murder.

Then he had seen a small child fall heavily. She was very brave and there were no tears until her mother hauled her to her feet and landed her an almighty smack, shouting, 'What did you want to go and do that for, Sandra?' Sandra, not having wanted to at all, dissolved into yells of outraged pain, only to receive a second slap, with 'What are y'crying for Sandra?'

Lowry had sadly watched the weeping toddler out of sight, pondering the oddness of the human race. 'How d'you account for it, Mr Marshall? How d'you account for there being more tension about these days than when people were less well off? Oh, I could have sat there all day – just watching the tension. That's why I enjoy drawing so much – you can get the tension between folk better in a drawing than in a painting.'

I remember Lowry standing in the sunlight one brilliant spring afternoon, as he gazed across the green lawns to the beautiful view of Wallington Hall in Northumberland, now owned by the National Trust.

In 1856 Sir Walter and Pauline, Lady Trevelyan, commissioned the painter William Bell Scott to decorate the new central hall with scenes from Northumbrian history. Bell Scott had come from London to Newcastle in 1844 to open the new Government School of Design. He was to become a great friend of D. G. Rossetti, who introduced him to the other Pre-Raphaelites. For many years Scott was made welcome at Wallington by the Trevelyans, as were Ruskin, the Millais brothers (until John Millais married Effie Ruskin), and many others connected with the arts and sciences. Frequently I had argued with Lowry that Ford Madox Brown was influenced in his painting by Bell Scott rather than the reverse as is always supposed. We had arrived at Wallington this day to settle the argument once and for all. Not that one ever settled an argument with Lowry, for he revelled in resurrecting them.

Lowry was more than familiar with Madox Brown's famous painting *Work*, of 1863, in Manchester City Art Gallery; we had often viewed it there with him. It is this particular painting which is always thought to have influenced Scott's splendid *Iron and Steel*, the last of his eight Wallington panels. Lowry decided that it was high time he saw the Wallington murals and here he was gazing across at the great mansion. Leaning back on his walking stick he sighed, 'My God! Those painters knew where to hang up their hats, didn't they?' I sensed some regret on his own part that he had failed to find so splendid a hatstand for himself.

When I pointed out to him that William Bell Scott's panels had been completed and exhibited in London in 1861 – whereas Madox Brown's *Work* was not completed until 1863, nor were any of his small replicas of the same subject, although he had certainly commenced them much earlier – Lowry showed some dissatisfaction, and still more so when he learned that each Wallington picture, when completed, had been photographed, and Scott had sent copies to Brown, who kept these by him. As Lowry had to agree, Brown showed a much greater diversity of style throughout his lifetime's painting than Scott ever did. And then Scott was not a man to feel he had much to learn from another.

There continued to be some dissatisfaction as Lowry walked around the interior of the wonderful house, not open that day to the general public. Moving about with his usual abrupt, slouching stride, walking stick tucked perilously through one arm, he almost swept a lovely marble head of Pauline, Lady Trevelyan, from its resting place on the grand piano in the great hall, and then just avoided poking a hole in more than one of poor Scott's paintings. He expressed approval of Thomas Woolner's large sculpture – rather to my surprise – but on seeing a watercolour by Ruskin he fancied the fellow should have stuck to his writing.

As we travelled homewards Lowry announced that people put too much emphasis upon the dating of pictures, and that he didn't envy anyone in the future who tried to prove a point from the dating of his own works. One had to concede him a victory there, for he would often inquire what date he should put on some work or other, and Micky would say that so-and-so was a good vintage year. . . . 'Oh yes, you're a good lad, we'll have that, Mr Marshall!' There would be no consistency, and any dating of a Lowry work can be plus or minus ten.

There were many drives out and about. Lowry loved Tan Hill,

rather to my surprise. This is the highest inn in England, situated in North Yorkshire and incredibly isolated. During one of Carol's vacations from Swansea College of Art, Lowry suggested that Simon and a friend should drive her over to Tan Hill for the day, it being a good place, in Lowry's opinion, for her to paint a landscape. Alas, when the three youngsters returned, Carol's little canvas was remarkably blank – and Lowry remarkably displeased.

No matter how late we would drop Lowry at his Seaburn Hotel, he usually had a walk along the front. In his shabby raincoat and battered trilby, he could look a pathetic figure as we waved goodbye to him. Photographs of the artist do not give a correct impression of his appearance, which was very run-down and virtually tramp-like. Indeed, had he looked more prosperous, one would have had fears for his safety on those late-night strolls, for he had various stories to recount of violence to which he had been a witness on these occasions. But he was a hard old nut, without, it would seem, any fear that he might be a victim of such an incident.

Very occasionally, should we arrive at the Seaburn Hotel with him rather earlier than the accustomed hour of return, we would sit for a while with him in the residents' lounge; this was on the southerly end of the building, with windows overlooking the front, and constantly illuminated by the neon lights outside. His bedroom, again overlooking the front, was always very neat and extraordinarily impersonal, with its single bed and his brown leather suitcase standing to attention. Latterly, in his bathroom, instead of a bath mat, two large paper 'footprints' were provided, on which he was supposed to alight when emerging from his bath – an impossible accomplishment for Lowry, but an idea in which he found enormous amusement. In his last years he found it difficult to get in and out of a bath, let alone land on a pair of paper feet.

It was on these occasions that the man whom we could find fearsome, bullying, boring, understanding, gentle, artistically knowledgeable, mischievous, trouble-making, fascinating – in short, the many-sided artist L. S. Lowry – could suddenly dissolve into the most pitiful of souls. Anger, irritability and mirth would suddenly give way to an enormous sense of pity for the elderly figure, as we drove away into the night. We would look back to wave a farewell and he would be standing watching the car so long as it remained in sight. This overruling sense of pity – once felt never entirely to be forgotten – seemed to have woven a cord which bound us to him.

8

After Pru ceased acting as our secretary, she was succeeded by a girl with the most extraordinary Pre-Raphaelite hair. As she bent over her desk she might have been Jane Morris herself. Lowry would murmour comfortably in his chair in the office, 'Ah, all's well with the world, there's *Proserpine* hard at work outside.' Then there was Susan, a charmingly pretty local beauty queen. She arrived for her interview one evening when Lowry was in the gallery. As Micky came out of the office with this young lovely, he introduced her to the artist, and to me and Ian who were sitting expectantly around the reception area. Introductions over, Micky said we would be seeing more of her, and Lowry, totally out of character, said yes, he hoped so; and, after agreement and the usual encouragement from Ian, Lowry added that as she was wearing trousers it was to be hoped that her legs would meet with their approval.

Ian gave a legal nod, adding, 'Indeed yes, sir – it is to be hoped so.'

Over all the years I had never seen Lowry quite so uninhibited as this on first meeting a young girl. Susan was not a beauty queen for nothing. Wrinkling her retroussé nose and showing her perfect teeth in a mischievous smile while she carelessly pushed back a mass of waving auburn-gold hair, she won all hearts.

Six months before Simon and Veral were married, our future daughter-in-law became our secretary. Veral is tall, well built, with curly dark hair, small features and large dark eyes. Hard working, and most reliable in any crisis, she always got along splendidly with Lowry, and when I was in London she would look after his every comfort.

Just three days before the private wedding in September 1972, Lowry decided that he would like to have a run out in the car with

Simon to see the flat they were to move into at Blagdon. They turned through the gates of the main entrance to Blagdon Hall, the home of Matthew and Anne Ridley. Lowry gazed up at the white bulls facing each other as they recline on top of the tall stone pillars on either side. 'Where are we now?' he asked, as ever. As they drove slowly along the deserted drive in the August afternoon sun, they passed the cricket pitch with its white pavilion. 'Ah, that's the place, is it?' he asked.

Simon explained that it wasn't, they were on their way to a flat in the courtyard. A lake lay on the right, with a small white bridge one end, which was surmounted along each side with stone busts of long-deceased members of the Ridley family. Beyond, the aged-looking and slightly green-moulding figures sculpted by Lough reclined or stood in the longish grass. Lowry had eyes for none of this. He saw a notice which read 'Private Beyond Here', and clutched Simon's arm.

'My God, Simon – stop. You mustn't go any further – we're not allowed any further.' Simon told him to brace himself if he wanted to see the flat. As they drove on through the archway of the clock-tower and arrived in the courtyard, Lowry was convinced their arrest was imminent. But over the next three years it all became very familiar to him.

They returned to the gallery and Lowry expressed great satisfaction at the prospect of Simon's new home being so close and convenient to the city. 'Oh yes, a very nice flat indeed – I shall enjoy going there.' And he did.

He returned to Mottram the next day, and Carol arrived the following morning. She looked happy and very chic, and carried an armful of red roses for me and a delightful present for Simon. No other girl of our acquaintance would have taken the trouble to fly in for the day from the Isle of Man and we loved seeing her.

Simon and Veral were away for three weeks. On the day they were due back, Micky and I, who had been doing various things at the flat in their absence, went out in the afternoon to put some finishing touches. We filled the fridge, set the dinner table and the drinks tray, and filled bowls with fruit. As I was arranging the last vase of flowers, the telephone rang. I heard Ella's laughing voice inquire, 'Guess who's here?'

'I don't know, Ella, who?'

'Mr Lowry!'

'Oh, Christ *no*! Not today of all days.'

'Yes, but don't worry, he won't have heard that yell. He's just in the "library" [Lowry's term for the loo]. But he wants to know where you are, what you're doing, and how long you're going to be.'

'But he knew Simon and Veral were due back today!'

'Oh yes, he hadn't forgotten, because he says he's going to have dinner with them.'

'Over my dead body. Oh, Ella, not on their first night home.'

'Well, you'd better get yourselves back here; I wouldn't like to try and talk him out of it. And you want your tea – don't you, Mr Lowry? I'll start it up.' I took the hint that he had returned to the office.

I broke the news to Micky as I put the last vase in place and surveyed the pretty sitting room as the early autumn afternoon sunlight filtered through the small square-paned windows. I could hardly credit that Lowry had chosen this of all days for his return. We had been looking forward enormously to welcoming the 'children' back, but in the meantime we hastened to meet the old man in the gallery.

How was he? 'Dying. Fed up. Absolutely bloody well fed up, Mrs Marshall. Always callers at that dreadful house of mine. I couldn't stay there a moment longer. There's never been a moment's peace there. Everyone always wanting something for nothing.' It went on and on.

I passed round the tea, and we tried to raise his spirits. 'How is Carol?'

'Well, I understand you've seen her since I have. She doesn't write often enough – and oh, dear me, I wish her handwriting were better.'

At about 5.30, I hardened my heart for the first and only occasion. Micky ordered a taxi for Lowry, and I must say he took his departure well, assuring us that he would be in the following day at his usual hour for morning coffee.

Next evening, in her strange kitchen, hardly aware of what was in which cupboard or drawer, Veral cooked her first 'private-house chicken' for Lowry. It was the forerunner of many. I suppose it was also the only time I recall him being receptive to beauty as most people are receptive to it. He remarked upon the flowers, asking who had arranged them. 'Tilly,' Veral told him.

'I think they're very beautiful,' he answered, and Tilly nearly dropped down dead.

He loved to arrive at the flat in the early evening and hurl himself into a huge armchair, reminiscent of the ones in his own sitting room at The Elms. He would recline almost flat on his back, his long legs stretched to the fire, winter or summer. He would demolish a dish of his favourite nuts and sip his orange squash. Simon's marriage put an end to eternal restaurants.

Veral had some embarrassing moments, of course, such as the night the vicar called unexpectedly. He was introduced to this elderly 'Mr Lowry', and obviously supposed him to be some unfortunately placed old relative to whom these worthy young folk were giving a little comfort and shelter. Lowry snored soundly in his chair while Veral prayed, as I had so often, that the heavy wink bestowed upon her from time to time might not be observed. At last there was a loud whisper from Lowry – was Veral sure the dinner was taking no harm?

He enjoyed the young Ridley daughters looking in. The three Hons. (Lowry was quite unaware he was using an old Mitfordism when he referred to them so) were extremely pretty and attractive girls: Cecilia and Rose tall and dark haired, and the youngest, Mary – nicknamed Miss Mary by her family – delighted the artist. Mary is a highly organized and efficient person with, as Lowry said, 'All her chairs at home.' And he was greatly taken with their Dandie Dinmont, boasting the name of Fuzz-Wuzz. 'Ah, that's a champion little dog,' he would smile, 'champion little dog.' He was not quite so fond of Moley, one of three chocolate labradors. Moley enjoyed visiting. She was an inveterate scavenger, and if she reached the newly delivered groceries before Veral she would quickly demolish a pound of bacon. Once or twice the chicken was served ungarnished.

Lowry enjoyed a trip across the courtyard to the hall for an evening drink. We had been asked to bring him for luncheon years before but, perhaps a little naughtily, I always made an excuse. Ten to one he might have called it off at the last moment, depending upon how he felt: I had reached the stage where I was prepared for his tantrums with us but no longer cared to inflict them unnecessarily upon others. An evening drink was another matter, however, for then he could move around at will, looking at the pictures. Hands in pockets, hitching his trousers, he could see again one of his own paintings hanging beneath a Rubens or, across the room, admire a favourite William Nicholson, for which Matthew's mother (a daughter of Edwin Lutyens) had been the model as a child. There were many works to interest him, and so for this short time he would enjoy himself.

He delighted in a tame collar dove called Hamish, who would perch himself on Anne's head, occasionally gently crapping on her dark hair. This enthralled Lowry. He would chuckle over the memory of it and once said that he would dearly love to make a drawing of it: *Woman with Bird on Head.*

'Oh you must,' I urged him.

'No, no – I couldn't do that. It wouldn't do at all. Why, she's not a woman – she's a viscountess!'

Matthew and Anne were in New Zealand when Lowry died, and the news of his death was one of the few items from Britain to be publicized there during the visit.

'We *shall* miss him,' exclaimed Matthew. 'He virtually lived across the yard.'

The time Lowry spent with us during his last four years was passed in gentler mood than the ten preceding ones.

In days of crisis when there were strikes, three-day weeks, electricity cuts and blackouts he would arrive hastily and unannounced from Mottram to be reassured, comforted, warmed and fed. Once we returned from London to find him chuckling agreeably in the candlelit office, delightedly warming himself before a newly acquired stove. Simon had gone out hastily to purchase it, unable to support the sight of the old man shivering over the small one which was enough for him.

We went less and less to Mottram. Someone had to be in London more frequently now, and when Simon and Veral were there Micky and I would stay at their flat so that we might care for Lowry during the evenings. Lowry had also made good friends at Seaburn with Mr and Mrs Earnshaw and 'Little Earnshaw', as he would refer to their daughter, at least until she was married. Mr Earnshaw very kindly drove Lowry home to Mottram on occasion.

We had another factor to consider at this time, for the painter informed us that he wished to clear most of his own paintings out of The Elms, as he had no desire for them to be found in the house when he died. The more found at the time of his death, the higher would be the charge upon his estate. Because of high taxation he had no wish to sell the works. He still maintained his attitude of 1968 when we had shown his final important paintings. So we took no part in this clearing out. Nevertheless he had decided to exchange a splendid painting called *Open Space* for the last Rossetti he was to acquire – a large pastel drawing, *Pandora*, which he wished to give to Carol in the spring of 1968.

He gave his last large mill scene, *Going to Work*, to Manchester's Reform Club (so he said). As he started this clearing up, he suggested that if Micky would go over to Mottram he would give him certain paintings. At the same time, he still moaned continuously, 'Everyone wants something for nothing!' Micky's attitude remained as it had been from the first – and he declined Lowry's offer.

He used to say that his mother's favourite painting of his own, *Yachts at Lytham*, which was the one I had taken down from above his bed and which he was aware Micky admired, was to come to my husband. But he made no arrangements for this, nor did we seriously suppose he had. He had given Simon a wedding present, of course, and later gave him a splendid drawing. Constantly, as he sat opposite where it hung in the living room of the flat, he would promise another to go with it, but none materialized.

We realized over the last two years that Lowry was feeling his age at last. No longer was his talk of being 'fed up' merely talk for the sake of it. Now we had to accept that he was genuinely sick of the world in which he found himself. Often after dinner, stretching out those long old legs as he reclined in his favourite chair, he would assert that he had lived too long; he had seen too much change for what he considered the worse. He failed to appreciate or even understand much of contemporary British life. He found unacceptable a nation forever faced with strikes and industrial unrest. It frightened him and he was not by nature a fearful man. Shipyards short of work disturbed him; he had always loved busy shipyards and docks. Lowry had a dislike of nationalization for the simple reason that it apparently failed to work to the greater good of the populace. He would have had no complaints had it been otherwise. His down-to-earth mind was unable to reconcile public ownership of certain industries and services with workers striking against themselves and their fellows.

‘ “Security is mortals’ chiefest enemy,” – you remember that, Mrs Marshall? Well, take it from me, the enemy’s within the door now!’

He had no stomach for unions calling their members out on strike, while the taxpayer footed the bill to support the families of those members. He suffered if he found himself without the light and heat necessary to his age and saw himself contributing, through his taxation, to his own misery. Postal services had been better and speedier in the nineteenth century. Railway fares were ‘fiendish’. Electricity was rapidly becoming too expensive for many to use for adequate heating. Lowry rated striking miners and electricity workers, or any who went on strike to the detriment of their fellows, little better than those who had run concentration camps. The end did not justify the means.

He loathed the violence of football mobs and always considered that it was only required to make an example of a few to benefit the many. He hated mugging and constantly congratulated the judge who gave two youths twenty years for this offence. He fancied the public benefited immediately from the legal gentleman’s courageous action in an era of muddled-thinking do-gooders whom Lowry despised.

He abhorred terrorism in every form. He considered that dictatorship had come to our democracy through fanatical leadership of the unions. He had no disapproval of the unions in their correct and proper function but it was his opinion that they were now a threat to democratic government.

It appeared ironic to him that a civilization sufficiently clever – ‘oh, fiendishly clever!’ – to travel to the moon could not solve the parking problems in its cities. This was no joke where Lowry was concerned as it became a perilous business putting him in the car at the gallery door. Countless Newcastle bus drivers have yelled at him, ‘What the hell are you doing, you silly old bugger?’ as they just avoided putting an end to Britain’s most famous living painter. And the poor old soul was only minding his own business. Three people have been killed on the road at our door. Quite simple measures would remove the danger but, as Lowry would say, ‘Whatever bureaucracy is or isn’t, it’s never simple.’

Constantly he mourned the rapidly diminishing individuality of city centres such as Manchester’s or Newcastle’s, in favour of mass uniformity. Night after night he would tell us of the days he had known when people had less money but greater happiness. There had been fewer divorces, less permissiveness, drug addiction, cigarette smoking, less terror and greater honour. This was not the most cheerful company at times for two newly marrieds. But, as the signs of genuine weariness and disillusionment continued, our son would admonish us all to be gentle and patient while he and Veral gave unstintingly of their own happiness.

Lowry would sit longer and longer, legs outstretched to the warmth, muttering his constant discontents until one or other of us would prompt him into some familiar and more pleasant remembrance. But before long he would be back, recounting the story of a friend who had become intolerant of the demands of his workpeople, for, in Lowry's opinion, it was quite unnecessary to strike for a second car and a holiday in his much-despised Majorca. One Friday his friend gave the order for his factory to close and it never went into production again. He failed to accept that the workers could have, and probably would have, staged a sit-in nowadays.

Micky would try to move the conversation to safer ground, recalling comedians both had seen long years before, and Lowry would explode with guffaws as he found himself referring to one of Gracie Fields's husbands as Monty Bloom and through bronchial splutters would demand of me, 'Dammit, what was the fellow's name?'

'Monty Banks.'

'Aye, that's right. What did she want to go and marry him for?' And at the thought of this non-British marriage he would sink himself back into a new gloom. 'Ah, dear me, I've lived too long, you know.'

We would try a little consolation by reminding him that it must have been nice to have a good innings and after all he had lived to see his own fame and success, unlike Van Gogh.

'Well, no – I should hope not – there was a fool if ever there was one. No time for him.' He would laugh again when he remembered sitting with Simon in the gallery office when a young painter rang to inquire whether we were interested in living artists. Yes, he was assured; it was suggested that if he cared to bring in a few works we would give an opinion.

'Oh, I know how Van Gogh felt now!' exploded the caller.

'Right, then go and cut off your ear,' retorted Simon.

Lowry never lost his sense of humour and his sense of the ridiculous – there was fun even during his last two years. There were far fewer trips out and about as he said he didn't want to go anywhere any more – he just liked sitting around the office where Micky and he would continue their nonsense. One day after luncheon they decided to give us a sample of a model TV interview. Holding out the microphone Micky asked [Marshall tape recording]: 'Mr Lowry, I understand that you've had one or two affairs of the heart?'

'Oh yes, two or three you know.'

'Tell us more.'

'I can't remember more – two or three was quite enough – they've faded now.'

'Can I jog your memory? Simon, fetch over the hammer.'

'I'm afraid it's no use – they're all gone now. It's years since I had a heart. . . .'

'You can say that again,' I laughed.

'I understand that you have in your home a colour television set in every room?'

'In every room, sir! And on the roof – don't forget the one on the roof.'

'Aren't you thinking of the aerial?'

'No, I like watching television on the roof – it's a deal more comfortable than m'sitting room.'

'Oh yes, how interesting. And do you keep your Rolls-Royce in the back garage or the front garage?'

'Oh, the back garage.'

'What d'you have in the front garage?'

'Another Rolls-Royce.'

'Another Rolls-Royce. Indeed. So would you say you were a man of means?'

'*No*!'

'Would you say you were a mean man?'

'Yes.'

'And I understand you're setting a new movement afoot for an increase in income tax?'

'I would like to see an increase in income tax, yes, sir. Undoubtedly. It would encourage me to paint more.'

'And consequently this would indicate that you are entirely satisfied with the present government?'

'My God, yes, *entirely* satisfied.'

'You are a supporter of Mr Wilson?'

'*Absolutely*, sir.' The interviewer was interrupted by terrible and ironic laughter from the interviewed.

'What are the qualities in Mr Wilson that you admire so much?'

'His integrity. And of course his slag heaps.'

'What is your earliest memory?'

'Chopping up m'mother's sideboard. Not all of it, of course – but the front panels.'

'Why?'

'Well, it was something to do, and I thought how nice it would look chopped up. M'mother didn't agree with me over that.'

'Was it perhaps of inferior design?'

'*No*! It was a very good design. Good God no, sir, if it had been of a bad design I wouldn't have bothered.'

'What are your plans for the future?'

'None. I'm expecting to demise very shortly, sir, so there's no point in going to the trouble of creating plans.'

'But have you not made plans for your demise? Are we to expect a big tea afterwards?'

'Oh, no tea, sir! No, I can't afford tea. No sir, oh, no tea.'

'But that would be a first charge on the estate wouldn't it?'

'Oh, I don't think there'll be any estate, sir.'

'If we knew when it was going to happen we could make an appointment to see the Madox Brown murals either before or after,' I interrupted. 'There's always been a fellow playing the organ or something whenever I've tried to see them.'

'Oh, but you've got to make an appointment, Mrs Marshall.'

'Yes, but Ian didn't. Princess Margaret was being entertained when he called – and he not only saw the murals but partook of free refreshment!'

'He was a very fortunate gentleman at that rate – but you forget, Mrs Marshall, he specializes in law – he can talk his way in or out of anywhere; but with that eternal dispatch case of his, which may well have a bomb in it, and that suspicious-looking raincoat – well, I'm sure they wouldn't have let me in, and I always look so well dressed!'

During the years Lowry brought Carol most frequently to the gallery she had two boyfriends. The first was a fellow student at Swansea College of Art. David lived in the town; he was every inch a Welshman. His parents died and left him a ready-made home. He had a car and, should Lowry be staying at the Dragon Hotel in Swansea, David would drive the three of them about. One summer he came to spend a week at Seaburn with Carol and Uncle. I gave a small dinner party for him to meet some young friends. He was quiet, unassuming, and very good looking, with an interest in rugby football. Carol considered him a little dull and I agreed with her.

When their student days were over, Carol saw no more of David, who promptly married. She now lived with her mother in a Rochdale council flat and taught art at a local school where she became very attached to a fellow teacher, a master of English. Sam was a real Lancashire lad. He called in to see us once or twice without Carol as he visited the gallery. He was not a particularly prepossessing young man to look at – but amusing. Carol found him fun. Lowry was perturbed. He had been permitted to meet David – why was he never allowed to meet Sam?

At the time when Simon became engaged to Veral, Carol became engaged to Sam. This engagement lasted a month. Lowry made a gift of twenty thousand pounds to Carol, and off she went to the Isle of Man to teach art in a Ramsey school. Lowry would go to the island for occasional visits – his energy was still remarkable. Carol told me that after these visits she felt worn out.

She originally stayed in a Ramsey guest house, then took a flat, having some of her possessions sent over, then between moves she returned to the guest house. Here she met a property developer, John Spiers. Originally from Kent, he was a tax exile, but not a Manx resident – which Carol now was. However, he was developing a property there, and Carol moved into a cottage he owned and lived with him. She wrote to me frequently; she did not hide the fact that she was living with John from either Lowry or her mother.

'My God! D'you think she's going to marry this fellow?' Lowry asked me.

'Yes, that's for sure,' I replied. It was. Carol became John Spiers's third wife. She told neither Lowry nor her mother that she was marrying until it was a *fait accompli*. From this Lowry never really recovered. He was not angry – only unbelievably hurt. The hurt remained. He reconciled himself to the loss of Carol's company; he would murmur, 'I've done the job as well as I could. She's seen a bit of the world, and can stand on her own feet now. If I hadn't taken a hand she'd probably have married at seventeen and had half a dozen kids by the time she was twenty-five.' A worse fate for a girl than that Lowry could not imagine.

After Carol's marriage the artist repeatedly affirmed that he intended to change his will. 'She's had all she's getting out of me!' He once met Carol's husband (before they were married), and he had not cared for the gentleman. The three of them had dined together and John Spiers had talked only about himself and his own affairs, which did not interest Lowry – who had been left to foot the bill! 'He can afford an aeroplane – he could have given me dinner,' announced the artist.

He would talk endlessly about making a new will. But what should he do now? I reminded him of his old intention to leave everything to the RA Benevolent Fund should such a situation as this arise. 'Oh, but not *now*!' he exclaimed in anger. 'That was before Fitton voted against my work being chosen for the postage stamp. I'll not have Fitton benefit.'

I suggested that James Fitton might not need to benefit. Lowry retorted, 'Aye – but again he might!'

Lowry no longer visited the Isle of Man. Carol and John went on a six-month honeymoon travelling abroad. To all intents and purposes Carol had gone out of Lowry's life.

We left behind us the densely shrouded moors in the early morning light. The wipers swished to and fro as the fog and mist gathered on the windscreen of the car. Micky and I were the passengers, Simon was driving.

Ten days before Lowry had rung Veral at the gallery to say he would be with us the following Tuesday – 17 February. Convenient or not, he was always with us at that time. The heavens might fall but Lowry would stick to his routine.

It was not the heavens that fell – it was Lowry.

He fell the evening of the day he had told Veral how guilty he was feeling; he had promised Mr Marshall to visit him in hospital and had failed to do so. To be honest, none of us had expected him. Lowry was not one for hospital visiting. Now it was Micky who was going to visit and Lowry who was in hospital.

If the artist were home, Philip Robertson would call every Thursday night for a chat, and 12 February 1976 was no exception. At about nine o'clock he pulled up his car at the door of The Elms and knocked. There was no reply. Seeing a light on in the sitting room, he knocked louder and then raised the flap of the letter box to see if all was well. He heard Lowry calling that he had fallen and could not get up.

Philip went quickly for Mrs Swindles and they found Lowry sprawled on the passage floor. He had apparently slipped on a mat, for it and his pocket book and other things were scattered about him in disorder. They managed to get Lowry into his chair in the sitting room but the painter refused to have his doctor called. It transpired that he did not have one. Eventually some first aid ambulance men arrived who considered that nothing was broken nor radically wrong, and Lowry insisted on staying in his chair. Philip called in the help of a mutual friend, Frank Whalley, and eventually the old man was persuaded to retire to bed at about two o'clock in the morning. Even as Philip followed him upstairs he turned irritably to demand, 'What are y'coming up here for?' He was assured that it was merely to see him safely to his room.

Two days later Lowry's condition had deteriorated, and Philip was successful in getting him admitted to the Woods Hospital in Glossop, only a matter of minutes from his home.

As we motored across to Glossop on Sunday, 22 February, my mind wandered again over the events of the last six days – days of continuous telephone calls. The first had come early on the Monday morning as I was taking coffee to Micky who was convalescing after a major operation. Apparently Philip Robertson had endeavoured to telephone us the previous day but, as our home number was ex-directory, had had to wait until the gallery was open on the Monday to reach us. It was Lowry's wish that only we and the Bennetts should be told of his indisposition. Neither Carol nor her mother was to be informed; but he had been due at Mrs Lowry's on the Sunday, so she had to be told.

Philip's information was that the artist was bearing up as well as might be expected, but pneumonia had set in and it was considered advisable to keep details of his illness from the press. The hospital was small and would scarcely have known what had hit it if the identity of its new patient leaked out. It was thought prudent, therefore, to announce that he was merely suffering from influenza.

That evening Carol contacted me to say that she and Mr Alick Leggat (an old friend and client of Lowry's) had come over together that day from the Isle of Man. She had seen Uncle and had been asked by the hospital not to visit for another week. However, she was determined to continue visiting each day and would stay with her mother in Rochdale meanwhile. I received another bulletin from Philip, who said that Lowry would like to see us but, on being reminded that Micky was also on the sick list, said how stupid of him to have forgotten. Nevertheless Philip urged me that if it were at all possible we should go over. I regretted that it seemed totally out of the question.

On Tuesday there were more phone calls and the latest news. Lowry appeared to be bearing up. On Wednesday Carol announced that Uncle wanted to see Micky, and she had assured him that Micky was totally recovered now and would undoubtedly be going to visit. I was shocked, but when I informed my husband of this development he looked wearily at me, saying, 'Then I shall go.'

'*Go*? What do you mean? You can't go – the doctor wouldn't allow it!'

'He won't know. Simon can drive us over, I shall go. If Carol's said that – I can't let him down.'

'But we hear conflicting reports – one moment visitors aren't allowed – the next he's seen various people. Mr Bennett was there Monday apparently, and his wife is going Saturday. Carol tells me that Mr Leggat went to The Elms today, contacted Mrs Swindles, collected up all the mail, and spent hours reading it to Lowry this afternoon. Well, that's daft for a start – the old boy didn't bother with his post when he was well!'

In fairness to the hospital I had considered it more helpful to learn of the artist's condition at second hand, but in view of Carol's assurance to Lowry I decided I should have to ring the matron myself the following morning. She told me that Lowry was very ill indeed, and allowed no visitors other than Mr Robertson and Mr Whalley.

'And Mr Leggat also?' I inquired.

'Oh yes, Mr Leggat, of course, because he's his executor, and as such he must visit.'

'Mr Leggat an executor? He's certainly not.'

'Are you sure?' I told the matron I was very sure. I then told her of my own dilemma and explained that the last thing I wanted to do was to subject Lowry to a visit if her decision was otherwise. I was constantly hearing that he wanted to see my husband, who had recently undergone a major operation, and so I'd no wish to subject him to this visit either, were it not absolutely essential. The matron said she would go at once and ask Mr Lowry if he did indeed wish to see Mr Marshall. She returned shortly to confirm that such was the case. I said that our son would take us over on the Sunday.

Now here we were, already over the Pennines, with the sun unexpectedly shining as we motored into Glossop. Philip had kindly suggested we call on them first; he and his wife Margaret made us most welcome. Over a cup of coffee we learned the latest news of the patient, who had appeared in good spirits the previous evening. Mr Leggat had caught a cold on Thursday and wasn't able to visit.

A short while later Philip took us round to the hospital and knocked on the matron's door. It was opened by a very efficient, precise, no-nonsense Irish lady. She failed to catch our name upon introduction, only grasping the essential fact that we'd come to visit her famous patient. Eyeing us sternly, she announced without more ado, 'Oh, if you're another lot come to fight over the old man's paintings – you can forget it!'

Later I was to wonder what on earth had been going on, but at this time I was in no mood to mince my words either. I snapped, 'We've come, I hope, to give – not to receive!'

Then, on hearing our name, her face cleared, 'Oh, I'm sorry – you're the people who rang up, of course.' She suggested that Mr Robertson show us to Lowry's room. We followed him along a passage, he opened a door and left us. The room was like a small cottage bedroom rather than a hospital room. It had two beds, but only the one near the window was occupied.

The old artist was propped high on pillows, his breathing very heavy, his arms stretched out straight before him. The fine hands, palms down, looked strangely small and stiff on the white cover. Even allowing for the absence of teeth, his face was startlingly shrunken. He seemed only half the size of the man remembered.

A nurse was giving him some nourishment from a feeding cup. She turned to smile and say, 'There, we're nearly finished – we shan't be a moment now.' I looked at the many get-well cards, and saw the humorous one we had sent. I longed to tear it up as I gazed at the sad wreck of the man we had known. As the nurse completed her task our friend turned his face to her with a savage grimace – as though to bite the hand that fed him.

The nurse left the room with another smile and a nod, and Micky moved to the bed. Lowry gazed up at him with a sort of awe. 'My God – so you've come . . . you've come. You always promised to be with me at the end, didn't you? Yes, you always promised.'

The years of fun and teasing dropped away; how seldom we'd met Lowry when he hadn't immediately talked of his end. This time it was for real.

'Oh, come now, I'm not here to keep that old promise, it's not time for that yet,' I heard Micky saying gently.

'You're wrong y'know . . . it is the end this time.'

'No, no, I've come to see you because you didn't keep your promise to visit me in hospital; so the mountain's had to come to Mahomet.'

'I fancy it's not such a big mountain as it was. . . .' Lowry tried a weak smile, then started coughing, eventually to repeat again, 'My God – you've come.' Solemnly he held Micky's gaze with his own, his speech was slow and difficult as they talked together. At the other side of the bed Simon moved nearer and the old man turned his head to see who it was. 'Well, I never – if it's not S-S-Simon. Oh, how very nice to see you, Simon.' Minus his teeth Lowry had a little difficulty with the name. Now the coughing was taking over, insistent and continuous. We waited for it to stop, but it just went on and on. He was far nearer death than any of his friends had led us to suppose. Aware of this, it never occurred to me to draw attention to the fact that I was there as well, as I stood at the foot of the bed listening to Micky gently talking, with Lowry unable to answer for his coughing. I heard Micky telling him he must rest now, he would be in again shortly to see him.

The sound of continuous coughing followed us down the passage.

Micky knocked again on the matron's door. He had come armed with a list of consultants and impressed upon the matron that he would personally take responsibility for calling in the foremost specialist opinion, should she consider this advisable. No expense must be spared.

Emphatically she shook her head. 'No, he will die here. He is terribly ill. He's had several strokes, he has pneumonia and, even if he were to recover from these, there is so very much wrong with him . . . so much wrong.' But she suggested that my husband return again in the afternoon for a few moments only, and again after six o'clock in the evening. He assured her he would do that. Then we were asked whether we knew this girl who called herself his niece, but who, she understood, was not actually related to him and was not his next of kin. We said we knew her well, and that was correct – his next of kin was an elderly first cousin, Mrs May Eddows.

On our return to the Woods Hospital in the afternoon Micky went alone to see our friend. He had a feeling that Lowry wanted him there for some particular purpose. In the winter sunlight the little place looked attractive set in its park-like gardens; I thought how much Lowry would prefer its atmosphere to that of a large city hospital.

Micky reappeared before very long; he was accompanied by Carol and a diminutive lady whom I surmised correctly to be her mother. Greetings over, we learned that Lowry was much the same as we had found him that morning. Mrs Lowry hoped that he would enjoy the little dish of trifle she had taken. After the memory of the feeding cup, I had my inner doubts, and while admiring her practicality was surprised at her insensitivity; these two ladies had not been expected to visit.

Carol insisted we return to Rochdale for tea. Following her hired car I found the distance to be further than I had supposed and felt more than a little anxious on Micky's behalf.

Aware only that Mrs Lowry lived in a Rochdale council flat I was totally unprepared for the small Aladdin's cave which met my eyes on entering, and no longer wondered that Lowry, despite his constantly caustic comments upon his hostess, enjoyed the comfort of going there for Sunday dinner. There was no Sunday dinner at The Elms, and precious little comfort at any time.

Often over the years Lowry would complain that Carol's mother talked too much and got on his nerves; however, he never failed to give Mrs Lowry full marks for what she had done for 'the kid'. Surveying her flat, the walls of which were covered with Pre-Raphaelites and Lowry's own works, I gave her full marks too. The light had long since gone from the large picture window with its open view across the urban landscape to Rochdale Town Hall – a view which must have delighted the painter as he sat at table there. I glanced at his finest carriage clock where it rested on the lovely old Welsh dresser he had discovered and bought for Carol. It was time to be on our way.

As we turned for the third occasion through the gates of Woods Hospital it seemed best that only Micky should visit but, as I watched him disappear slowly and now very wearily through the door, I got out of the car, telling Simon that I thought after all I'd better go with him. Walking through the passages, passing the patiently waiting visitors to the wards, I arrived at Lowry's room to find Micky already backing quietly out of the door. On seeing me he said, 'He's sound asleep – I'm sure it would be wrong to waken him.'

Through the half-open door something disturbed me about the figure in the bed. No longer propped back on the pillows, it was slumped forward and to one side in an unnatural manner – the mouth hanging open, the body still. I moved past Micky and went close. After the laboured and difficult breathing of the morning, the constant coughing, there was now not the slightest sound or movement; an oxygen mask lay abandoned on the bed, a canister on the floor; there was the appearance of someone having left the room hastily to get help.

The get-well cards mocked from the walls. The trifle was still in its little dish. I remained only a moment, when I was certain that all that could be done for Lowry had been done. In life we had tried not to fail him – in death we could only be in the way. Time for visiting was past.

'I think he has gone,' I murmured to Micky. At the door I turned to look back for what I knew would be the last sight of our friend – and clear as a bell I seemed to hear Lowry's voice, 'No camera could get it you know.' I felt his spirit surging and resurging through that little room, and seemed to hear him again. 'Daumier and I – we could get it!' And only later was I to wonder – was that pitiable husk of humanity the ultimate subject Lowry would have chosen for his talent? Was that the answer to his constant and inexplicable preoccupation with his own death?

The following morning over the radio it was announced that L. S. Lowry was dead.

9

Lowry's solicitor rang to inform us at Carol's request that the artist's funeral would take place on the following Friday afternoon at two o'clock in Manchester Southern Cemetery. We had already had a telephone call to this effect from the Reverend Bennett, who had told us that he had been asked to conduct the service, and, should Micky think of anyone who would like to be there, then it would be a good idea to tell them when and where it was to take place. My husband was surprised that Lowry's old friend should apparently be disregarding the artist's wishes for a private burial and made it clear that we would inform no one.

On the Thursday afternoon we, with Simon and Veral, went to Manchester so that Micky could rest before the following day. On the Friday morning, 27 February, I spoke to Carol on the telephone. Neither of us knew where the cemetery was but an official car was to come to the Midland at 1.15 for the Bennetts; Carol, her husband (who had come over from the Isle of Man), and mother would arrive about the same time and we could all follow in our respective cars. A second official car was to collect a Miss Brooke, sister of Lowry's late picture restorer from Huddersfield. We had often heard of her brother from Lowry and were aware that, until Mr Brooke's death, the painter used to spend Boxing Day with them. Carol had arranged for ten or so of us to gather at the Midland for a cup of tea after the service and I suggested that the Robertsons should be included.

After speaking to Carol, I picked up the *Daily Telegraph* to read:

In private, as he had wished, Mr L. S. Lowry, the artist, who died on Monday, aged 88, is being buried today in the grave of his parents, whose only child he was. . . . Mr Harold Riley, the Lancashire artist who was one of his inner circle of friends, said: 'He was well aware of death duties and had it all worked out on the best advice . . . a lot of civic bodies and some individuals will benefit as well as groups of bodies and also establishments. He has been very fair with what he has done regarding his will but I respect his confidence that only the executors, in due course, will reveal the nature and details of the will. It is understood that there is no single beneficiary.' Mr Riley added, 'Some of his work and possessions are bequeathed to art galleries and some items will go to auction. He felt things should find their own way into the world.'

I felt that in due course a few people were going to get a hell of a surprise.

During the many years we had known Lowry his philosophy had been a resolute one: 'Never do today what you can put off until tomorrow, Mr Marshall.' Neither Mr Lowry nor Mr Marshall ever did do today what might be put off until the morrow and, although since Carol's marriage the artist had repeatedly affirmed that he intended to make a new will, we knew he had not done so.

He had continued to make it clear that his resentment against public galleries was still what it had always been, because they retained in their cellars important works which should have been on occasional, if not permanent, exhibition. Public galleries were also an integral part of the state, and Lowry intended to leave nothing to the state. It had already filched too much from him over the years in the form of taxation which he fiercely resented. Works which took him years to paint promptly put him into the surtax class when sold at an exhibition. On 27 July 1968 the *Sun* printed a piece which began:

Taxman Stops Sale. . . Artist L. S. Lowry explained yesterday why he has not put price tags on his new paintings, which go on show for the first time at the Stone Gallery in Newcastle-upon-Tyne. 'If I sold them the taxman would get a lot more out them than I would, despite the fact that it is I who put all the work into them.'

Lowry's attitude never changed. Capital transfer tax at his death could not be avoided – the state would therefore get something, but not 'the whole damn lot', if he could help it.

Lowry had got enormous enjoyment and amusement from holding out the carrot of his estate – but he only held that carrot out to donkeys. No-one more than he would have revelled in the public confusion and speculation as to how he had left his affairs, and in the arguments that ensued between various directors of public galleries in the Manchester area. None would have appreciated more than Lowry the sight of the vultures gathering, the acrimonious argument in the press between one public gallery director and another. His will was in perfect order and why it was thought necessary to wait some five months before the executors made a statement to the press is difficult to comprehend. Certainly no value could be placed upon his estate at the time of his death, but some announcement as to the beneficiary would have been helpful to men in public office whom Lowry had mischievously led up the garden path.

Although could Manchester City ever seriously have expected to inherit any part of Lowry's estate? In June 1968 we visited, in the company of Lowry, an exhibition at Manchester City Art Gallery entitled 'Art and the Industrial Revolution'. The works on view were all of an earlier date than Lowry's own, but the introduction to the catalogue gave our friend a great feeling of resentment towards his home city, when he read:

> The only artists in Britain whose work retained something of the observation and wonder of an earlier age were the journalist illustrators of the *Illustrated London News* and the *Graphic* and the photographers, faithfully recording the great engineering feats of the later nineteenth century. It was their spirit that was recreated in the second quarter of the twentieth century in the documentary film movement under the guidance of John Grierson. . . .
>
> Many of todays painters have retreated further than ever from reality. . . . Will those of our time ever come to terms with the manifestations of our technology?
>
> *Arthur Elton, May Day, 1968*

Not one word of the painter of the industrial scene who had emerged from the city of Manchester – L. S. Lowry. But worse – as we looked around the City Art Gallery that day in his company, in no part of it hung a work by Lowry.

Ten years later a well-known painter visited Manchester and the City Art Gallery for the first time; his reaction was similar to that of Lowry's own ten years before, 'Lowryland is still there for all to see – but my God, there's no sign of Lowry. Has the city forgotten him already – or has it never heard of him?'

How the painter would have hated, fumed over and exploded at the opportunity given to Manchester City Art Gallery when, by courtesy of his estate, his collection of Rossettis was shown under the title, 'A Pre-Raphaelite Passion', and the introduction to the catalogue read:

> Lowry's art is so familiar, so often imitated, reproduced and over-exposed, that his pearly-grey industrial compositions, 'match-stick' figures and caricature 'down-and-outs' are almost artistic clichés.

During the morning, we decided to stroll across to Manchester's Town Hall in the hope of seeing, at last, the Ford Madox Brown murals which for so many years had evaded us but which I had in fun only assured Lowry we should try to see, come his funeral.

As usual, we were informed that it would not be possible to see them. The following day a large gathering was due to meet Mrs Thatcher there, and the caterers were making the great hall ready for the occasion. With surprise I heard my husband telling the uniformed attendant who barred our way that we had permission from Councillor Higginbottom to view the murals that morning. The man called to a fellow employee, 'Hi, George, this party says it's got permission from Councillor Higginbottom to see the murals – I haven't heard of Higginbottom, have you?'

'Oh, he's very newly elected,' explained Micky (he was indeed!) At any rate we were successful and were at last confronted by Madox Brown's many years of work in and for the city of Manchester.

I had always found it difficult to accept Lowry's enormously high regard for Brown's genius. Although the murals were extremely fascinating and interesting in that setting – a splendid example of Manchester's nineteenth-century foresight and patronage – I still could not accept Brown as the greatest painter ever produced by this country, as Lowry would affirm. We looked at one another in fright and horror, however, as fiendish laughter suddenly echoed throughout the great hall. It came again and again, peal upon peal of monstrous, demoniacal mirth. Simultaneously the thought occurred to the four of us – Lowry! Only Lowry could laugh like that. I decided that he was disagreeing yet again with my opinion of Madox Brown. The attendants assured us it was only someone testing the 'mike', but we returned to the hotel a little unconvinced.

We lunched in company with the Reverend and Mrs Bennett who had just arrived by train from Carlisle. As I demolished the last of my omelette, Mrs Bennett leaned forward and fixing me with a firm eye said, 'I think I should tell you categorically that Carol is Lowry's sole beneficiary.'

'But, of course,' I agreed, 'we've always been fully aware of that. In a way we helped him make his will years ago. But your husband's getting his clock, and Mrs Swindles gets something – perhaps not very much (it was one thousand pounds) – and, of course, Lowry's solicitor gets one of his Rossetti pastels.'

'Oh, does he now? I didn't know about that. You know, Lowry used to talk about making a new will after Carol married – but I used to say to him that one wouldn't cut out a favourite child who'd displeased one; and I said to him, "She gave you a lot of pleasure – didn't she?" And he agreed, oh yes, she'd given him pleasure. Well then. . . .' I nodded agreement.

After lunch I took Mrs Bennett to my room to prepare for the afternoon. As she went up a short flight of stairs ahead of me she turned back to smile. 'But there's one thing, we're all the better off for having known him, aren't we?'

Remembering the large and important collection of Lowry works owned by the lady and her husband, I stopped in my tracks to roar with laughter. 'My God! You may be – but we're not. Our accountant is always telling me we're thousands the poorer – and no holiday all these years!'

It was Mrs Bennett's turn to stop in her tracks. 'But that's not possible. What about all the financial aid he gave the gallery? We never knew how much it was, of course, although he inferred about a hundred thousand. . .?' Her voice trailed away in a question mark.

'*What*!' I exclaimed. 'It was the vast sum of three hundred pounds to be precise.'

'Oh no!'

'Oh yes!'

'But Lowry always implied it was *thousands*.'

'Ye Gods, did he? No wonder some folk have never been very fond of us. Oh, no! When the gallery company was formed, each shareholder, other than family, put in the identical amount. It was restricted to three hundred pounds because that was all the youngest man could afford. We'd been accused by certain local public bodies of being an élitist concern – the old Marxist war cry – and these ten or so people joined us as a token of disapproval that certain committees had not stood by the promises originally given. Good heavens, with the sort of capital you suggest, Micky couldn't half have made the region hum.'

Goggle-eyed, Alice Bennett stood static on the stairs. 'Well, Lowry always claimed he'd done so much for the gallery.'

'The old blighter. The gallery did much for Lowry. At any rate, financially we'll be better off now he's gone. You know, as a family, it was sometimes a hell of a strain the expense he put us to.'

'Well, why did you do it?'

'You may well ask – and it's not an easy question to answer. I suppose we got caught in a sort of trap. When we first met him he kept repeating, "Everyone wants something from me for nothing." And I'm not saying that a lot of people didn't. At any rate we set out to prove that we were the exception. We'd no idea we were going to know him all those years. Then we simply continued as we'd begun, like long-distance runners forever trying to break our own record. You knew Lowry well enough – he was a *committed scrounger*, and we were a good touch. As he played his "po'r lorn critter" role he could make one feel so damned sorry for him. And we didn't drop our responsibilities when we put the bolts in the gallery door.'

When it was time for the departure of the official car taking the Bennetts to the cemetery there was still no sign of Carol and her little party, but we thought it best to leave with the Bennetts.

We turned through the imposing gateway of the main entrance to Manchester's Southern Cemetery. On the other side of the road stood a 'Marble and Art Centre, James Hilton, established 1867, Monumental Sculptor'. Lowry would have fantasized for hours around that particular art centre. As the cars drew up, the Robertsons were already waiting by the laurels and evergreens. Well-kept grass and neat flowerbeds bordered the wide tarmac road running through the cemetery; office buildings stood just inside the gates to left and right, those on the left surmounted by a fine clocktower. There was no sign of graves here – only the appearance of a well-maintained park.

Small attaché case in hand, Mr Bennett with his wife left us to walk quickly down the road to the Anglican Church so that he might change into his cassock and surplice. With some relief we welcomed the arrival of Carol, her husband, whom we were meeting for the first time, and her mother. 'Oh,' laughed Carol, pointing at Micky's black tie, 'what on earth are you wearing that for? You've got nothing to mourn.'

'It was always agreed with Lowry I'd be wearing a black tie at his funeral,' he murmured, slightly taken aback. Nothing daunted, Carol moved over to denounce Simon's.

'Why, look! There's Uncle Laurie come to his own funeral,' Carol exclaimed. While I sincerely hoped that he was indeed coming to his own funeral, I had not expcected him in the guise of the grey squirrel to which Carol was pointing as it sat in a branch of a small tree above us. We all gazed up at the unperturbed little creature as it ate with relish some tit-bit it held between upraised front paws. Carol laughed again, 'Oh yes, that's Uncle Laurie all right – in his grey suit, as usual.'

We proceeded in double file down the wide tarmac road towards the church, when suddenly there appeared a number of men with busily clicking cameras. They fell back along the road in front of us to get better shots of this oddly assorted procession. Veral appeared to be leading the way with Micky and Carol following; her husband was walking with me, and Mrs Lowry kept pace with Simon, beside whom she looked even more diminutive than usual.

We approached a diamond-shaped flowerbed surrounding a cypress tree in the centre of the road, which now divided left and right. A miniature black signpost with fine gilt lettering directed to the left 'Non-Conformist', to the right 'Roman Catholic', straight ahead 'Church of England'. Bearing left around the cypress tree we continued straight on down the road which was still bordered by trees and rhododendrons. Suddenly the view opened out revealing a huge circular lawn with flowerbeds interspersed with large and impressive tombstones and monuments. As far as the eye could see there were apparently Pre-Raphaelite-inspired stone memorial figures hovering over the graves of long-buried loved ones.

Here was a Burne-Jones lady sitting in her stone drapery, eyeing with some disappointment the closed book of life resting upon her knee while she held a stone quill hopefully at the ready to add some more names. There was a Rossetti-type girl, gentle, dreamlike, her white marble grace garbed á la Lizzie Siddal. Sadly she reclined against white marble steps, a small wreath in one drooping hand, her brow rested on the other. The lowest step bore the inscription 'May every morning seem to say, There's something happy on the way.' Nearby was a Frederic Shields angel of death with shuddering wings, reluctantly raising a curtain upon some family roll-call, and away over the grass a kneeling Millais beauty. A little further down the road another Rossetti blessèd damozel held a spray of lilies, caught for ever in the act of discarding an unwanted bloom.

Row upon row of figures, some of gentle countenance, some more menacing; flight upon flight of graceful angel wings, upraised arms and family scrolls; flower and bird-wreathed stones, charming cherubs; and over this mass of marble mourning hung the amazing all-pervading atmosphere of nineteenth-century progress and wealth. Lowry would not have exchanged this for Westminster Abbey itself.

Still the wide road circled on towards the little church among the trees – and as we came to the clearing around it we were suddenly faced with a great crowd of people and many more photographers. So this was Lowry's private funeral.

The desire of many to pay their last respects is understandable but not in the face of disrespect for the dead man's wish. The executors had made it very clear through the press that the funeral was to be private. A few were making a social occasion of it; a few were making it a business one; for one or two it was obviously a distressing one. A beautiful dark-haired girl was in floods of tears. Knowing Lowry, it was impossible to regret his dying when he had. To have lived on incapacitated, an invalid, dependent, was the last thing he would have wanted. He had been fortunate.

A hush fell over all the gathered company except for Mrs Martha Lowry, who was too diminutive to see the hearse advance slowly towards the church. With solemn tread the bearers carried the coffin through a side door. Carol with husband and mother went through the main entrance first and were shown by an attendant into the front row on the left, we to the front on the right, with the Robertsons directly behind us.

Upon the impressive brass-handled coffin rested the laurel wreath, tribute from Lowry's fellow academicians. It was perfect for the occasion. There had been a request for no flowers, the artist had always insisted that there should be none, but there was a floral arrangement in a plastic holder from Tommy Steele and a cellophane package of strange shape containing two bunches of violets at either end of a paint brush. These two items spoiled the dramatic effect of the Academy's laurel wreath.

We had lived through this funeral so many times with Lowry; whenever life was a little dull he would cheer himself up by going through the routine for the umpteenth time and never omitted to assure us with a mischievous smile 'I'll be there of course – but unfortunately only in a passive capacity.' Little or nothing was sacred to Lowry – certainly not his own funeral, but he had wanted it kept private.

The green pastures of the twenty-third psalm had me worried – Lowry never cared for green pastures; if a table was being prepared I doubted not that our friend would be demanding a white cloth upon it, and it was to be hoped there would be egg and chips.

The reverend gentleman referred to his long friendship with the artist. Lowry had expected this, and once even wished that Mr Bennett would make it clear that he also painted – and had a few works for sale.

The large number of people filed out of the church and took the wide road to the right. Gradually the headstones became smaller and less impressive, of the kind to be found in any graveyard and in no way like the glorious memorials admired earlier. It was in this modest area that Manchester's famous citizen was to be laid to rest. Press and television men were everywhere; the cameras continuously clicked away. Faintly I heard '. . . earth to earth, ashes to ashes, dust to dust. . .' as Mr Bennett proceeded with the committal. Later he put in for a small extra fee for this over and above that due in respect of the church service conducted for his old friend; this cost him the transport price of his inherited clock – Carol decided that if Mr Bennett could charge the estate, the estate could charge Mr Bennett.

The grass was cold and damp, and the sky overcast. I leaned against a convenient headstone and seemed to hear Lowry's voice again. 'Oh, isn't it laughable? What have they all come for? What are they hoping to see? Humanity is the lowest form of animal life – oh yes.' With a sigh I turned away and began to walk down the road. I glanced back and saw people still pressing forward to peer into that hole while the cameras clicked busily.

We drove to the back entrance to the cemetery, and Simon walked down to Lowry's grave with a large wreath of spring flowers and carnations which students of Newcastle University had asked him to bring. This he now placed with the other tributes.

Returning to the Midland we found ourselves to be the first arrivals. We were shortly joined by Carol, who told us that tea would be waiting in the Narrow Boat Coffee Shop. With others of the expected company we gathered around the doorway; Carol took my arm. 'Now come along Tilly and do a Tilley's – you're always so good at seating people.'

But, fearful lest this lead to misunderstanding, I replied, 'No, no, Carol. This is your day, dear. I must just get rid of this coat. I won't be a moment.'

When I returned the company was seated at two long tables. Only one chair was still vacant between my husband and Veral. I had arrived in the doorway at the same moment as Mr Andras Kalman, a London art dealer, and stood aside for him to take the seat. Mr Kalman declined it, and it transpired he was not of the party, but was meeting someone else.

I sat down. Just beyond Micky was a gentleman representing Manchester's Academy of Art and opposite to him in the corner was a thin, serious looking man whose name I did not catch, but he was obviously the undertaker as he was sitting next to Mr Hume, Lowry's solicitor. Lowry had always told us what to expect – his solicitor would be present, and the undertaker – and, bless them, here they were. Next to the legal man and directly facing me was Miss Brooke, a gently retiring lady; and next to her I was delighted to see Sheila Fell, whom Carol had included when she had seen her at the funeral.

Sheila leaned towards me and asked whether Ann had been at the funeral. Miss Brooke said no, there'd been no sign of her. Nor, I added, had there been any sign of Lowry's cousin May. Someone asked who cousin May was. My husband then asked the solicitor whether, as Lowry's next of kin, she had been officially informed of her cousin's death. He turned a blank face. Micky called over to Mr Bennett. Surely he was aware that May lived just outside Burford? To our surprise Mr Bennett knew nothing of her. He had known Lowry's cousin Grace, but Grace was long since dead. Lowry had told us that she had died of cancer in 1949. I explained that there had been three sisters (the daughters of Lowry's Aunt Mary): Ruth, Grace and May. The last named was the youngest and she was still alive. At that moment I decided to go find Cousin May at the first opportunity. How should I feel if I constantly read in the press that I did not exist? For so many years now it had been publicly maintained that Lowry had no living relative.

A hush had descended upon our table, and, feeling that I had a social obligation, I turned towards the professionally mournful gentleman in the corner who had not as yet spoken. Lowry's funeral had been so thoroughly rehearsed that I felt he would have relied upon me to make the undertaker welcome. Leaning foward, I addressed the gentleman. 'What a wonderful cemetery you have here in Manchester. The north-east certainly has nothing comparable. You are to be much congratulated. I've certainly never seen anything like it before. It's positively Pre-Raphaelite in parts. You must be jolly proud of it.' I saw a blank expression in his eye and thought that he probably didn't know what Pre-Raphaelite meant, nor was jolly perhaps the right word to have used. Doing my bit as best I could, I added with what I intended to be a charming smile, 'You must almost enjoy funerals there.' He made no reply. After a further little encouraging smile in his direction, I thought he might have reacted more pleasantly. Maybe I'd used the wrong word again – funerals weren't intended to be enjoyed – but they were his *trade*, and he could have concealed his disappointment at the lack of a good ham tea. If he had known Lowry, he would have been prepared for no ham. We were very fortunate to be given this cup of tea and piece of toast at Carol's restricted 50p a head. Afterwards, she asked Micky if he had the money to pay for it – she only had Manx money. Micky was firm – he had not!

The Bennetts caught their train back to Carlisle; Miss Brooke offered Sheila Fell a lift on her way; Carol's husband left to repatriate the hired car as they were returning to the Isle of Man early the following day. After some chatter and gossip, only Mrs Lowry and Carol were left with us in the hotel foyer.

'Oh,' laughed Carol, making a dive at Micky's tie, 'I can't stand that another moment – there, that's better.' She wrested it from him, unfastened the top button of his shirt and eyed his tieless state. I thought it looked much worse: middle-aged and very weary of countenance, he resembled some awful would-be whizz kid.

'I can't see what you've got against it, Turnbull and Asser's best – look, nice orange lining,' smiled Micky.

'I told you before – you've got nothing to mourn.'

'And I told you I promised the old man I'd be wearing a black tie. What I think you're trying to tell me is that I've nothing to celebrate. We've always been aware of that, you know.'

As we met together for an evening drink, I announced to the family, 'I say – I do think it was a bit of bad luck that we had to have the undertaker at our table. You and Carol seemed to be having a hell of a good time, Simon!'

'I didn't know the undertaker was there,' said Micky.

'Of course he was there – Lowry always said he would be. That fellow in the corner next to the solicitor.'

'You fool – that wasn't the undertaker – that was the representative from the executory division of the bank – Lowry's second executor.'

'My God! I thought he was the undertaker!'

'Silly Tilly,' comforted Veral. 'Simon, give her another glass of champagne – she looks as though she needs one.'

However, Micky explained that I wasn't so far off the mark, for the man in question would be undertaking for Lowry's estate for a long time to come and, as banks don't do such jobs for nothing, he prophesied that the bank might well do better in the end than the beneficiary. I thought he was joking.

'I hope he's not,' smiled Simon, 'after all, that's a very pleasant thought. "You're making me very happy, sir," as our late friend would have said. Don't forget my recently inherited great-grandmama's shares in that particular bank!' Simon raised his glass. 'Here's to our late friend, his estate and my bank shares!' Oddly enough, he had raised his glass to extraordinarily good purpose.

The following morning we decided to visit the City Art Gallery before leaving for home. As we moved from room to room, looking at familiar Pre-Raphaelite works, I seemed to hear Lowry's voice again. 'My word, but they could do it, couldn't they? I don't care too much for that Millais. He couldn't paint hands. Remember those hands he gave Ruskin, Mrs Marshall? I fancy he painted them from Effie.'

'Of course he didn't,' I would reply. 'They weren't seeing each other then. She was away in Scotland, waiting for her divorce from Ruskin. Anyway, you're not very good when it comes to hands.'

'Aah – but then I'm not trying to paint hands like that – I could, y'know, if I wanted to. I see they've had that Arthur Hughes restored. They needn't have bothered. You only want the first raters. You agree with me there, don't you Mr Marshall? You and I don't rate Arthur Hughes – too pretty. That thing in the Tate – what's it called?'

'*April Love. . . .*'

'That's the thing – very overrated. No battle of life. Of course, when it comes to the Pre-Raphaelites you've no discrimination, Mrs Marshall, you like 'em all. What d'you think of that?' We might be standing before Millais's *Autumn Leaves*, and I would claim it as a great favourite. Lowry would disagree. 'Uhm, too pretty. And he became much worse. Oh, my word, yes. I blame Effie, she was the ruin of him as a painter, and the making of him as a wealthy man.'

'I don't agree with you, as well you know. Everyone always blames Effie – but Millais painted for money when he was only a student. Even his parents were horrified when they found he'd contracted himself to some dealer to paint a picture for him almost every day. It was lucky for Millais the contract wasn't legal. Oh no, he used to say to Hunt, "It's the money in our time that matters – we won't be here to enjoy posterity." He was a bit like you.'

'Oh, I don't think I care for that, Mrs Marshall.' Lowry would laugh, and we would move on. 'And talking of Hunt, he was very great but I wouldn't want one. Always teaching and preaching. Colourful? Oh yes – too colourful – hard. I can't say I've ever seen the Hunt I'd want to take away on a dark night.

'Aah, here we are now – this is one of your favourites, Mr Marshall – *Manfred on the Jungfrau* – good old Madox Brown. And here's *Work*. I think Mrs Marshall likes that better.' He was quite right.

Lowry's favourite Madox Brown was not *Work*, however, it was either *The Body of Harold brought before William the Conqueror*, or *Cromwell, Protector of the Vaudois*. . . . I think he liked these equally well. He would moan again, 'Oh, why can't they have my favourite Maggots Browns up? Always in the cellar.' Then, catching his breath with his usual reverse sort of hiss, he might exclaim, 'Ooh – just look at that. My God – to think I can't ever have that. Don't you think they might be permitted to give it to Little Laurie?' We would be standing before Rossetti's *The Bower Meadow*, and he would continue, 'Oh, you don't eh? Well, I call it very mean of them, very mean. Just look again at that line. . . .' He would trace an outline in the air with his forefinger, then moan, 'To think – even if I was Getty – I couldn't get it.'

Moving away and on, for Lowry never wasted a great deal of time in any gallery but ours, he would say, 'Ah now, that's what we want to see. Isn't she wonderful? *Astarte Syriaca* . . . forerunner of the Symbolists. You're right there, Mr Marshall. Just look at those hands; look at that face – those eyes. By God, sir, but Rossetti could do it. No Victorian sentimentalism there. Pity she's too big for m'house, or I might have tried to get her out of here one night

– don't think they'd miss her.'

Lowry would slouch on in his fine leather slippers. 'Ah now, *Jolie Coeur*. She's not so good as some, but a lot better than others. I wouldn't mind having her to go with my *Loving Cup*. No one could get what Rossetti gets. Did I ever tell you that I once heard Wyndham Lewis being interviewed on the radio? And, although he said it was really an impossible question to answer, in his opinion Ford Madox Brown was the greatest painter we've ever had, then Hogarth, then Constable.' We would hear again how much he approved his hero signing his work F. M. Brown. Lowry heartily enjoyed this lack of affectation. 'I like Burne-Jones, wonderful painter, but I don't like that hyphen of his, nor his title, come to think of it.'

Again and again I seemed to hear Lowry's voice until, moving into the final room, I came to two of his own paintings. In the corner of one I saw a tiny self-portrait. I had a sense of dreadful inner sadness. The inconveniences of the years fell away and I was left only with the sensation of loss. Only now perhaps was I fully conscious that he had gone from us for ever. Life would never be quite the same again.

Hastily I found it necessary to put on my sunglasses and rush from the building. I heard my husband following me down the steps. 'What's the matter?' I didn't answer. I was overpowered for the moment by the knowledge that Lowry was dead and aware of an enormous affection for the man who had gone.

During luncheon, I asked the family whether they would mind very much if we returned to 'Manchester South', as Lowry used to call it, that afternoon? A little surprised, they were nevertheless agreeable. This time we went to the back entrance to the cemetery. The sun was shining warmly from a blue winter sky. We walked the short distance down the road. This day all was wondrously quiet and orderly; not a living soul in sight other than ourselves. Only the newly turned turf and flowers resting on it showed which plot had so recently received its occupant. Tall trees were bare and stark, slim branches and trunks shadowed across the headstones so closely grouped that these in turn shadowed across each other.

I had been unable to approach the grave for the crowd the previous afternoon, but now I saw the solidly simple rough grey stone cross, with the names of Lowry's father and mother and the dates denoting their span of life inscribed on the base. When I returned the following year, Lowry's name had been added on the right-hand side of the base, but I had to look closely to find it. On the grass stood a tiny black marble urn, empty of any flowers. It carried the inscription, 'L. S. Lowry'. Nothing else. I recalled the Rossetti grave at Birchington with its memorial stone designed by Madox Brown. I looked again at Lowry's and wondered. Was it enough?

And each year when we return, one wonders again.

I had not forgotten my decision to go in search of Lowry's cousin May. At three o'clock precisely on Sunday, 11 April 1976, just six weeks after Lowry's death, my husband and I drove into the village of Carterton.

We were aware that Mrs Eddows lived in this village near Burford, and we had hoped that it might be a small and typical Cotswold hamlet. Situated as it is, close to the air base of Brize Norton, it proved to have a large bungaloid growth and was quite unlike any Cotswold village with which we were familiar. How were we to find the good lady amid this conglomeration?

There were no shops open so we called at the police station; there was no reply to our knock. We drove slowly here and there through this rather depressing place; and were about to leave when we spotted a police car and signalled for it to stop. It seemed a singularly stupid question to ask the young policeman: whether by any chance he knew of an elderly lady living in Carterton by the name of Mrs Eddows. He shook his head, then suddenly paused. 'Wait a moment, you don't mean the lady related to that famous old painter who died recently?' He fancied she lived in Swinbrook Avenue, but had no idea where. He directed us to the road in question, a lengthy one of many bungalows.

According to Lowry, his cousin May could not afford a television and, despite all my chivvying of him over the years, he had remained adamant in refusing to buy one for her. Her bungalow, therefore, would not be sporting an aerial. That narrowed the possibilities. She had spent some time in Rhodesia and it was just feasible she might have given her home an un-English-sounding name. Being hard up, there was little likelihood of an immaculate appearance. As we motored slowly up the avenue I spotted the very place. No aerial, funny-peculiar name, run-down exterior.

How many people have been hanged on circumstantial evidence?

No one of that name lived there. A little further up the road, we were told, lived a retired policeman and there was a possibility he might be able to assist. His wife, it transpired, worked for the local social security adminstration and knew of Mrs Eddows but she couldn't recall off-hand the name of the bungalow, or the road, but it was on a corner and we couldn't miss it.

There appeared to be many roads with many corners. It had been suggested that, being elderly, Mrs Eddows might well be resting during the afternoon as she had not been too fit recently. One bungalow on a corner had the curtains of one window drawn, so we decided to try there, but whoever was resting was not letting on. Across the road was another house with curtains drawn and a note pinned to the front door requesting callers to go round to the back. We did but it availed us nothing. We made inquiries, but drew a further blank. We drove round and round – it seemed a hopeless quest. But my husband refused to give up now; we had run to earth two people who had heard of her. Again we trailed round the same corners. We must have been everywhere in Carterton six times. Near the first bungalow we had tried on the first corner we saw a young man working in a garden and we asked him.

He knew no one of that name, but wait – there was an elderly lady lived around the corner, about six bungalows away (not on a corner). She was in the habit of taking a little stroll in the evenings and he accompanied her home occasionally if she'd walked a little too far and had become weary. She had a nice cat. (Charles was dead.) We thanked him, got into the car again, turned and drove back into another long road and saw a lady walking toward us. Micky stopped the car, I got out quickly and asked her whether, by any chance, she knew if a Mrs Eddows lived in the vicinity? 'Why yes,' she replied. 'You're standing at her gate.'

We walked up the path of the small semi-detached bungalow. As I had expected, it was all rather run down and, knocking on a plain glass front door, over the interior of which hung a shabby curtain, I received no reply. The lady I had just spoken to was talking to another a small distance away. 'You'll have to knock harder, she's a little deaf,' I heard her call. I did as directed.

'Be patient, be patient,' I heard a voice say from behind the door. Oh yes, that was Lowry-ish.

I called back, 'Yes, we'll be patient,' adding, lest she might be nervous, 'we're friends of your cousin, Mr Lowry.' The door was flung open at once and there stood a small female edition of our old friend. No need to ask whether she was his cousin, the family likeness was startling. I felt I had known her for years as, indeed, at second hand I had. There were the same very blue eyes, her now grey-white hair had once been sandy-fair like his, her features were finer than the old man's but, as I saw when she clutched her dressing gown more closely about her, her hands might have been Lowry's finely boned hands, only smaller.

'Oh, I'm so sorry,' I heard her say. 'I'm in bed today, I've been in bed all day – it's warmer there.' She was wearing an old blue nightdress beneath the soiled blue dressing gown, and old slippers.

I repeated, 'We're friends of your late cousin, Mr Lowry.'

'You *are*?' she exclaimed, delighted. 'You're friends of *Laurie's*? Please come in.' Inside the little hall she asked, 'I wonder if you'd mind coming into my bedroom, it's warmer there and, look, I can put on the fire.' And, suiting action to words, just as Lowry used to, she bent to switch on a small electric fire.

There, however, the resemblance between the two homes ended. The Elms had been grim but this was worse. I had not seen such apparent poverty since I visited poor families in Gateshead fifty years before.

'Now,' I heard her voice saying, 'we must find some chairs.' Over in a corner was a small upright, hard, wooden chair, another by her bed, and Micky was instructed to bring another such from the kitchen. There was no carpeting upon the bare, unvarnished floorboards. Against the wall, just inside the door, was newspaper spread on the floor upon which rested four saucers, one with the remains of some cat food on it. In the centre of the room was a single bed from which she had just risen and in the middle of this there slept a very large tabby cat. Only one thing in the room was familiar – the small carved oak chest against the wall opposite the foot of the bed.

We sat ourselves before the tiny fire and, drawing closer to it, she said, 'Oh, do tell me, do tell me about my cousin.'

'You haven't heard from his solicitor since he died?'

'No, no, nothing from anyone. I only know what I read in the papers sometimes. And if you read those,' smiling pathetically, 'then you'll know I don't exist. Sometimes I think I must have died a long time ago. They always say Laurie had no living relative. But I'm his first cousin, you know. His mother and my mother were sisters. Laurie and I were very close. There was only a year or so between us. My sister Ruth, she was the eldest, and she died a long time ago. Grace has been dead for years. And they were much older than Laurie and I. That's how Laurie and I were thrown together so much when we were young.

'My mother and his used to meet – oh, two, three, yes sometimes three, times a week for tea, at one or other's home. Unless there was illness they took it in turns. Laurie and I played together so he was more like an elder brother in many ways. And he loved playing with little figures.' She made an expressive movement with her hands.

'Soldiers?' I prompted, rather stupidly.

'Oh *no*, not soldiers, not Laurie. Laurie wouldn't have cared for soldiers, never. Soldiers weren't Laurie's line of country at all. No, they were little figures that belonged to me. I suppose they were dolls really, but when you talk of dolls you usually think of something larger and these were just tiny. I could pack them up and take them with me if we were visiting them. Oh, dear me, here I'm talking, but it all comes back to me, you see. And I want to hear about him. D'you think he remembered me? Or did he leave everything to the girl?'

It was useless to raise her hopes. Micky looked uncomfortable, so I drew closer to her. 'There has been no statement from anyone but, yes, I'm afraid Carol has inherited everything. But I'm sure, as his next of kin, you should have had some word from Mr Lowry's solicitor, only perhaps they don't bother with things like that nowadays. I'm afraid I just don't know.'

Cousin May fixed me with very familiar blue eyes. She had a few teeth left, I noticed as she smiled, 'You must understand that, even though my cousin left everything to the girl, he was an honourable man; you know what I mean, don't you?'

'Oh, yes.' I agreed at once.

She continued, 'I was always very sure, though, that he would leave me *something*. It would have helped. I've always been independent and I worked as long as I could but, of course, I can't now.' Indeed she could not. 'With everything so expensive it's so much more difficult now.' Her voice trailed away. Then, turning those blue eyes on me again, and pulling her shoulders back, for she stooped somewhat, she said, 'Dear, dear Laurie. I should so like to have gone to his funeral. I wrote to his bank. He always said he would leave his bank in charge, you know. I put my name and address on the back of the envelope, so that they would know who was writing to them, but it was returned unopened. I had a friend post it for me.' She certainly appeared too frail to have attended the funeral, in any case.

'You see, my father and mother are buried in the grave next to Laurie's mother and father, at right angles to it. When my father died both the sisters went and bought adjacent plots, so we'd all be together. My sister Grace would be at Laurie's funeral.' I thought her mind must be wandering – a moment ago she had remembered that Grace was dead – but I misjudged her. 'Yes,' she continued, 'Grace was there, in what Laurie would have called "a passive capacity" for she's buried with father and mother. You know,' she said, 'those graves are so close together, side by side and head to foot!'

'Yes,' I smiled, 'they are, aren't they?'

'Now, I'm going to tell you something,' she went on. 'I've always believed in God. But, just lately, everyone forgetting me, never hearing from anyone since Laurie died, and always reading that he had no living relative, I've begun to think there can't be a God at all. So yesterday afternoon, I got down on my knees beside that bed and I prayed. I prayed that God would let me know that I wasn't forgotten. When I got up I didn't feel anything, I still wasn't sure there was a God. And now, today, you two have come and I know that I shouldn't have doubted. I know now there's a God – I'm ashamed I doubted – and what a good God he must be to send an answer so soon. It won't really matter now if Laurie didn't leave me anything, it's just so *good* to know that I'm not forgotten.'

How dreadful, I thought, how quite dreadful. If only we had been able to give her some good news. Micky leaned forward. 'I'll tell you one thing,' he said, 'I shall ring up Mr Lowry's solicitor first thing in the morning and anything I can do for you will be done. Even if your cousin has left you nothing outright, it is possible there might be copyrights. I don't want to raise your hopes, but at least I'll find out for you.'

'Oh, how good of you,' she smiled her thanks which Micky shrugged away, saying that it was probably a forlorn hope. She told us what a nice cup of tea she had just made for herself before we had arrived but there was no sign of her having had anything and, when later she insisted on showing us around the little bungalow, she opened cupboards in the kitchen and there appeared to be no food. It was all sad and distressing. Possibly she lived with the assistance of meals on wheels.

We stayed with her almost three hours. Pointing to the carved chest in her bedroom, I said that her cousin had had an identical one. Yes, she told me, the two chests had belonged to the two sisters, her mother and Laurie's. As she said the name 'Laurie' I was aware that she drawled it slightly, quite unlike the pronunciation given it by Carol and her mother, who appeared to be referring to a heavy vehicle when they said it. Cousin May pronounced it as Lowry had done, although her accent was altogether more educated than his and never slipped for a moment.

We were shown the bedroom her cousin had occupied when he used to stay with her. I said he had missed Charles after he died. 'Oh,' she exclaimed with delight, 'he even told you about Charles! I think he'd have liked this one, too,' she said, returning to the bedroom and pointing to the large feline creature just stirring in the centre of the bed. As though he were aware he was under discussion he made a tremendous leap and, in a flash, made his exit through the top of the window.

'How amazing,' I laughed in admiration.

'Wait till you see him return,' said Cousin May and, sure enough, before very long he leaped back in the manner of his going.

'Laurie always used to come and stay in the old days, during September. Of course, I asked him for Christmas – I asked him last Christmas, but he wrote to say he'd come in the spring when his bronchitis would be better, but he left it too late.'

I felt an inner anger as I recalled the presents I had seen Lowry give over the years; luxury holidays for which he had paid; the financial independence for Carol which we ourselves had advocated. It was well into the evening before we took our departure. As we drove back to London I turned to my husband, 'Ye gods! That explains a great deal. We used to suppose that Lowry took advantage of us but, if that was the yardstick, I can only suppose he imagined we had untold wealth.'

As he had promised, early the following morning Micky rang Lowry's solicitor in the forlorn hope that something might be due to this cousin. He described the circumstances in which we found her, but there was no provision for the lady and nothing could be done. He then consulted Rubinstein Callingham, the copyright specialists – to no avail.

Within a matter of days we received a letter from the friend of Mrs Eddows who had posted the letter for her to Lowry's bank. She said that she would like to meet us so, when next we went to visit Cousin May, we called first upon her friend. She wished to show us an early Lowry oil, dated 1912, given to her some years previously by Mrs Eddows. She wanted us to value this work, which she kept wrapped in brown paper under the impression it was worth a fortune.

'Could you tell me,' she asked as we were leaving her, 'who was Charles?'

'Charles?'

'Yes, I've read some correspondence belonging to Mrs Eddows, in which her cousin says in one letter how sorry he is to learn that Charles has died and I can't think what relation this was?'

'Why,' I laughed, 'Charles was Cousin May's cat!' I wondered later why she had not asked Mrs Eddows.

On our second visit to Lowry's cousin she was up and dressed and delighted to see us again. When Micky broke it to her that she had, indeed, been left nothing, nor was there any hope of copyrights, she took the news like the lady we found her to be. She said that we were not to worry, she had no recriminations but was delighted to know that she had not been forgotten by his friends. Her hurt, she told us, was when she had supposed that none of his friends were aware that Laurie had a cousin in the land of the living. It seemed meagre compensation, but she took comfort from our visits.

'Did Laurie tell you what a lovely touch his mother had?' she asked, moving her hands over an imaginary piano. 'She was really up to concert standard, you know. Of course, she didn't take it up like that but sometimes acted as accompanist for people if someone had let them down.'

In her living room hung a photograph of an exceedingly handsome man in First World War uniform. She told us that he was her second husband. 'He was handsome, wasn't he? Unfortunately, he died as a result of the war only months after we were married.' Near his photograph was a framed letter from Earl Haig on the occasion of the husband's award of the DSO.

'Your cousin didn't go to the war?' I asked.

'Oh, *no*,' was the shocked response. 'Laurie could never have stood anything like that. Oh, no, no.' She paused for a moment's reflection. 'You see he was an only child and *very* spoiled . . . his mother adored him.'

'His father, when he died, must have left them fairly comfortably off?' I asked.

'Laurie's father? Oh, dear me, no. He left only a hundred or two, if that. You see he was. . . .' Her voice trailed away, she looked at me a little sharply, giving me the full concentration of those blue eyes. 'Laurie's father – oh, well, never mind Laurie's father,' and quickly she changed the subject. I gathered Laurie's father had not rated very high.

Strolling round the back of the bungalow with her, I pointed to a little field beyond, saying, 'That's where Charles arrived from?'

'Why, yes! You've got it all quite right. I would put his food down here for him just by the door and then, one day, when I was in the kitchen, there he was rubbing round my legs and purring. I could do anything with him after that but he was very fierce with anyone else. Laurie was very frightened of him but enjoyed it. My word he told you all about everything!' (No, he didn't, I thought).

That evening, as we said goodbye, she pointed to a few daffodils growing in the small front garden and asked me to pick them as she would like me to have them. Gently, I said it seemed a shame, they looked so pretty there and they would last longer if we left them. 'Oh, how nice, you're like me, I think it's nicer for flowers to be growing.'

I took her hands in mine and told her again how like Mr Lowry's they were. I had always admired his hands; hers were smaller, of course, but his had been very fine and small for his size.

She stood at the gate waving as we drove away into the evening sun. Inwardly we cursed our helplessness. The simple remembrance of her existence, a few chocolates and kind words, hardly seemed lasting comfort.

When Carol came to visit us in London, to tell us that she was Lowry's heir, and that probate would be granted for something in the region of two hundred and ninety-five thousand pounds, I pressed Cousin May's cause but to no avail.

Lowry's cousin only outlived the artist by two years. She died in a home after her mind had become sadly confused. Perhaps they were more alike than even I had supposed. May Eddows did not die penniless. She was not in the same league as her cousin – but she managed to leave forty-four thousand, eight hundred and thirty-two pounds, which included the value of her bungalow.

It had of course been suggested that there should be a memorial service for Lowry. The decision rested with Carol. She waved the idea aside in view of the expense it would incur.

It is no use pretending that over the years I had not sometimes wondered what effect Lowry's excessive spoiling of Carol during her formative years would have upon her later. During the summer after the painter's death, when she visited us very frequently in London, I had my answer.

One afternoon she sat on the floor of our sitting room, legal-looking documents spread around her. She looked delightfully childish, no older than the day I first met her – but much more attractive. She sighed, 'Oh my goodness, I'm the most unfortunate girl alive.'

'I beg your pardon?' I held the teapot aloft – dumbfounded.

'I'm the most unfortunate girl alive,' she repeated.

'I should be a little careful if I were you dear,' I suggested, 'or you might just tempt the Lord.'

'Lord who?'

'I was referring to the Lord God Almighty. After all, not many girls would consider themselves unfortunate just to have been left two hundred and ninety-five thousand pounds!'

'Oh, but think of all the work it's putting me to – and all the tax I shall have to pay.'

How that smacked of the old man.

Others have said that as a family we held a unique position in Lowry's life during his last fourteen years. Not only did we work for him, and also with him, but so much of our leisure was spent in his company. There were others who worked for him, or worked with him, or spent leisure time with him to some extent. There were some who ran from him as from a plague. I can think of three who moved their homes to escape his attentions. Much has been written of Lowry being pestered by persons who wanted something from him – but it must not be overlooked that Lowry also pestered. There were those who made a good deal of money from the publication of his signed reproductions; a few more in the Manchester area chivvied him with regard to how he intended leaving his estate;

certainly during his last months this may well have contributed to an earlier death than might otherwise have been his. On the other hand, he delighted in encouraging expectancy of this sort, and would deliberately raise false hopes.

In retrospect, I fancy few, if any, understood the element of absurdity in Lowry's character like my husband, who was quick to recognize this element. The rest of us were much slower, if indeed we ever came to terms with it. In his correspondence with Micky he enjoyed such nonsense as, 'I come over to you on the 28th if my creditors will let me. I mustn't let them know I'm coming.' Or again from Mottram, 'I have a feeling I want to see the ships coming and going in South Shields. There are no ships in this terrible village.' Or, 'I'm doing very good work, I think, encouraging one or two young artists to work about fifty hours a day. That is the way to do it, I tell them.'

In October 1966, 'I went to the south coast for about a fortnight – the weather was dreadful, never saw so much rain in my life – my friends told me I was as unpleasant as the weather, this to a certain extent cheered me up a lot. . . . I went to Portsmouth twice – it cheered me up enormously – reminded me of Warrington – it did me a lot of good, did Portsmouth.'

From the Dragon Hotel, Swansea, when visiting Carol, 'These ships seem to be little ones compared to those on the Tyne. Give me North Shields! I'll be leaving Swansea on Friday, thank God. I much prefer Blyth and, of course, Hebburn and Wallsend. I look forward to coming into civilisation and will bring the child along.'

I remember him deciding to write his first letter to the press on the evening of 31 August 1968 as he sat at the familiar table in Tilley's with Micky and me, tears of helpless laughter running from his blue eyes as he recalled an art review from that day's *Guardian* in which the critic was comparing his exhibition at our gallery with an avant-garde one at the ICA at the end of London's Mall. There was a large photograph of Lowry in front of one of his oils, taken in the Stone Gallery. But the sub-headline ran, 'The nonart of "Cybernetic Serendipity" signifies more for the future than the high art of L. S. Lowry. . . .'

'Oh,' he was gasping, 'it was dipity all right!' He pulled himself together sufficiently to compose a very terse little missive on the back of an envelope taken from the bulging pocket book, and, handing it to Micky, commanded him to return to the gallery forthwith and type it for him . . . no, no, tomorrow wouldn't do at all – he might have cold feet by that time – it must be done immediately. I remained at the table to the refrain of 'Good for babies and young children.' Upon Micky's return, Lowry's mood changed and pulling a face he growled, ' "Cybernetic Serendipity" – oh my God, isn't it simply ridiculous? *Ludicrous*? What the devil will they think up next?' After reading the short letter he announced, 'They'll take no notice of me, they'll think it's just sour grapes. You must sign it, Mr Marshall!'

Micky remonstrated that he couldn't possibly do that – he knew the art critic well, and what on earth would he think if he received such an opinion as coming from him? But by that time there were few lengths my husband would not go to for the old man, so eventually he resigned himself to the inevitable, as Lowry looked sideways at me to announce, 'Mrs Marshall doesn't approve of it – wouldn't do for her and *The Times*!'

As it transpired, it didn't do for the *Guardian* either. Lowry was mightily disappointed when it failed to be published. Needless to say he had not trusted Micky to post it, but did this himself on leaving the restaurant.

There were the absurd occasions when he would persuade Micky to read from *Beachcomber* (J. B. Morton). 'Let's have that one that reminds me of an early lady friend I had.'

'The one with the large hands and feet – that real love of your life?'

'No, no, sir, not that one – the other.'

'Oh, the one you've been putting in your paintings for years.'

'Yes, that's the one. I think I'll have egg and chips tonight. Yes, a nice lightly fried egg and chips.'

'Well, that'll make a change. Why not have *oeuf à la Lowry*?'

'No, no, it's got to be an English egg. Come on now, haven't you found that yet?'

'Yes. . .

> 'Life has its problems for us all.
> Our dreams must go beyond recall,
> The future's chill and black.
> The girl I loved was so cross-eyed
> That every single time she cried
> The tears ran down her back.

'Prodnose: Who on earth wrote that?

'Myself: George Eliot, I think. No wait. It was surely Henry James. Or could it have been Mr Ruskin?'

Lowry never tired of this sort of thing, and however fed up, near to death, or suffering from one imagined complaint or another he was when he came to see us, Micky could have him forgetful of everything but the fun of the moment in no time at all. I never saw anyone else have this kind of relationship with Lowry.

Lowry always laughed at others' misfortunes. Whenever, so it seemed, anyone felt ill in Woolworth's they came into our shop next door for speedy medical attention. We got a little tired of it. One morning a pregnant lady decided that her time was imminent, and I dialled 999 before helping a helpless husband deliver a splendid baby boy. I was more than a little distrait when I joined Lowry for luncheon in the gallery. He was entirely uninterested in my morning and when I asked him how he was, I received the familiar moan, 'Oh, I'm dying, *dying*.'

'How jolly!' I announced, 'First a birth – and now a death – I do think you might have waited until after lunch!' Suddenly he saw the absurdity, collapsed with the usual guffaws, now demanding to know every detail.

'You're too young,' I retorted, but he had me laughing as well.

Another day one of our own customers fell down several stairs to break open the worst varicose veins I'd ever seen; in no time the shop floor was awash with blood. The lady herself remained calm saying that upon occasion this happened, while my manageress collapsed in hysterics, other customers fled the ever-deepening pools of blood and my assistants decided it was their lunchtime. Again 999. When the ambulance had removed the poor sufferer, I calmed the manageress, and set about clearing up the mess.

When I retailed this woe to Lowry later, his immediate reaction was prolonged and awful mirth. As he wiped his eyes, he kept repeating. 'Oh, what a subject for a painting! What a merry picture it would make – woman with burst varicose veins, pools of blood, hysterical lady looking on. And I could call it *A Fall*.' He laughed and laughed, just as he had laughed uproariously at the death of eight of Atkinson Grimshaw's children. But I do not think it was just a black sense of humour – it was rather the absurdity of a woman going shopping in Woolworths, and producing a baby in the process; the absurdity of constantly breaking open one's varicose veins; the absurdity of a father not discovering the bad sanitation at his home until he had lost eight children as a result. Lowry's recognition of the absurdity of human nature left him no recourse but to laugh at it all.

After the painter's death in 1976, John Read decided to update his 1956 BBC television film about Lowry. He met us in our London flat in the course of his research. We held back nothing of our knowledge of our friend; nothing of the fun and laughter. We offered the assistance of the lengthy tape recordings Lowry made for us but the offer was not taken up and Lowry remained the shadowy figure he'd always been. Read was apparently unable to accept that the man he had met twenty years previously was not the Lowry we knew.

Let me not for a moment give the impression that the Read film is not good. Lowry's art is accurately presented but in my opinion the man's character is not. Once again this is a case of the original story being carefully prepared and rehearsed by the artist, years before, approved by Lowry, but not proof of the man.

Lowry would have been heavily on his guard with John Read – a son of the influential critic of modern art and advocate of Henry Moore, whose work our friend never admired. Lowry was not against modern art; he would merely say, 'I don't understand it,' and that was an end to it. Lowry did not give a thought to his position in art on any time scale. To him, time was irrelevant to the art of Giotto, Hogarth, Turner, or himself. They were all simply painters – doing 'the job' as well as they could.

Twenty years previously Lowry had no hesitation in talking, and talking well, of his work and method, but he would be careful to give away as little as possible of the private man. This can be the only explanation for statements in Read's commentary such as: 'Lowry kept everyone at arms' length – his friends never knew one another,' or: 'Lowry became more and more withdrawn. . . .' The situation was the reverse. As he eased up on his work he became less and less withdrawn, for at last he had time on his hands. Read also said, 'He found little consolation in fame – Lowry would have preferred the respect of his fellow artists.' If there was one thing Lowry revelled in it was his fame. He loved to be recognized in a restaurant or anywhere else. He delighted in being asked for his autograph; he enjoyed one piece of publicity after another. None would have been happier at the enormous press he received at his death than he, could he but have read it and heard and seen the media's tribute to him. Lowry might have been heard occasionally to say that his fame had come too late. This meant he wished it had come earlier – not that he wished it had not come at all.

As for the respect of his fellow artists, this appeared to mean the least of all to him in the years of our friendship. I can bring no living painter to mind for whose opinion and respect Lowry cared one jot.

John Read quoted Lowry's pet expression as being 'the battle *for* life', which can be construed as a Marxist preoccupation. Lowry's involvement was with 'the battle *of* life' – an entirely different matter. It was this element he looked for in every great work of art – hence he cared nothing for the Impressionists, whose works, for him, were too pretty and showed nothing of 'the battle of life'.

He always set great store by education; he enjoyed classical music up to a point. He was delighted with the honour of the special birthday concert given for him by the Hallé Orchestra in 1967 to celebrate his seventy-seventh birthday – although he was at a loss to understand why that particular year had been chosen, unless, as he said, it was not expected that he would live to see another. Considering his continuous claims that he was dying, this should not have surprised him. Although he maintained that the Hallé was 'a jolly good band', he still had to have his little grumble – he was very disappointed that the programme failed to include his favourite *Norma* after he had particularly asked for some part of this Bellini work. 'But then,' he would add, 'there's no one can sing it nowadays – no one can do it justice.'

He would certainly not have approved Read's choice of the delightful Vera Lynn at the conclusion of his revamped film, singing, 'We'll meet again, don't know where, don't know when, But I know we'll meet again some sunny day.' In life, Lowry didn't care much for sunny days, and in death I doubt he counted on meeting any of us again.

Three months after Lowry's death, Robert Tyrrell, the producer of the 1968 Tyne Tees Television film *Mr Lowry*, telephoned to ask whether we were aware, and, indeed, had we always been aware, that Lowry had a working life other than that of a painter?

We laughed at such a suggestion. However, Bob insisted that his informant had proof that early in life Lowry had become a rent collector for the Pall Mall Property Company in Manchester and, remaining with the same firm, had finished up as its chief cashier to retire on full pension at the age of sixty-five. 'And Tilly! Lowry *evicted* people!' Bob added with horror.

Again we laughed; it was totally out of the question, and we couldn't suppose what motive anyone had for suggesting such a thing. Lowry himself had told us a hundred times that it was unthinkable that he could ever have held down an ordinary job and, knowing him as we did, we could not have agreed more.

Indeed, I had occasionally supposed that had the term 'autistic' been in use in Lowry's childhood, it might well have applied to him, as for instance when he chopped up his mother's sideboard for no apparent reason. It was as a consequence of this subconscious feeling one had with regard to his personality that we so frequently made allowances for him when he flew into his sudden and terrible rages, for no reason and without warning, losing control to the extent of becoming incontinent. Ella would often have to wash the cover of the chair upon which he had been sitting, until at last we replaced it with a leather one . . . but his incontinence only occurred when he became unduly excited or angry.

Indeed he did refer to himself as 'a Sunday painter who painted every day of the week'. But because of the manner of his delivery of the phrase it was not accepted as it would have been from an acknowledged 'Sunday painter', but as from a man whose work had for too long been considered only that of a 'primitive' painter. He was sick, he would shout, of being described as a 'primitive' who painted matchstick figures.

Many times he had recorded in detail – as reported in the press by Edwin Mullins, Michael Hardcastle (of the *Liverpool Daily Post*), and many others – how he had loathed his schooldays and how after leaving school his aunt Mary had said to his parents, 'What on earth are you going to do with Laurie?'

'Well, he's not good for much,' they had replied, 'but he used to like drawing little ships – he'd better go to an art school and learn how to do them properly. You never know, they might make something of him.'

Hence had begun his long years of academic art training, of which he was immensely proud. Only after his death was it discovered that this art training was at night school.

In the Tyne Tees Television film where he is his own commentator, Lowry says, 'I could never have stood a nine-to-five job, bowler hat, dispatch case and umbrella! Oh no, no, I could never have stood anything like that.' And to Edwin Mullins he had said, 'It was suggested that I went in for art as I was fit for nothing else . . . at school I had few friends, and I never passed any exams. Time went on and on. . . . It was any port in a storm. There's nothing in my life but what I've said. . . .'

But there was. From Tyrrell's inquiry, it now emerged that on leaving Victoria Park School, Manchester, Lowry had joined the firm of Thos. Aldred & Son, Chartered Accountants, Mosley Street, Manchester, in 1904 at the age of seventeen. After three years there he moved to the General Accident, Fire & Life Assurance Corporation, in Cross Street, as a claims clerk. In 1910 he moved again and began work as a rent collector and clerk with the Pall Mall Property Company Ltd, in Manchester, and forty years later he retired from that firm on full pension; he had risen to the rank of chief cashier. (No wonder he looked forward to and never missed a Stone Gallery Annual General Meeting!)

Poor Robert Tyrrell – how much easier his job as producer would have been had any of us known of Lowry's full working life as a businessman. How much more there would have been to talk to him about, as Veral was to point out, during those endless dinners she gave him.

That splendid collection of clocks ticking away in his little house – a collection supposedly made by his mother – what a story each clock might have told if the truth was that they'd been taken in lieu of rent. How much more interesting to learn that Lowry was a teetotaller because his father drank too much and that Lowry's miserly instincts were the outcome of his father having died in debt, as I was to learn eventually from his cousin May and from Carol, after she had seen his estate papers.

We had certainly sensed that somewhere there was a well-guarded secret in the artist's life; he was forever on his hostile guard with the press. But it certainly never entered any of our heads that he was successfuly hiding a full working life as rent collector and cashier. When faced with the proof of this, Veral and I looked at one another in total astonishment, to exclaim simultaneously, 'The old *fraud*!'

It was not the work for which we condemned him but the deception. Lowry had attached himself to us for so long, not merely as friend, but professionally. His deception was our deception (Tyrrell implied). We had fought tooth and nail the idea that he was ever an amateur or primitive painter (and essentially he was not).

All the greater honour to the man for painting throughout the long reaches of the night, by artificial light – so that there are no shadows in a Lowry painting. But it would have been good to know the reason while he lived and to have talked with him naturally of his life.

Once he wrote to a friend, 'I'm just off to the Marshalls again – they're the only thing that keep me alive.' But our efforts in his cause were not enough for him to trust us, apparently. I doubt if he ever trusted a human being in all his life.

In retrospect it was no wonder he had a jealousy of Norman Cornish, whose reputation as a painter was made while he still worked as a miner. Rent collecting and evicting folk would hardly have found the same emotive response.

Many people paint, but few achieve in their lifetime such fame as Lowry's. Of those few, fewer still are remembered for long after their own time. Occasionally discussing with us whether or not his reputation might survive into posterity, Lowry would maintain that he did not care either way. The odd penny or two in his lifetime was more important, and keeping his creditors at bay was all that mattered!

Lowry, it must now be remembered, had been a businessman first; he remained one for a man's normal span of working life. When he reiterated that he would like to have been a stockbroker, puzzling though it was, there appeared some genuine regret that he had not achieved this height. So, after his office retirement, he was to bring a small businessman's experience to the final running of his life as a painter.

John Read wrote in the *Listener* on 16 June 1977, 'He could not be bothered to promote himself in the art world.' But during his last years Lowry devoted himself to little else. Hence all the signed reproductions which earned him money so easily, and the advertising of which made an ever-wider public familiar with his work. A sight easier to sign his name than paint a new picture; easier to receive a cheque for forty thousand pounds for copyrights than paint a new picture. Granted the constant interruptions at his home (when he was at home) must almost have precluded the possibility of working there in those last years. But he had brought these interruptions upon himself by taking over to a large extent the business of dealer as well as painter. (For taxation purposes Lowry was registered as a dealer.) It was shortsighted.

Lowry had a London gallery which must always be given the credit for having discovered him. But he chose to keep the directors of that gallery in total ignorance about how he intended leaving his estate. Micky and I were present when Carol broke the news to Mr Gerald Corcoran and his son that she was Lowry's beneficiary. Their reaction was one of enormous surprise, they had assumed from the press that the painter's works and his collection of pre-Raphaelites and other artists' work had been left to the nation.

John Read also wrote in the *Listener* in that same article, Lowry 'had a profound suspicion of the "establishment" of his particular profession. It is a miracle that he ever consented to become an RA.' This was no miracle if one was familiar with the real Lowry. An organization which would market his works and retain for itself no commission was totally irresistible. But Mr Read is correct when he says that Lowry had a profound suspicion of the art world, and unfortunately he taught his heiress to have the same suspicion. At the time her inheritance was being publicized, she was quoted in the *Daily Telegraph* as saying that 'Uncle' called people in the art world 'sharks' – and she knew exactly what he meant. Micky advised her to keep such views to herself as the publication of them would not assist Lowry's standing in the years to come. A jockey can ride a horse to win, or he can ride a horse to lose.

Lowry was fully aware that he was not what is termed a critic's painter. For want of a better definition he was a people's painter. If the critic, as he suggested, is without influence – people are fickle. All the same, it was the artist himself who would constantly remind me that Ruskin's opinion of Rossetti's work is still influential. But Lowry, the lone wolf, was irrevocably convinced that he, and he alone, knew what was best for his artisitic career, and certainly that served him well enough while he lived, for he died wealthy and famous. As he looked forward to good art reviews, as was only natural, increasingly in the last years he would insist that it mattered nothing what any critic wrote about him, and he would repeat, 'What does it matter? It's only the work that matters – the work will speak for itself.' And yet as late as 16 June 1975 he asked me to write in *The Times* correspondence columns, 'With reference to his own work, L. S. Lowry admits that he sees on an average about two fakes a fortnight. This being the case with the work of a living British artist . . . etc'. How came Lowry to be so shortsighted as to overlook the fact that, after his death, fakes would also speak for him?

We have perforce had to stand by while one wrong Lowry was published as genuine. We have watched fakes sell in small dealers' galleries; fakes sell at auction; three wrong works were shown in the painter's Retrospective Exhibition at the Royal Academy. We have to stand by because of threatened litigation should we speak out. Lowry was aware while he lived that there existed a ring of pasticheurs; he was even visited by police in an effort to clear this up. Lowry had no knowledge of who these persons were and the matter remains unresolved.

With my family, I recently recalled the long years Lowry spent with us – how the hell, I wondered, did we manage to continue giving comfort to the elderly man?

Simon said, 'Ah, but mother, what compensations there were also. Lowry could bring a place alive for me. In his company everything looked different – as I sat beside him as he sketched, looked at places and things I wouldn't have given a second thought to but for him – I suppose I learned more about painting and drawing from Lowry than from any other source.'

Did Lowry ever suppose that the woman in whom he placed his final trust, the one who received so much from him, would see fit to publicize what have been termed his quasi-erotic works? Many painters indulge in so called pornographic subjects. After his death, Turner's were destroyed by Ruskin, rightly or otherwise, on the assumption that they would be injurious to the artist's reputation. It is public knowledge that, for the same reason, Sir Alfred Munnings, ex-PRA, was instrumental in getting Stanley Spencer's erotic and bizarre paintings burned. I am not suggesting that Lowry's should of necessity have been destroyed, only that they should have been kept private, since he considered them unsuitable for the public while he lived.

Lowry's erotic works are not of the normal kind; certainly not expected of this painter. His drawings and paintings of young girls dressed as ballet dancers, dolls or puppets in revealing costumes are not out of order – but there are others that are. Young girls in agony and torture, some decapitated by knife, sword, axe or guillotine – blood flowing, hands tied and chained, the male executioner represented only by the presence of the hand that wields the weapon – these are disturbing works coming from an artist with a known preference for young girls. Now these paintings and drawings speak for Lowry. Did he ever in his wildest imaginings suppose they would?

I have a letter from Carol confirming my husband's introduction to her of an ex-*Daily Mail* reporter, an introduction Micky regrets having made. With the cooperation of Lowry's heiress, this journalist publicized these works. Again with Carol's cooperation, an attempt has been made to associate them with the girls in whom Lowry took an interest – Pat Cooke, Sheila Fell, Carol herself – as the outcome of the hurt done to him by one or all of these, possibly adding up to an image of Ann, Lowry's *Dark Lady of the Sonnets*, who it is suggested did not exist except in the painter's mind.

As might be foreseen, many newspapers took up this sensational aspect of an unknown side of Lowry's character.

Should such interpretations of Lowry's quasi-erotic works be acceptable, then it must also be accepted that the painter was well on his way to being a psychopath with paedophilic leanings. But to those with a deeper knowledge of the man and his art other explanations are possible.

Years before Lowry's death Micky was asked to persuade Lowry to accept a commission to produce designs for a ballet. The idea was not new to the painter. The two men discussed the project in detail; both had long admired the work of Leon Bakst and together they pored over his designs. Eventually, however, Lowry decided against the commission. There would be criticism because the type of design he had in mind did not fall in line with his life's work. But there is little doubt that Lowry's studies of young ballet dancers have a close relationship to the work of Bakst.

With regard to the nature of his much more disturbing paintings and drawings, we well remember Lowry being appalled, and at the same time fascinated, by the case of the Moors Murders. He always claimed that he attended the trial, as did several well-known writers. On a number of occasions our friend and I discussed the particular plight of the young girl who called on God to help her in the agony of torture resulting in her death. Lowry was obsessed with this particularly dreadful murder, maintaining that it shook his faith in God. One dark night Micky and I were returning Lowry to his home very late, when he suddenly asked my husband to stop the car in Hyde, and shortly the three of us were standing outside the perfectly normal-looking house where the crimes had taken place. Perhaps it was its very normality of appearance, or the extreme lateness of the hour, or the dark windy night with a strange moan in the wind as it swept across the unremarkable housing estate, which evoked my overwhelming feeling of terror and depression – but, whatever it was, I urged the two men to return to the car. I continued to shiver with a sense of sordid evil as we motored the short distance to The Elms.

Lowry's fascination with the Moors Murders continued, and he certainly *said* he had made drawings and commenced certain paintings around the subject. So were the more innocuous of his 'erotic' works the outcome of the suggestion of a commission for ballet designs? Were his bloody and violent ones the result of his interest in the Moors Murders – committed not very far down the road from his own home, the bodies buried on the Saddleworth Moors so familiar to him?

As he sat the hours away over the years in the gallery office, how often Lowry would recall the accepted pattern, after a popular painter's death, of rise, decline, then the inevitable fall into obscurity, after which occasionally one rises again for recognition fifty or a hundred years later. One new piece in this pattern certainly never occurred to him. Hating pop groups as he did, he would have been outraged to find himself the subject for a song that went to the top of the pops. His immediate reaction to 'Match-stalk Men and Match-stalk Cats and Dogs' would have been a fierce demand of the perpetrators, 'What's in it for me, eh?'

I see him sitting again in the big wing-back chair across the room where I write. I seem to hear him sigh again, 'Ah well – it's the way of humanity – the lowest form of animal life. But where will it all end?'

I hear myself laughing again as I quote to his comfort four lines of Beachcomber. The last two I used to add – they pleased him:

Meditation Among the Moderns

Pleasure that most enchants us
Seems the soonest gone;

How short and sweet are Epstein,
And Nevinson, and John.
Lowry's was a sadder tale
His art may well live on.